110–111 **Face Off: Sergeant Robert Chester**
112 **Bravest of the Brave: Sepoy Ishar Singh, VC**
113–121 **True Stories: WO Matthew Tomlinson**
122–123 **Bravest of the Brave: Trooper Mark Donaldso**
124–125 **Beating the Boredom, Counting the Hours** by
126–129 **Medicine and War**
130–131 **Face Off: Sergeant Liam Varley**
132–135 **Entertaining the Troops** by Alan Grace and Angie Avlianos
136–137 **Heroes of the Silver Screen**
138–144 **True Stories: Lance Corporal Sally Clarke**
145–147 **An Excellent Mess: Soyer's Field and Barrack Cookery for the Army**
148–149 **Face Off: Flying Officer Robin Fowler**
150–151 **Fighting Fit**
152–155 **Against All Odds**
156–157 **Face Off: WO2 Matthew Campbell Henry**
158–159 **My Heroes** by Fergal Keane
160–161 **Angels of the Air** by Georgina Reid
162–163 **Bravest of the Brave: William Rhodes-Moorhouse, VC and Andrews Fitzgibbon, VC** by David Willetts
164–171 **True Stories: Corporal Carl Thomas**
172–173 **The Art of War** by Sun Tzu
174–175 **Face Off: Sergeant Robert Wiseman**
176–179 **Civilian Courage**
180–183 **Homeward Bound: Stranger in the House** by Julie Summers
184–185 **Bravest of the Brave: Charles Lucas, VC** by David Willetts
186–189 **Sangin: Crucible of Courage** by Colonel Stuart Tootal, OBE
190–191 **Our Losses Are Not in Vain** by Lieutenant Colonel Nick Kitson
192–193 **Recon: Helmand**
194–197 **Global Hot-Spots**
198–199 **Face Off: Trooper Adam Hanger**
200–203 **Invisible Battle Scars** by Michael Upchurch
204–205 **Bravest of the Brave: Rorke's Drift** by David Willetts
206–209 **Christmas Boxes: A Piece of Home on the Front Line**
210 **Acknowledgements**

How to use this book

There are references throughout *Real Heroes: Courage Under Fire* to external websites. All these sites can be accessed in the usual way, by typing the address into a web browser, or by using your smartphone to scan the QR code printed by each web address. On a QR code-compatible smartphone, you will need to download a QR code reader first. To scan the code, launch the reader and hold the camera lens over the bar code in a good light.

HarperPress is not responsible for the content of any of the external sites mentioned.

HarperPress
An imprint of HarperCollinsPublishers
77–85 Fulham Palace Road,
Hammersmith, London W6 8JB
www.harpercollins.co.uk

First published by HarperPress in 2010
in association with
News Group Newspapers Limited, a subsidiary of
News International Limited in 2010
News Group Newspapers Limited is a subsidiary of
News International Limited
The Sun and The Sun Logo are registered trademarks
of News Group Newspapers Limited

Visit The Sun website at: www.thesun.co.uk

Comic artwork on pages 14–19, 40–46, 64–71, 113–121,
138–144 and 164–171 by Yibi Hu www.m-i-e.co.uk
Comic words for 'Sally Clarke', 'Wayne Owers', 'Alex
Duncan' and 'Matthew Tomlinson' by Ben North
All other words by HarperPress

1

A catalogue record for this book is available from the
British Library

ISBN 978-0-00-737903-3

Design by seagulls.net

Printed and bound in Germany by Mohn Media

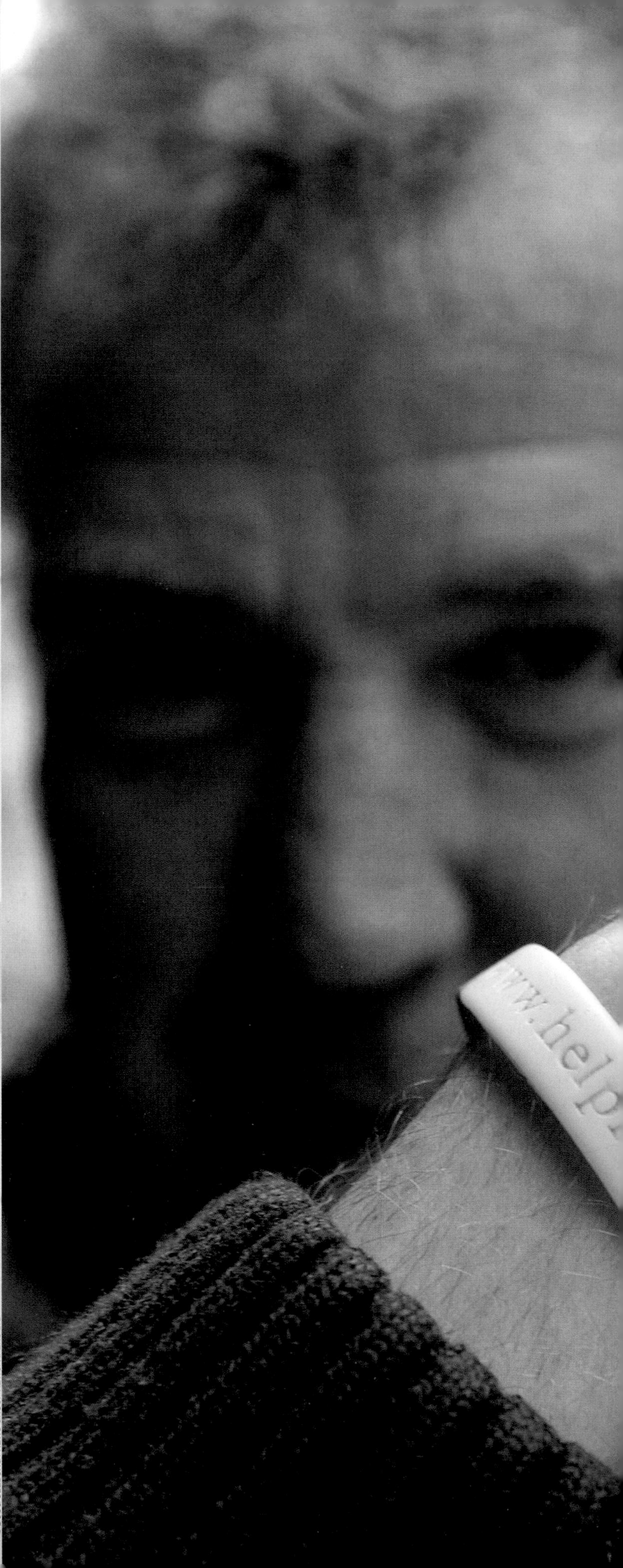

PREFACE

Let's face it: although I enjoy explosions and violence (especially if it involves caravans) I'm not really cut out to be a soldier. But real Army, Navy and Air Force people like fighting and it's what they are trained to do. Loosing off 6,000 rounds a day to them is just part of the job.

In recent years, Help for Heroes has helped to swing public opinion on our troops from apathy through sympathy to outright admiration. These are special people, who go through hell on our behalf – and they need our support.

Yet, even among these special people there are some extra-special ones. The real heroes. Many – too many – of them will go unsung. A few will receive the recognition they deserve – whether it's a Millie from *The Sun* or an award from the Queen. Even fewer will be awarded the Victoria Cross. This deliberately simple cross – made from the bronze of cannon captured during the Crimean War – is the Commonwealth's highest award for gallantry, and the ultimate medal.

A few years ago I made a TV programme about the VC and one of the astonishing people who was awarded it. In 1944, Major Robert Cain held off the advancing German Panzers at Arnhem armed only with a 2-inch mortar held in his arm like a Western gunslinger. His action saved the lives of the men of the South Staffordshire Regiment. It was said to be the finest VC of the Second World War.

Cain was one of the select band of Victoria Cross recipients who lived to tell the tale. Although, of course, like so many others, he didn't tell the tale. He left the Army after the war and went back to his pre-war job at Shell. He died in 1974 of cancer. Which means I never met him. Which is a shame for two reasons. Firstly, I am fascinated by Victoria Cross winners. Secondly, I married his daughter.

She did not know her father won the VC until after he died – he never thought to mention it.

We have a warped sense of what constitutes bravery these days. We even call premiership footballers heroes for scoring a penalty.

When you compare that to the stories you will read in this book … well, enough said.

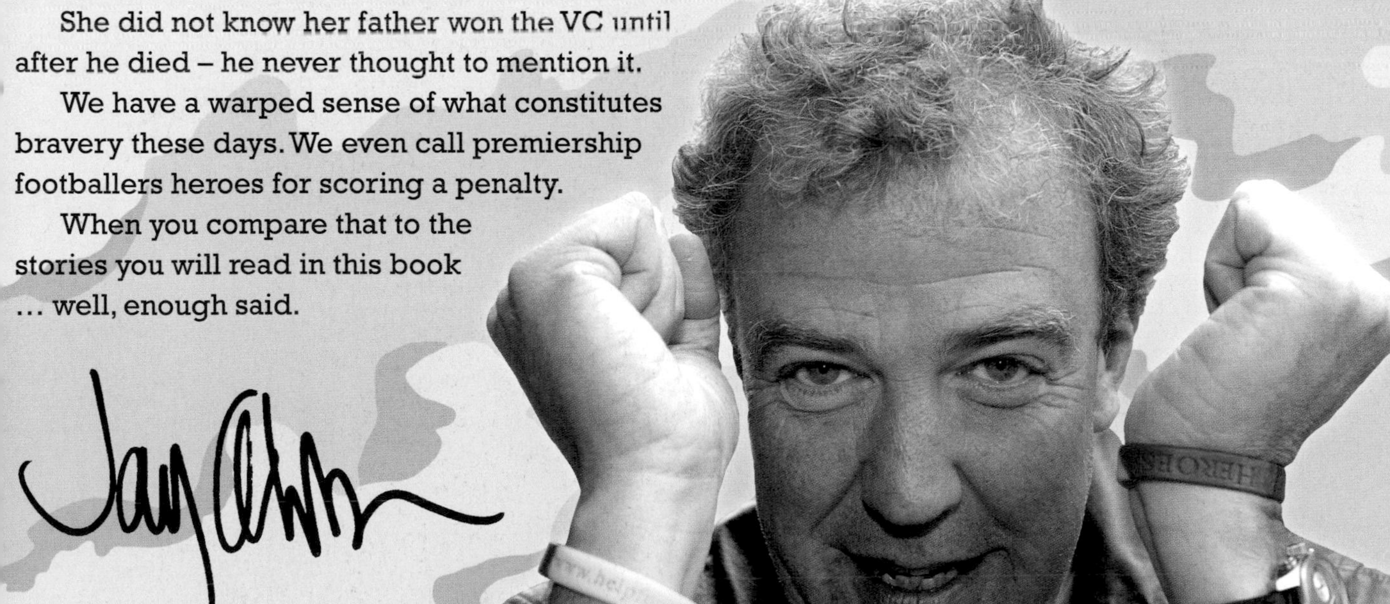

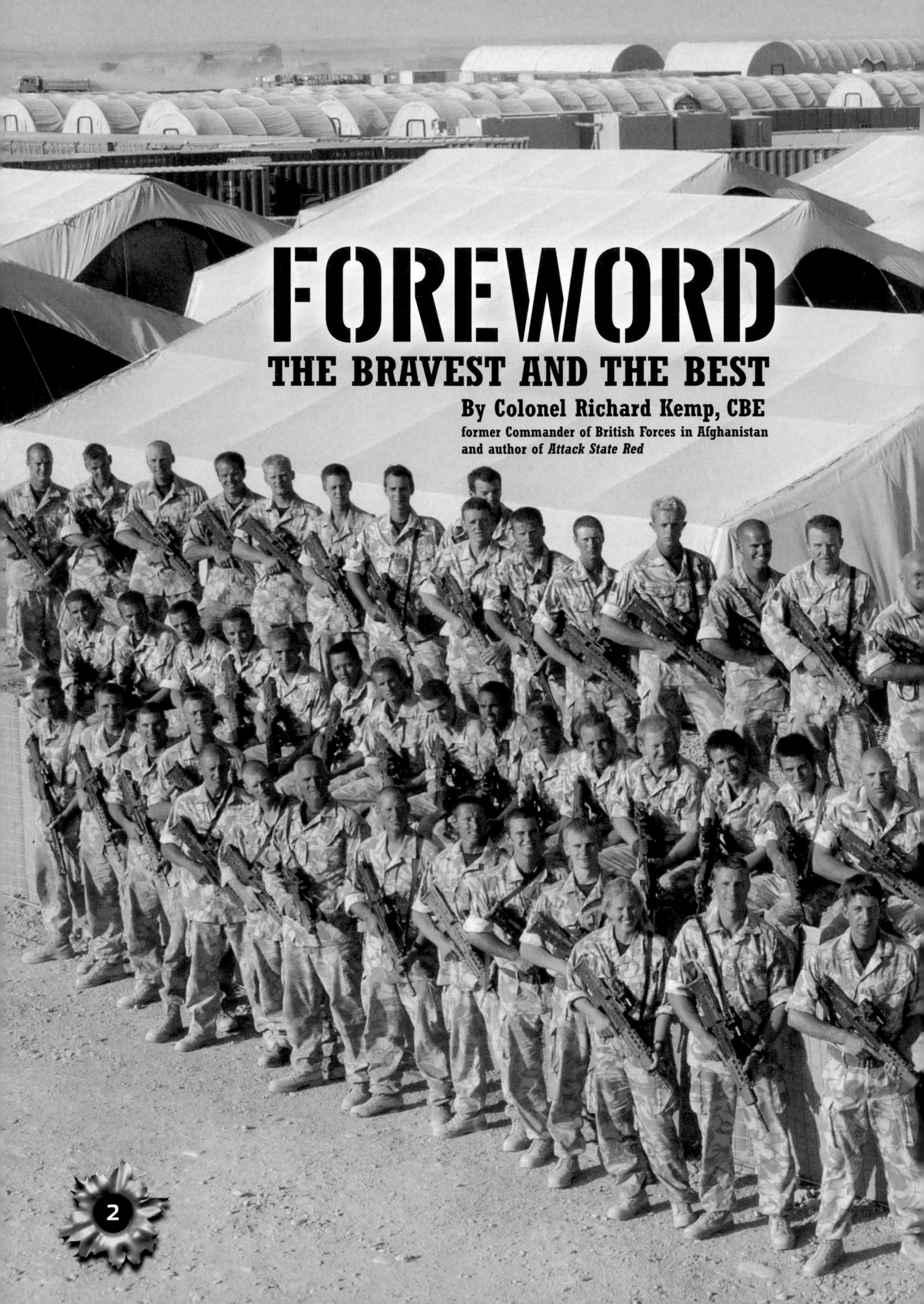

FOREWORD

THE BRAVEST AND THE BEST

By Colonel Richard Kemp, CBE

former Commander of British Forces in Afghanistan and author of *Attack State Red*

From the muddied fields of Agincourt to the quagmire hell of the Somme and the sun-scorched deserts of Afghanistan, the British soldier has overcome his opponents in countless bloody and hard-fought battles. The Armed Forces' fighting spirit, renowned throughout the world, is founded above all on courage – the supreme and eternal military virtue.

It has been my privilege, during almost thirty years in the British Armed Forces, to witness many awe-inspiring acts of bravery. One of my corporals, Andy Rainey, won the Military Cross in Bosnia, exposing himself to lethal shell and sniper fire so that he could machine-gun the enemy and allow his fellow soldiers to find cover. This was no isolated incident. The brave men and women of our Armed Forces have frequently played Russian roulette with their own lives to safeguard the lives of others.

In Helmand today, bravery of an order that most people will never be called upon to muster is a daily part of life for our troops.

The infantry point man has perhaps the most dangerous job in the world – and is the embodiment of undiluted courage. Normally a young private of eighteen or nineteen, weighed down by a massive ninety-pound battle load, pouring sweat in temperatures spiralling to 55°C, the point man leads his patrol through territory laced with deadly improvised explosive devices and the risk of ambush round every corner. He does so knowing that his next step could be the last he ever takes.

Are our fighting troops without fear? The point man is usually gut-wrenchingly terrified and most soldiers readily admit to being afraid in every battle. That reality makes their actions in combat truly courageous, because without fear there can be no courage.

Gallantry medals are the nation's recognition of extreme bravery. The accounts of heroic actions by medal-winners in this book are truly inspiring – and humbling. Decorations for valour are greatly prized throughout the Armed Forces. But no soldier will run forward into the teeth of enemy fire in order to win a medal. Courage is an individual and a personal attribute. But it is cultivated by strong leadership and the British Armed Forces' historic regimental system, which bonds and shapes its new recruits – some forged by council estates, care homes, sink schools and frequent visits to police stations – into powerful fighting units that are equal to any challenge.

Courage is also fostered in the crucible of violent and intensive combat, in which soldiers are bound together more closely even than brothers. If your mate needs someone to watch his back or his flank, if he needs to be rescued from enemy fire, if he's wounded and needs to be dragged to safety, then you'll do it, however much effort it takes, whatever the danger you face.

This book will give you a unique insight into many fascinating aspects of our Armed Forces over the years, and especially their courageous fight in Helmand today. The arguments about whether we are right to be in Afghanistan, whether the blood price is worth paying, and whether we can win the war, are raging as never before. But one thing is certain: we can be proud and grateful that so many of our young men and women are prepared to follow the heroic traditions of their forbears, putting their lives on the line in the defence of this country.

They are the bravest and the best.

A MATTER OF LIFE AND DEATH A SOLDIER'S SURVIVAL GUIDE

By John 'Lofty' Wiseman, author of the *SAS Survival Guide*

Man is an animal who, in his natural state, can only survive in the tropics. If he is to live anywhere else in the world he must recreate a tropical environment by wearing adequate clothing and creating good shelter. The hardest of all places for man to survive are cold areas, especially those at an altitude where, without proper clothing or equipment, life can be measured in minutes. Extremes of heat or cold create their own life-threatening risks, such as hypothermia or heat stroke.

Generally speaking, man can survive for three minutes without air, three days without water and three weeks without food with no lasting ill-effects, and some people have been known to have endured longer periods with the aid of drugs and medicines. Soldiers are deployed in all theatres and all conditions and must rely on their training to survive anything they may encounter.

Afghanistan is unique as it has all the ingredients for disaster: searing heat by day under a cloudless sky and freezing cold at night. In the mountains, which dominate the landscape, temperatures drop so low that water freezes at night. Located just above the Tropic of Cancer, Afghanistan is geographically classified as an arid area. Water, the most precious of all commodities, is scarce and jealously guarded. The population is scattered over a wide area, often in remote places, making access and evacuation difficult.

To be able to exist effectively in such conditions, soldiers must be taught the six

Dust devils and sand storms are just some of the challenges facing the soldier in Afghanistan.

A Chinook kicks up a blinding dust cloud in Musa Qaleh, Helmand.

Sleep is grabbed between patrols.

© PANOS

Soldiers gather around a fire at their campsite as night falls.

URST/AFP/GETTY IMAGES

© THESUPE87 / FOTOLIA

elements of survival: food, fire, shelter, water, and a good knowledge of medicine and navigation.

The art of surviving such an environment is to keep out of the heat, drink plenty of water, avoid exertion, get a good night's sleep, and maintain a healthy diet – completely the opposite to what soldiers on the ground actually do. In Afghanistan, the soldier is patrolling by day, weighed down by heavy equipment, wrapped up in body armour under a merciless sun. Sleep is grabbed between patrols or sentry duty, disturbed by gunfire, both outgoing and incoming. Soldiers curl up where they can for warmth, exactly like every other creature, and snakes, spiders and scorpions can become their bedfellows. Because of the heat and limited water, appetites suffer. Food is often seen as an inconvenience. Anything that is easily prepared is wolfed down, calorific value meaning nothing. Over a short period this is sustainable, but at the end of a six-month tour, health suffers.

In the desert, sight is the most important sense as visibility can be almost limitless, especially on high ground, and the eyes must be looked after, as vehicles – especially helicopters – create huge dust clouds. Flies carry germs that cause trachoma, an infectious eye disease that is the biggest cause of blindness.

The desert is a dangerous place and the biggest threat of all is one not yet mentioned: man. Animals are very predictable in their behaviour but man isn't. The average soldier comes from a large city, thousands of miles away from the theatre of war and is used to a more gentle, more temperate climate. In the desert they must clash with an enemy born in these harsh conditions who knows the ground intimately. Fortunately, the British soldier is the best in the world at adapting and learning new skills, working closely with the local population to hone soldierly instincts that have taken centuries to evolve. These men are true survivors.

If you have an iPhone, you can download a free SAS Survival Guide app here **http://bit.ly/bxT2M4** or by using your smartphone to scan this code:

FACE OFF

MAJOR TIM HARRIS

Age	35
Hometown	Harrogate
Unit	A Company, 3 Rifles

What is your job and what do you do?

I'm a Rifle Company commander and I am responsible for the command of 160 men and women in the south of Sangin. My headquarters is at a FOB, and I have my Riflemen in six other locations, ranging from patrol bases in the Green Zone to sniper observation posts in the urban areas. I spend a lot of time working with the Afghan Company commander, discussing possible joint operations to help improve security in the south of Sangin.

What was your best day?

Success in counter-insurgency tends to be a gradual affair with progress often so glacially slow that you hardly notice it. But after several months you look back and think how Sangin was and compare it to now and realise how much you have achieved.

The busiest time was when I took part in a battle group operation to build two new patrol bases in the Green Zone. The operation took three days and involved over

300 troops. The best thing was that our arrival in such force completely surprised the enemy, who were unable to stop us from doing what we needed to do. Despite various setbacks (the bridge we used to get into the Green Zone collapsed) we managed to push on through and achieved the mission.

What was your hardest day?
There were a number of dark days when we took casualties – these men were our comrades and, more importantly, they were our friends. But we always tried to stay positive; we knew that we had to keep going to honour their memory. When the chips are down you see the very best of British soldiers.

What is your favourite bit of kit and why?
I love the Jackal vehicles; they have so much utility and my company uses them for surveillance, resupply, heavy weapons fire support, escorts, casevac and as a command post. Plus the fact that they are open means that you can still interact with the local people – a vital element in winning their trust.

Please list the last 3 books/magazines you read.
1. Italy's Sorrow by James Holland – an account of the war in Italy 1943–1944
2. War in Val D'Orcia by Iris Origo – a diary of war in Tuscany
3. Kim by Rudyard Kipling.

THE JACKAL

The Jackal is a light patrol vehicle which fulfils a number of different roles, including surveillance, escort, rapid assault and fire support. It combines versatility, speed and manoeuvrability with unparalleled cross-country performance over Afghanistan's harsh terrain.

There are three models of Jackal currently in operation. The original Jackal was improved in the form of the Jackal 2. The latter holds four crew members to the former's two, and the vehicle's main armament has moved forward in the later model. The chassis has also been upgraded allowing the Jackal 2 to carry a heavier load than its predecessor.

The Jackal 2a is an enhanced version of the Jackal 2. The most significant difference between these two vehicles is the new cab design of the 2a, which provides integrated mine blast protection. In June 2010, the Ministry of Defence awarded a £45-million contract to the manufacturers of the Jackal for the production of 140 Jackal 2a vehicles to support operations in Afghanistan.

What do you miss most when away from home?
My family and proper fish and chips.

What is the best thing about being in the military?
It's an exciting job with lots of responsibility. There's always lots of variety – I have served in over twenty countries including Sierra Leone, South Africa, Kenya, Jordan, Cyprus, Gibraltar and the US. But the best thing is the people you work with – your mates, and the soldiers you are privileged to command.

Who do you most admire/who is your hero?
There are many people who inspire me every day – all of the lads I work with. I couldn't possibly pick one person out!

THE CONFLICT TODAY

By Duncan Larcombe, *Sun* Defence Editor

The war in Afghanistan is fast approaching its tenth year and, since the attack on the US in 2001, much has changed on the ground. Afghanistan today has its own elected government and a national army in the process of taking on responsibility for its own security – a far cry from the country ruled by the Taliban in 2001, where ordinary citizens were oppressed and where terrorism was fostered. But the war is not over, violence is ever present and the Taliban are not yet beaten. The fighting has reached its most crucial stage yet.

At the end of 2009, US President Barack Obama ordered a troop surge in a bid to stabilise what had become an increasingly volatile situation in the country. There are now more boots on the ground than ever before, with more than 9,500 British troops serving as part of the International Security Assistance Force (ISAF).

Duncan Larcombe reporting from the ground.

At the beginning of 2010, the Allies launched Operation Moshtarak – a joint operation between British, Canadian and American and Afghan troops aimed at asserting government authority in Helmand Province and securing the capital, Kandahar. The operation was a short, sharp, focused attack which centred on Nad'Ali and Marjah – both western regions of Helmand Province – in a bid to secure the last few remaining Taliban strongholds. The operation was to have three main phases: firstly to rearrange troops around Kandahar in order to secure it and to establish security for its inhabitants; secondly to secure central Helmand Province; and thirdly to move troops back to the capital, Kandahar, to support the government and police presence in the city.

The operation involved Afghans from the outset. President Hamid Karzai was fully briefed before the operation, the Afghan National Army and Police were involved in the planning of the operation, and Helmand Province Governor Gulab Mangal held meetings with local community leaders beforehand.

Even before the operation began, planning and shaping operations were taking place. In preparation, a US

ANA soldiers arrive at Camp Shorab, near Camp Bastion, during the second day of joint Operation Moshtarak.

taskforce secured a key canal, locking off a crucial junction. Meanwhile, the Household Cavalry and Danish Leopard tanks undertook operation in the Bolan desert to secure the area around Lashkar Gah, limiting the insurgents' movement towards the east. The Scots Guards cut off key areas in south Nad'Ali and Taskforce Leatherneck worked to isolate Marjah in order to secure key lines of communication which would help them in the main operation.

In the early hours of 13 February 2010, with the groundwork laid, 1,500 British soldiers climbed into 46 helicopters to launch what would be the biggest air assault of its kind in military history. Along with a *kandak* of the Afghan National Army, a company of 1st Battalion, The Royal Welsh, infiltrated the triangle around Chah-e Anjir from the air. A Company Group, also of 1st Battalion, The Royal Welsh, entered western Babaji, and a combined force of ANA and US Marine Corps conducted air assaults in central Marjah.

These air attacks were launched simultaneously with corresponding ground attacks. The Coldstream Guards, in partnership with another ANA *kandak*, attacked the area around Babaji; the 1st Battalion Grenadier Guards and a further ANA *kandak* moved into the area around Chah-e Anjir, to the west of Babaji; while a third force made up of the US Marine Corps and the ANA moved into northern Marjah.

All in all, about 1,000 troops were activated in each movement, the numbers on the ground matching those in the air. The night passed almost without a shot being fired, and by the next morning British Forces were in control of the Nad'Ali district. The Taliban were nowhere to be seen.

In the months that followed Operation Moshtarak, the work of bringing security to the region continued. British Forces were instrumental in putting Afghan soldiers and police in position on the ground and training them to secure their own country.

But by the middle of May, the Taliban struck back. From the Sangin district of Helmand Province, they launched hundreds of IED attacks and, in five weeks of bitter hostilities, twenty-four British solders were killed and dozens more injured.

At the same time, ISAF launched the latest major military operation in Helmand Province – Tor Shezada. Led by 1st Battalion, The Duke of Lancaster's Regiment, backed up by the ANA's 3rd Brigade, 215 Corps, the primary aim of the operation was to capitalise on the work of Operation Moshtarak, pushing the Taliban out of the region and restoring government leadership.

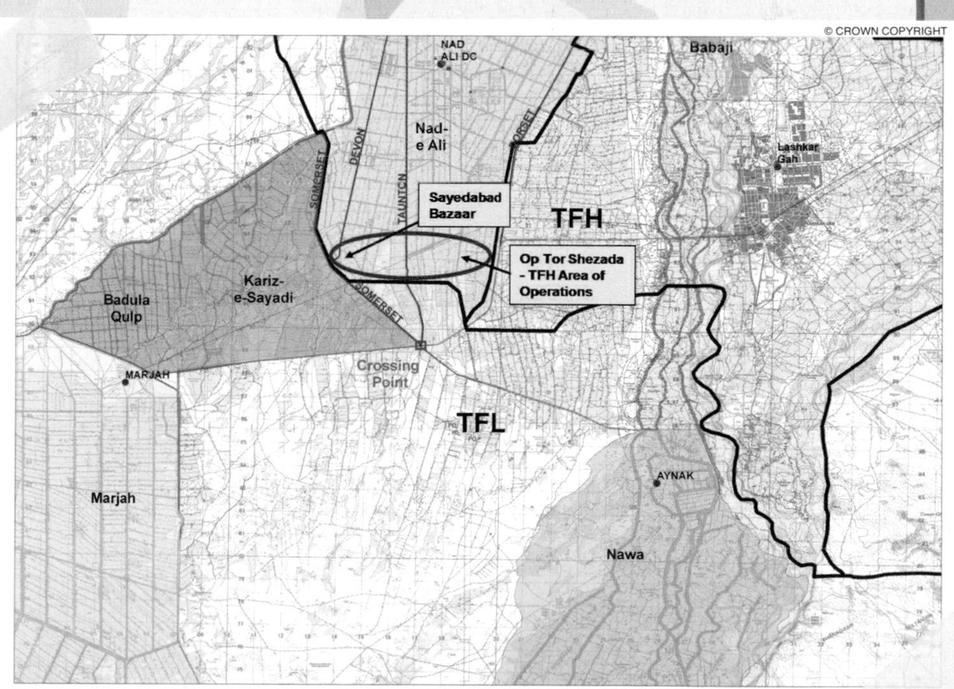

Op Tor Shezada area of operations.

The town of Saidabad was the operation's main target. Situated in central Helmand, between Nad'Ali and Marjah, this once relatively peaceful place had become increasingly dangerous; a highly corrupt police force, an abusive local government and the growing presence of insurgents had all taken their toll on battle-weary residents. After the response to Operation Moshtarak, it was crucial that troops break the power of some 200 insurgents who used Saidabad as a base while they encouraged locals to join the fight against the British military.

As the operation launched, hundreds of British and Afghan Forces made their way to Saidabad. The Brigade Reconnaissance Force (BRF) led the attack. This elite unit launched an assault from the air, deep into insurgent territory.

Previous attempts to enter had been met with strong resistance, however this time troops faced little opposition. The enemy remained at a safe distance from the battlefield, though they left a grim reminder of their presence in the area: IEDs peppering the town had to be carefully searched out and dismantled.

In a welcome development, the entire operation was completed without British casualties and the inserted troops were able to establish patrol bases to ensure that the newly cleared areas were kept free of Taliban fighters.

Before the op, the BRF's commander, Major Marcus Mudd, had stressed to his soldiers the importance of winning over the civilian population of Saidabad. He also warned them to be careful: 'If we fail to protect the population, we will fail in our mission.'

And certainly it seems that Tor Shezada has conformed to this injunction.

But wars of insurgency and 'hearts and minds' initiatives are seldom so clear-cut. While soldiers tour the region's residents, polling their views of the ISAF effort on their behalf, the potential remains for miscommunication and misunderstanding across languages, cultures and experiences. For instance, the Afghan culture of hospitality insists that locals make the troops feel welcome, even when they might not be, which makes gauging a genuine response to the operation all but impossible. Even as many Afghans insist they are happy to see ISAF soldiers, they admit that if given a choice between the deeply corrupt Afghan National Police (ANP) and the insurgents, they would prefer the latter.

And while the relative ease of the operation, in military terms, has allowed soldiers to adopt a more culturally sensitive approach in their interactions with locals, the potential for insult – in a country where to walk uninvited into the presence of women is profoundly taboo – is enormous.

So how to measure success in a murky world where it is almost impossible to gauge the long-term results of an operation that, from a military point of view, could not have gone more smoothly?

In the wake of Tor Shezada, most of the towns and villages in the area are no longer under direct Taliban control. However, civilians insist that the insurgents are still operating as close as two kilometres away.

An officer issues orders as US marines advance against Taliban on the northeast of Marjah.

Their security concerns are exacerbated by the knowledge that troops will likely be withdrawn in the coming years.

In July 2010, military chiefs announced that British Forces would be pulling out of the now notorious Sangin district and handing control of the area to the Americans. In four years of fighting, the tiny area known as the Valley of Death has left an indelible mark on the British. One in three of all troops killed in the war in Afghanistan died in Sangin. At the time of writing, over a hundred men have lost their lives there.

Recently, British Prime Minister David Cameron said that British troops might withdraw entirely from Afghanistan as early as 2011, depending on conditions on the ground. As a result, many residents of Saidabad believe that force is not the best way to deal with the crisis in their region.

Long-term, however, commanders hope that the operation will allow a safe environment in which to launch development projects in the region, such the refurbishment of health clinics and the Saidabad school, as well as the town's bazaar.

As more troops continue to be transferred to the area, whether the British military have won over the people of Helmand remains to be seen. And yet one thing is certain: in a war which continues to divide opinion at home, the bravery of the men and women on the ground remains the keystone of our efforts in that country.

Brigadier James Cowan addressing ISAF troops prior to the commencement of Operation Moshtarak.

Brigadier James Cowan, the Commander of 11th Light Brigade, spoke to his troops – including soldiers from Australia, Canada, the United States, France and Estonia who are partnering with the Afghan National Security Forces – at Camp Bastion prior to Operation Moshtarak

'We stand here today as partners. In the past few weeks we have trained to be a combined force.

'Soon we will be part of an operation the like of which has not been seen since the start of this campaign: Operation Moshtarak, or, in English, "Together". I can think of no better name to describe this venture. For we are in this together: we have planned it together, we will fight it together, we will see it through together. Afghans with Allies, soldiers with civilians, government with its people.

'In the last few weeks we have seized the initiative from the enemy. Day after day for six weeks we have killed and captured the enemy's leaders, shaping the conditions for success. Soon we will clear the Taliban from its safe havens in central Helmand. Where we go, we will stay. Where we stay, we will build. We will establish security so that the people are free once more to live their own lives under their own government.

'The next few days will not be without danger. To reduce the risks, you must know your enemy. Avoid the places they would expect you to go. Stay off the tracks. Check vulnerable areas before you enter them. Watch out for propaganda traps. Be first with the truth.

'Above all else, protect the people. Defeat the enemy by avoiding civilian casualties. Hold your fire if there is risk to the innocent, even if this puts you in greater danger. That kind of restraint requires courage – the courageous restraint you have shown throughout our time in Afghanistan.

'Offer an open hand in friendship to those who do not wish to fight. They can join the people of Afghanistan and their government in rebuilding their society. For those who will not shake our hand they will find it closed into a fist. They will be defeated.

'With my Afghan friends, I am proud to be one of your commanders. Together, Operation Moshtarak will mark the start of the end of the insurgency. I wish you god speed and the best of luck.'

BRAVEST OF THE BRAVE

PRIVATE JOHNSON BEHARRY

Beharry on duty in Iraq, before the ambush.

Private Johnson Beharry is the most highly decorated serving soldier in the British Army – and is responsible for a legendary act of gallantry.

The Grenada-born soldier of 1st Battalion, The Princess of Wales's Royal Regiment showed incredible grit to save his comrades not once but twice after they were ambushed in Iraq.

On 1 May 2004, Private Beharry was the lead driver in a patrol of Warrior armoured vehicles rolling through lawless Al Amarah.

Suddenly the patrol was ambushed and a hail of machine-gun fire and Rocket-Propelled Grenades (RPGs) poured onto the vehicles.

Beharry's vehicle was engulfed in a number of violent explosions which physically rocked the 30-tonne Warrior.

As a result of this ferocious initial volley of fire, the platoon commander was knocked out cold, presumed dead, and the gunner was wounded and burning in the turret.

Due to damage sustained to the vehicle's radio systems, Beharry had no means of communication with either his turret crew or any of the other Warriors in his patrol.

He did not know if his commander or crewmen were still alive, nor how serious their injuries might be.

In this confusing and dangerous situation, he closed his driver's hatch and moved forward through the ambush position to try to establish some form of communication.

The vehicle was hit again by sustained RPG attack, causing it to catch fire and fill rapidly with thick, noxious smoke.

Private Beharry opened the armoured hatch to try to clear the smoke, only for another RPG to smash the hatch right out of his hand, simultaneously destroying the vehicle's armoured periscope.

He was forced to drive the vehicle through the remainder of the ambushed route, some 1,500 metres long, with the hatch open and his head exposed to enemy fire.

During this long surge through the ambush, the vehicle was again struck by RPGs and small arms' fire.

Beharry was directly exposed to the enemy fire and was hit by a 7.26mm bullet, which penetrated his helmet.

Despite the harrowing weight of incoming fire, Beharry continued to push on, and led the convoy to the British base in the centre of town.

There he climbed on to the turret of his burning vehicle, oblivious to enemy fire, to rescue his platoon commander. He then returned for the gunner and yet again for the soldiers in the back, before driving the burning Warrior away so it would not fall into enemy hands.

Private Johnson Beharry VC returned to visit his Warrior after his recovery.

Only then did Beharry collapse from the sheer physical and mental exhaustion of his efforts. He was subsequently evacuated.

But that was not the end of his outstanding bravery.

Just five weeks later, on 11 June 2004, Beharry was once more leading his convoy through the town of Al Amarah when his Warrior was ambushed a second time.

An RPG struck the vehicle just inches from Beharry's head, causing severe shrapnel injuries to his brain and face, while multiple rockets assaulted the vehicle.

Wounded, with bone splinters in his brain and his eyes filled with blood, Beharry still drove eight comrades from the 1st Battalion, The Princess of Wales's Royal Regiment to safety. He then fell into a coma and was rescued by comrades. At hospital, he required brain surgery for his head injuries.

Beharry survived but, despite his desire to, has never been able to return to active service. His citation read: 'Private Beharry carried out two individual acts of great heroism by which he saved the lives of his comrades. Both were in direct face of the enemy, under intense fire, at great personal risk to himself (one leading to him sustaining very serious injuries) … Beharry displayed repeated extreme gallantry and unquestioned valour, despite intense direct attacks, personal injury and damage to his vehicle in the face of relentless enemy action.'

He has since been promoted to the rank of lance corporal.

By David Willetts

Private Johnson Beharry's helmet showing where the bullet entered.

Between 1858 and 1881 the Victoria Cross could be awarded for actions taken 'under circumstances of extreme danger' not in the face of the enemy. In 1881, the criteria were changed and the VC became available only for acts of valour 'in the face of the enemy'. As a result of this change in criteria and the increasing prevalence of remote fighting techniques, it has been suggested that in future fewer VCs will be awarded. Since 1940, military personnel who have distinguished themselves for gallantry not in the face of the enemy have been awarded the George Cross, which ranks immediately after the VC in the Order of Wear.

ALEXANDER DUNCAN

MAY, 2008, AFGHANISTAN. THE START OF A VITAL MISSION TO TRANSPORT GULAB MANGAL, GOVERNOR OF HELMAND PROVINCE, BACK TO THE PROVINCIAL CAPITAL LASHKAR GAH.

A CHINOOK FROM 27 SQUADRON RAF LOADS UP.

THEY FLY LOW TO AVOID BEING SPOTTED...
...BUT SOMETHING SPEEDS TOWARDS THEM.
THEY ARE OVER TALIBAN TERRITORY...
DUNCAN TURNS THE CHINOOK TO GIVE HIS MACHINEGUNNER A CHANCE TO FIRE.
BUT THE INSURGENTS BLAZE AWAY...
BWHOOM!
...AND A ROCKET STREAKS TOWARDS THEM.
WE'RE HIT!
OH S***, WE'RE GOING IN.
BUT THE CONTROLS STILL RESPOND.
RIGHT! WE'RE GETTING OUT OF HERE!
IF MANGAL DIES THE TALIBAN WILL HAVE WON A PROPAGANDA COUP.

ANOTHER REASON TO KEEP THE CHINOOK SWERVING THROUGH THE LEAD-FILLED SKY.
BRANG!
BWRANG!!
CHOOM!

SPEEDING OVER A RIDGE THE CHINOOK NEARLY HITS A COMMS MAST.
@*$!! THAT WAS CLOSE!

STILL IN TALIBAN TERRITORY, THEY CAN'T LAND DESPITE THE DAMAGE - INSURGENTS WOULD LIKELY KILL THEM.
THEY MUST CARRY ON TO THE BRITISH BASE NEAR MUSA QALEH.

AFTER 30 MINUTES OF NERVE-SHREDDING FLYING...

SHUP
SHUP
SHUP

...BOTH AFGHAN OFFICIALS AND RAF CREW ARE **SAFE** AT LAST.

WHOOOOMPH
WOOOOMPH

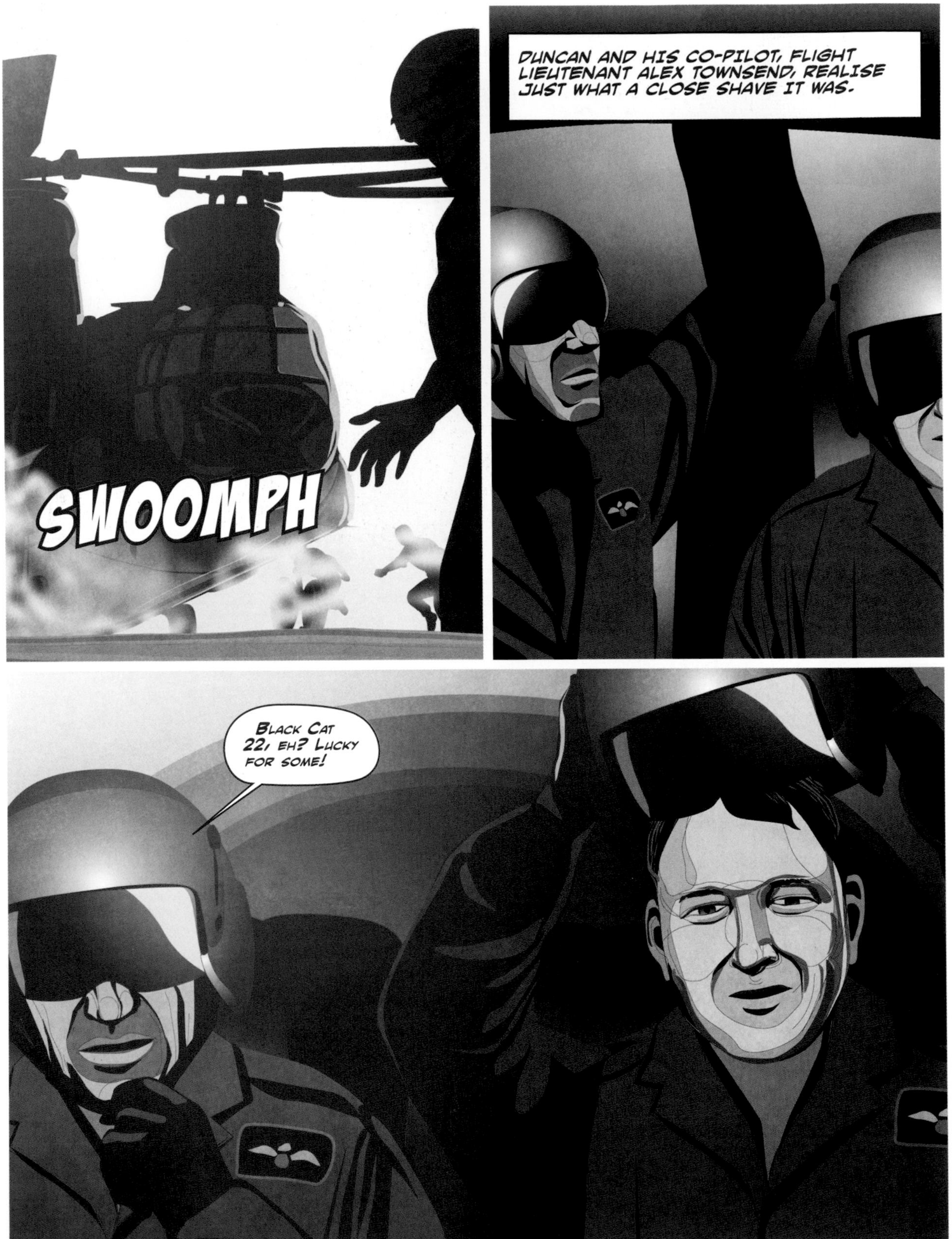

BLACK CAT 22, EH? LUCKY FOR SOME!

AND THEY ARE LUCKIER THAN THEY KNOW - THE TALIBAN ROCKET WENT STRAIGHT THROUGH THE CHINOOK'S REAR ROTOR BLADE WITHOUT DETONATING.

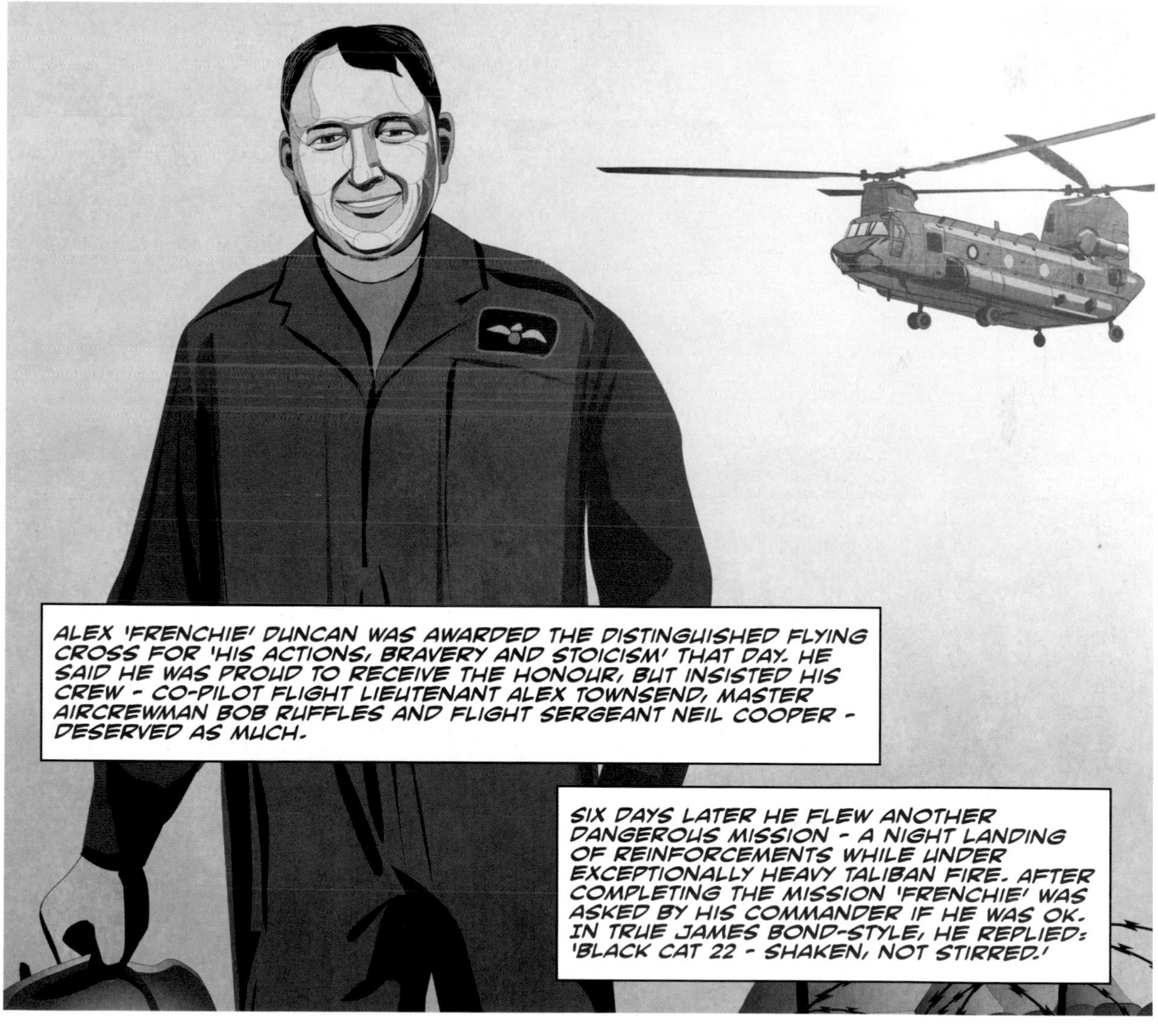

ALEX 'FRENCHIE' DUNCAN WAS AWARDED THE DISTINGUISHED FLYING CROSS FOR 'HIS ACTIONS, BRAVERY AND STOICISM' THAT DAY. HE SAID HE WAS PROUD TO RECEIVE THE HONOUR, BUT INSISTED HIS CREW - CO-PILOT FLIGHT LIEUTENANT ALEX TOWNSEND, MASTER AIRCREWMAN BOB RUFFLES AND FLIGHT SERGEANT NEIL COOPER - DESERVED AS MUCH.

SIX DAYS LATER HE FLEW ANOTHER DANGEROUS MISSION - A NIGHT LANDING OF REINFORCEMENTS WHILE UNDER EXCEPTIONALLY HEAVY TALIBAN FIRE. AFTER COMPLETING THE MISSION 'FRENCHIE' WAS ASKED BY HIS COMMANDER IF HE WAS OK. IN TRUE JAMES BOND-STYLE, HE REPLIED: 'BLACK CAT 22 - SHAKEN, NOT STIRRED.'

THE WORKHORSES

A fleet of sturdy vehicles provides vital aid to the troops on the ground. Platoons of support vehicles are regularly deployed to transport not only soldiers, but also building materials, water, fuel and other essential supplies to and from base. Below are just a few of these tough-as-nails workhorses on whose humble efforts so many lives depend.

CLOSE SUPPORT TANKER

The Oshkosh Wheeled Tanker is a highly mobile vehicle that is deployed in the logistic support regiments and transport regiments and forms the backbone of the British Army's bulk fuel and water transportation. It has been deployed on operations in Iraq and Afghanistan and can be fitted with enhanced blast-proof armour for driver and crew protection.

Oshkosh Wheeled Tankers come in three variants:

- a 15,000-litre Tactical Air Refueller
- a 20,000-litre Close Support Tanker (Fuel)
- a 18,000-litre Close Support Tanker (Water)

In Helmand, the tankers travel in the combat logistic patrols that ensure that the soldiers who man the FOBs across the province are fully supported with essential kit and equipment.

The patrols see upwards of 500 tons of food, water, fuel, ammunition, building materials and engineering supplies moved out to the FOBs across Helmand Province, as well as the all-important post sent from home.

SPRINGER

The Springer is a multipurpose all-terrain vehicle which is extremely mobile and agile. In Afghanistan it is specifically used for moving combat supplies from helicopter landing sites to the forward operating bases.

The small two-seater vehicles carry a crew of two and can recover loads of up to three-quarters of a ton in weight. The Springer has been designed specifically for rugged, desert conditions and is well-matched to the operational environment in Afghanistan. It is the first vehicle of its kind to be used by British Forces in theatre and has been ordered specifically for its role in Afghanistan.

QUAD BIKE

Quad bikes and trailers are being used on front-line operations in Afghanistan to deliver vital combat supplies to troops on the ground. Together with purpose-built trailers, the quad bikes are used to deliver food, water and ammunition to the front line in difficult-to-access areas, or where larger vehicles are not suitable, effectively running alongside those who are on dismounted operations.

The quad bikes can reach speeds of up to 75 kmph and can carry up to almost 160kg with the trailer attached. They can operate in water up to half their wheel height.

A dual stretcher fit-on trailer also allows the bikes to be used for the swift simultaneous evacuation of up to two casualties from the battlefield, thereby speeding up emergency aid.

Operators using the all-terrain quad bikes are protected by wearing Osprey body armour and Mk 6 helmets.

DEMOUNTABLE RACK OFFLOAD AND PICKUP SYSTEM (DROPS)

Demountable Rack Offload and Pickup System vehicles (DROPS) form the logistic backbone of the British Army. The eight-wheeled DROPS vehicles are capable of carrying loads of up to 15 tons and loading and unloading them in seconds.

Travelling in combat logistic patrols, the DROPS vehicles are used to supply essential equipment and supplies to the soldiers who man the FOBs across Helmand Province.

DROPS include two types of vehicle – the Leyland Medium Mobility Load Carrier (MMLC), and the Foden Improved Medium Mobility Load Carrier (IMMLC). Both have the ability to tow a long-wheelbase trailer. This is a force multiplier as it means the vehicle can carry two loads using only one driver.

Both MMLC and IMMLC are 8 x 6 load carriers with a 15-ton flatrack payload, allowing the rapid loading and unloading of flatracks or containers. IMMLC is used primarily as an ammunition carrier in support of AS90 155mm self-propelled guns. MMLC operates solo or towing a skeleton trailer.

CORPORAL RONNIE GREGORY

Age	25
Hometown	Glasgow
Unit	RMP/1RGR

What was your best day?
I am currently working with A Company, 1 RGR, so my best day so far was being introduced to my new Gurkha family who really looked after me and made me feel at home.

What was your hardest day?
My hardest day so far was 13 July 2010, when A Company sadly lost three extremely brave soldiers who will never be forgotten.

What do you miss most when away from home?
A glass of ice-cold Irn-Bru.

What is the best thing about being in the military?
Travelling and making new friends wherever you go, like my Gurkha family.

What is your job and what do you do?
I am currently serving in the Royal Military Police. My job is to go out on patrol with the battle group, assisting and advising on detainee handling, forensic awareness and biometric data collection.

What is your favourite bit of kit and why?
My favourite bits of kit are my MP3 player and nail varnish for my toes! The MP3 player because no matter how bad a day you're having, listening to your favourite song always makes you feel better. The nail varnish because when you're surrounded by so many guys all the time it's nice to feel a little bit girly!

Who do you most admire/who is your hero?
My mum is my hero, she is an amazing woman and my best friend.

What food do you eat and cook?
Being with the Gurkhas, the boys prepare all of the food. We have goat or chicken curries mostly; rice is also a big part of their diet.

What are your toilet facilities like? How often do you get to have a proper shower/bath?
They are pretty basic; we have to go in bags which are later burned. However, we do have a shower tent so I manage to have a proper shower at least once a day.

How do you wash your clothes?
We wash our clothes in a cement mixer, which works really well.

How heavy is your equipment and what do you have to carry?
My kit is fairly heavy. I carry evidence kit, biometric kit and detainee handling kit. On top of this, I will carry water, rations and spare ammunition.

FALLEN HEROES

In July 2010, three British soldiers – Lieutenant Neal Turkington from Northern Ireland, Major James Joshua Bowman from Wiltshire, and Corporal Arjun Purja Pun from Nepal – were killed in Nahr-e Saraj, Helmand, by a renegade Afghan soldier. The men were serving with 1st Battalion, The Royal Gurkha Rifles. Four other soldiers were injured in the attack.

Major Bowman's commanding officer, Lieutenant Colonel Gerald Strickland, MBE, said: 'Our Battalion has lost a brave leader. Major Josh Bowman commanded A Company with a rare determination. The tragedy of his loss is beyond words.' A hugely popular soldier, Corporal Arjun Purja Pun was described as 'the consummate professional; intelligent, determined and brave.' The youngest of the three men killed was Lieutenant Turkington, aged twenty-six. Captain John Jeffcoat of The Royal Gurkha Rifles said the lieutenant had loved his men as much as they loved him, and enjoyed 'every single moment of leading his men through thick and thin'.

LIFE ON THE FOB

For many servicemen and women on operation in Afghanistan, the reality of battle has less to do with the ordered life of Camp Bastion than with the rough-and-ready conditions and relentless hardships of life on the forward operating bases (FOBs).

FOBs are temporary bases used to support tactical military operations, often set up in existing compounds that have been abandoned or that are rented from local Afghans. It can be difficult to find a local resident willing to rent a property though – many are too frightened of Taliban reprisals to want to deal with the coalition forces, even when relatively large sums of money are on offer.

At the FOBs, troops sleep on the floor or, if they're lucky, in cots. They must be careful to store their boots off the ground at night as Afghanistan is home to all manner of creepy-crawlies, including a breed of scorpion which can kill in fourteen minutes and likes to climb into soldiers' boots during the night.

Food is supplied in ration packs, mostly in boil-in-the-bag form. There is often little to no fresh food available, and on longer ops the cooks struggle heroically to stretch some variety out of the ration packs. Troops often resort to buying whatever they can from locals – whether it's fresh vegetables or even the odd goat.

The troops are supplied with bottled water, but if this runs out before it can be resupplied, they drink whatever warm water they can find, which they must treat with chlorine tablets to prevent infection.

British soldiers of 3 Rifles work out in their improvised gym at FOB Jackson.

3 Rifles Battlegroup based at Patrol Base Airport Lounge near Sangin.

A British soldier relaxes in his accommodation at FOB Sangin.

Hygiene is a constant concern. Troops on the move use 'wag bags', but even at more established bases latrines are often little more than plywood planks suspended over stinking holes in the ground, permanently surrounded by clouds of flies. Despite rigorous hygiene regimes, there are frequent cases of 'D & V' – diarrhoea and vomiting – which can cripple a fort's fighting strength.

FOBs frequently come under fire, making it vitally important that the troops remain protected at all times. The roof of the FOB is frequently made into an observation point. If the troops plan to be in position for long, they will construct a grid of 'sangars' – lookout posts made of sandbags – to protect big guns and snipers.

The relentless heat, basic conditions, constant strain of incoming fire and daily, nerve-wracking patrols make life on FOBs a gruelling challenge for the men and women of the British Armed Forces.

An Afghan man leaves his family home after it was bought out by Coalition Forces.

A five-mile-long convoy that travelled from Camp Bastion to re-supply coalition bases in the Sangin Valley.

Body armour and helmets belonging to members of Recce Platoon.

British soldiers of 3 Rifles enjoy some downtime together watching DVDs in a communal room at their patrol base.

British soldiers of 3 Rifles play volley-ball with their interpreters and counterparts at FOB Blenhein.

BRAVEST OF THE BRAVE

CAPTAIN CHARLES HAZLITT UPHAM

Captain Charles Hazlitt Upham was a New Zealand soldier and one of only three to have ever been twice recognised with a VC, and so been awarded the VC and Bar. The captain in the 20th Canterbury-Otago Battalion of the 2nd New Zealand Expeditionary Force won his first VC in Crete in May 1941 when he was a second lieutenant. At the head of his platoon, Upham fought his way forward for over 3,000 yards unsupported by any other arms. During this operation, Upham's platoon successfully destroyed a number of enemy posts. When one of his sections was held up by

⮜Upham as a POW took delight in making life difficult for his captors.

⮝New Zealand's most celebrated war hero, Captain Charles Upham, is pictured in battle dress after the campaigns of Greece and Crete.

two machine guns firing from a nearby house, Upham placed a grenade through a window, destroying the crew of one of the guns as well as several others. He also carried a wounded man to safety under fire and rallied further men to help others who were injured. His citation declared that 'this officer performed a series of remarkable exploits, showing outstanding leadership, tactical skill and utter indifference to danger.'

Upham, now promoted to the rank of captain, won his second VC during 1942 after his actions in Egypt. Twice wounded – once when crossing open ground swept by enemy fire to inspect forward sections guarding Allied minefields, and again when he completely destroyed an entire truck load of German soldiers with hand grenades – he insisted on staying with his men to take part in the final assault. Upham then destroyed a German tank and, although he had been shot, took up a forward position and brought back a number of his men. As soon as his own wound was dressed, he returned to his men and stayed with them for the whole day under enemy fire and was severely wounded once more.

He was later taken prisoner of war, but survived to live into old age, dying in 1994. He is the only combat soldier ever to have received the VC and Bar.

By David Willetts

Upham in old age.

Commander-in-Chief General Claude Auchinleck speaks to Upham after the presentation of his first VC.

There is a widespread myth that all ranks must salute a bearer of the Victoria Cross. There is no official requirement to this effect, but tradition dictates that this occurs and the chiefs of staff will often salute a private who has been awarded a VC or GC.

BROTHERS IN ARMS
THE AFGHAN NATIONAL ARMY

In the fight against the Taliban, victory cannot be achieved without strategic co-operation between the coalition nations. So British troops and ISAF have been working closely with the Afghan National Army (ANA), a branch of the Afghan military, in order to defeat the insurgents. The ANA, under its chief of staff Lieutenant General Sher Mohammad Karimi, is currently being trained by the coalition forces to take part in land-based military operations in Afghanistan and has approximately 120,000 active troops as of May 2010, a figure which is expected to rise to over 170,000 by autumn 2011, as coalition forces prepare to leave the country.

HISTORY

The ANA was established in the 1880s, prior to which it was a combination of tribesmen and militia forces. It was trained and equipped by the Soviet Union from the 1960s to the early 1990s until the Taliban came to power in 1996 and dismantled the ANA. After the Taliban were removed from power in 2001, the ANA in its current form was established with the help of the USA and other NATO nations.

WEAPONS

Since 2002, the ANA has been provided with both financial and military support, from NATO countries. They have been given hi-tech weaponry including 4,500 High Mobility Multipurpose Wheeled Vehicles (Humvees), over 100,000 M16 assault rifles, M249 squad automatic weapons, M203 grenade launchers and M240 B machine guns. A national command centre is also being constructed, with bases across the country, and thousands of army trainers from NATO countries including the UK have provided advance warfare training to the members of the ANA.

An ANA soldier looks on during an operation with British soldiers of F Company (Fire Support) 1 Royal Welsh during Operation Moshtarak.

REPORT ON EQUIPMENT DONATIONS

RH/01/01

AFGHANISTAN / NATO SINCE 2006

© REUTERS / STRINGER
An ANA soldier surveys the effects of an attack by the Taliban.

Bulgaria	50 mortars, 21 million rounds of small arms ammunition, 500 binoculars
Canada	2,500 small arms, 6 million rounds of ammunition and equipment
Czech Republic	12 helicopters (attack and utility)
Estonia	4,300 small arms, 5 million rounds of ammunition
Finland	1,400 field telephones, 60 generators
France	personal equipment
Germany	clothing and equipment
Hungary	21,000 small arms, 150,000 rounds of ammunition
Lithuania	4 million rounds of small arms ammunition
Luxembourg	2,000 body armour kits, 2,000 helmets
Montenegro	1,600 small arms, 250,000 rounds of ammunition
NATO	heaters, cargo nets
Norway	100 field weapons, 100 mortars, 400,000 rounds of ammunition
Poland	uniforms, 4 million rounds of ammunition, weapon spare parts
Slovenia	60 mortars, 10,000 small arms, 2.2 million rounds of ammunition, Compact 200 Bridge, tools, equipment & training
Switzerland	3 fire trucks, spares, medical equipment
Turkey	24 howitzers, ammunition, clothing equipment, academy supplies

Transportation for the above equipment donations was facilitated by the following countries: Canada, Denmark, Finland, France, Germany, Iceland, Luxembourg, Norway, Slovenia, the United Kingdom, the United States.

Source: NATO. Accurate as of April 2010.

© SSGT MARK JONES / AFP / GETTY IMAGES

STRUCTURE

The ANA is divided into seven combat corps which are deployed throughout the country. These are the 201st Corps in Kabul, the 203rd Corps in Gardez, the 205th Corps in Kandahar, the 207th Corps in Herat, the 209th Corps in Mazar-e-Sharif, the 215th Corps in Lashkar Gah and the ANA Air Corps.

OPERATIONS

The ANA has formed a crucial part of several major operations in Afghanistan, including the Battle of Musa Qaleh, which the ANA and ISAF Forces retook after the town spent ten months in the hands of the Taliban; Operation Panther's Claw, which targeted members of the Taliban who were involved in the drug trade; and Operation Khanjar, an ongoing US-led offensive in southern Helmand Province.

An Afghan National Army soldier in Camp Bastion.

Sgt Ajab Han, an IED expert with the ANA demonstrates how to spot an IED.

WORKING TOGETHER

The alliance with the ANA is making a difference on the ground every day.

Ajab Han, a sergeant in the Afghan National Army working with British troops from 1st Battalion, The Royal Regiment of Scotland (1 SCOTS) at a patrol base in the Sangin Valley, has found 177 IEDs during his three years in Helmand.

'I know where they put them now,' said Sergeant Ajab. 'It helps to know the terrain. I can also think like the insurgents, stay one step ahead of them, and keep my soldiers and ISAF soldiers safe. But we can make it better.'

While detecting equipment is very useful, he says just staying alert can be equally effective. 'I can just see them,' he said. 'There might be a telltale trace, or something just not quite right, or a piece of wire or wood showing, and that is when I know I have found another one. IEDs often come in many parts so we have to find all the bits in the ground,' he added.

His successes are etched on a beam on a watchtower next to the place where he sleeps, along with his army number and the description 'IED Team Sangin Special Force' written in English.

Captain Will Wright, the platoon commander from the 1 SCOTS mentoring team, said, 'Patrolling with the ANA gives us such an advantage. They see things we sometimes don't, they are brave beyond words, and we learn so much from them every day.'

Members of the 1st Batalion The Royal Welsh's Fire Support Group negotiate with an Afghan tribal elder near Shawala.

FUTURE

The current goal of the Afghan Ministry of Defence is to expand the ANA to about 260,000 troops at a cost of $20 billion. This is

ANA soldiers heavily armed on a joint patrol with British soldiers of 3 Rifles, near to the town of Sangin.

supported by US President Barack Obama. All costs of expansion of the military, including pay and new, modern equipment, will be paid for by the American government. The quality of troops has also improved considerably since the ANA was set up, with 90–95 per cent of troops graduating from basic training passing a weapon qualification test.

British Secretary of State William Hague said, 'The NATO objective in Afghanistan is simple – to assist the Government of Afghanistan in exercising its authority and influence across the country, paving the way for reconstruction and effective governance. This requires the protection of the population, the provision of more effective governance at every level, and the creation of an Afghan Security Force able to maintain security. This is the strategy that UK forces are helping to implement, through their training and partnering of Afghan troops, and their efforts to create the opportunity for more effective local governance in Central Helmand.'

ANA soldiers attached to US Army B Company, 2nd Battalion, 12th Infantry Regiment guard the Korengal outpost.

The ANA aren't the only ones fighting alongside British troops. The Afghan National Army Air Corps (ANAAC) and the Afghan National Police (ANP) also play their part...

ANAAC

Current Strength: 2,876 men and women, plus 34 rotary-wing and 12 fixed-wing aircraft

Target Strength: 8,000+ personnel and 152 rotary and fixed-wing aircraft by December 2016

Capacity: Flew 90 per cent of ANA air support missions in 2009 (compared to 10 per cent in mid-2008).

ANP

Current Strength: 104,459

Target Strength: 109,000 by October 2010; 134,000 by October 2011

Primary organisations include:
- Afghan Uniformed Police: 81,842
- Afghan Border Police: 14,494
- Afghan National Civil Order Police: 3,964
- Afghan Counter-Narcotics Police: 2,695

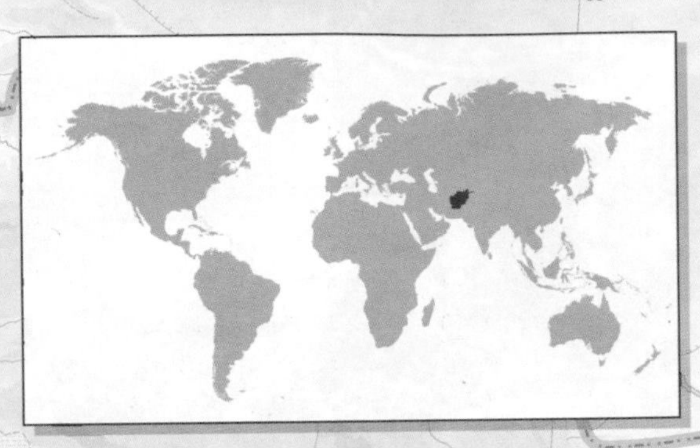

AFGHANISTAN

Conventional long form: Islamic Republic of Afghanistan

Conventional short form: Afghanistan

Local long form: *Jomhuri-ye Eslami-ye Afghanestan*

Local short form: Afghanestan

Formerly called: Republic of Afghanistan

Flag: Three equal vertical stripes of black, red and green, with the national emblem in white centred on the red band. The central emblem shows a mosque and minaret with flags on either side. Below the mosque are numerals for the solar year 1298 (1919 in the Gregorian calendar, the year of Afghan independence from the UK). The image is bordered by a circle consisting of sheaves of wheat on the left and right, and in the upper centre is an Arabic inscription of the Shahada (the Muslim creed). Below this are rays of the rising sun over the Takbir (an Arabic expression meaning 'God is great'). At lower centre is a scroll bearing the word 'Afghanistan'.

TAJIKISTAN
EKISTAN
CHINA
BALKH
Mazār-e Sharīf
QONDUZ
Qonduz
Tāloqān
TAKHĀR
Feyzābād
BADAKHSHĀN
Āybak
SAMANGĀN
Pol-e Khomrī
BAGHLĀN
PANJSHIR
Bāzārak
NŪRESTĀN
Nūrestān
KUNAR
PARWĀN
KAPISĀ
Chārīkār
Maḩmūd-e Rāqī
LAGHMĀN
BĀMĪĀN
Bāmīān
Asadābād
KĀBUL
Mehtar Lām
Meydān Shahr
KĀBUL
Jalālābād
WARDAG
NANGARHĀR
LOWGAR
TAN
Pol-e 'Alam
Gardēz
Ghaznī
PAKTĪĀ
KHOWST
GHAZNĪ
Khowst
Sharan
PAKTĪKĀ
BUL
Kalāt
PAKISTAN

© EROS HOAGLAND / THE TIMES

A British officer on mounted patrol in Afghanistan.

Altitude
Metres / Feet
6000 / 19686
5000 / 16404
4000 / 13124
3000 / 9843
2000 / 6562
1000 / 3281
500 / 1640
200 / 656
0 / 0

International Boundary
Province Boundary

Miles
0 50 100
Kilometres
0 50 100 150 200

LANCE CORPORAL CHRIS WALTON

Age	22
Hometown	Blackpool
Unit	1 LANCS

What is your job and what do you do?
Section 2iC at a patrol base – I act as guard commander and look after the Kingsmen's admin and I act as the platoon sergeant's right-hand man – helping him out with tasks.

What is your favourite bit of kit and why?
My favourite bit of kit is the platoon weapons we have: the SA 80 (Rifle), UGL (Underslung Grenade Launcher), LWMG (Lightweight Machine Gun). They are good bits of kit and really reliable.

What is your favourite sport/and or sports team?
Football and badminton. I play for my local team and support Blackpool FC.

What do you miss most when away from home?
Food, family and mates.

What is the best thing about being in the military?
The unique experience, it's something you'd never do at home.

Who do you most admire/who is your hero?
My mum.

How heavy is your equipment and what do you have to carry?
It's probably between 60kgs and 70kgs, depending on what we are doing. As section 2iC you carry extra kit, like ladders or extra ammo.

SA 80

The SA 80 series are selective fire, gas-operated firearms. When introduced, these weapons proved so accurate that the Armed Forces' marksmanship tests had to be redesigned.

The British Armed Forces' standard combat weapon is the SA 80 A2, which is made up of the Individual Weapon and the Light Support Weapon. These fire NATO-standard 5.56 mm x 45 mm ammunition. The rifle has a forward-mounted pistol grip in keeping with a 'bullpup' layout, so the action and magazine are located behind the trigger and next to the firer's face. Soldiers with a dismounted close-combat role use rifles equipped with SUSAT (Sight Unit Small Arms, Trilux) optical sight with a 4 x magnification and an illuminated aiming pointer. The SA 80 A2 can also be fitted with an Underslung Grenade Launcher system. The SA 80 A2 is the most reliable weapon of its type in the world; they are dependable, accurate and highly versatile.

MILITARY MAPPING
A Brief History

'We are not fit to lead an army on the march unless we are familiar with the face of the country – its mountains and forests, its pitfalls and precipices, its marshes and swamps.'

So wrote the great military tactician Sun Tzu in 500 BC. Since ancient times, military leaders have known that mastery of the landscape is vital to victory. Armies on the move need to know which routes present the least danger, where they can safely set up camp and where they are likely to find fresh water and supplies. In battle, the troops who know where their enemy lies and which features are likely to present obstacles to an attack are far more likely to carry the day.

Today, armed forces on the front line benefit from cutting-edge technology that can provide rapid and accurate information about the landscape. Satellites beam down information from cameras and sensors, and computer programmes generate 3-D models that help soldiers prepare for combat.

But these are merely the latest in a long line of cartographic developments that have been driven by military need. Defence or conquest, the policing of a territory, decisions as to where to garrison troops or lay down lines of communication – each of these military considerations relies implicitly on detailed, accurate mapping.

Some of the earliest military maps in Britain, dating back 500 years, were the result of military anxiety. In the time of Henry VIII, England's coastline, in particular its harbours, was seen as extremely susceptible to enemy attacks and so was amongst the first areas of the country to be properly charted.

By the latter part of the eighteenth century, much of Britain had been surveyed but often only on a local basis, with funding for the maps coming from subscriptions. These maps were not suitable for military purposes as they were lacking in essential relief data, while the scales used were far too small to be useful for engineers in the field. The Jacobite rebellions in Scotland and the recurring threat of French invasion meant the need for an accurate, national survey which could support military operations was of great national importance. The Duke of Cumberland and his generals who led the government forces against the Jacobite rebels were said to have been 'greatly embarrassed for the want of a proper Survey of the Country'. As a result, in 1746, King George II authorised a military map of Scotland to be drawn. This was intended to help prevent further uprisings in that country. The principal surveyor on the project, William Roy, would

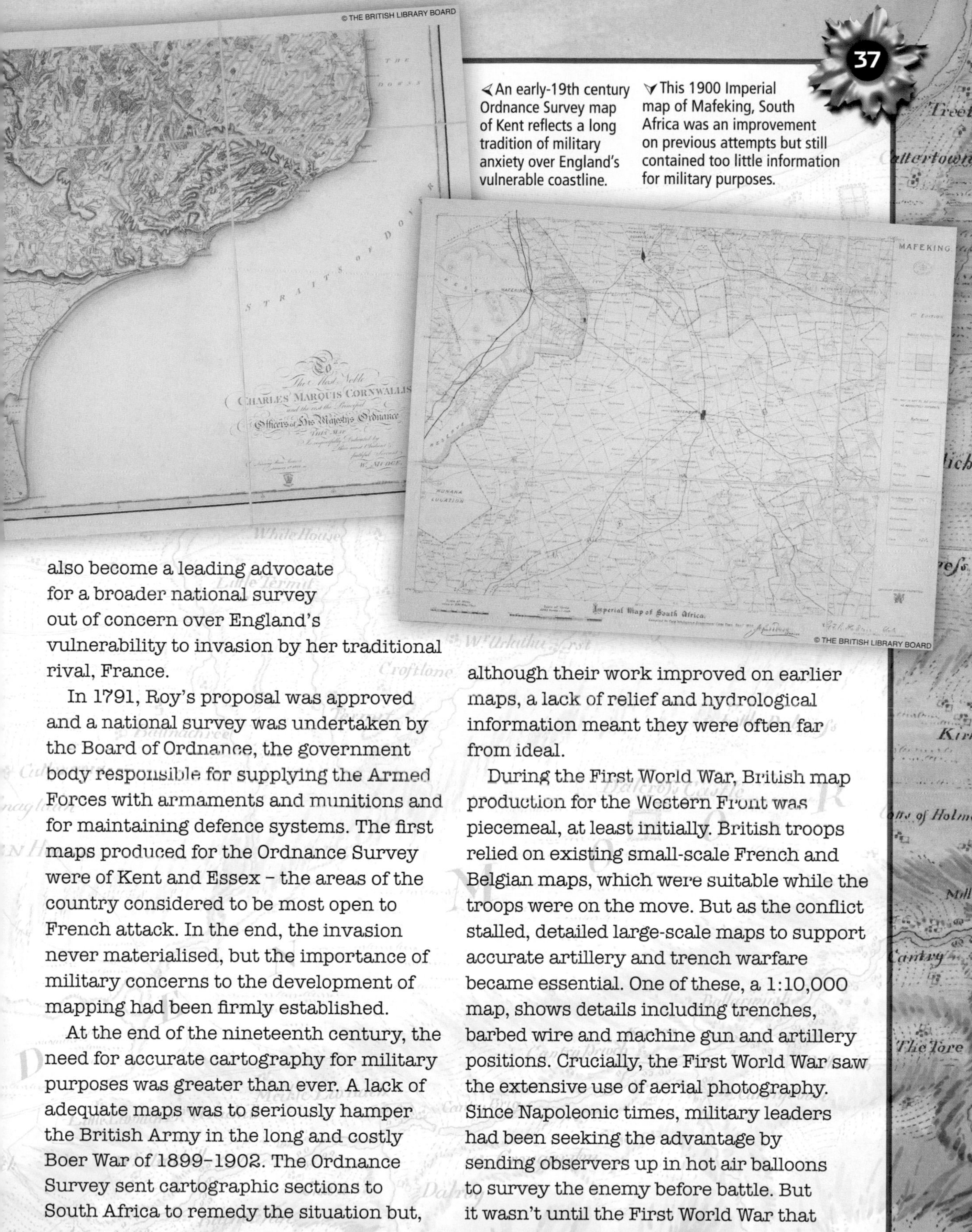

◀ An early-19th century Ordnance Survey map of Kent reflects a long tradition of military anxiety over England's vulnerable coastline.

▼ This 1900 Imperial map of Mafeking, South Africa was an improvement on previous attempts but still contained too little information for military purposes.

also become a leading advocate for a broader national survey out of concern over England's vulnerability to invasion by her traditional rival, France.

In 1791, Roy's proposal was approved and a national survey was undertaken by the Board of Ordnance, the government body responsible for supplying the Armed Forces with armaments and munitions and for maintaining defence systems. The first maps produced for the Ordnance Survey were of Kent and Essex – the areas of the country considered to be most open to French attack. In the end, the invasion never materialised, but the importance of military concerns to the development of mapping had been firmly established.

At the end of the nineteenth century, the need for accurate cartography for military purposes was greater than ever. A lack of adequate maps was to seriously hamper the British Army in the long and costly Boer War of 1899–1902. The Ordnance Survey sent cartographic sections to South Africa to remedy the situation but, although their work improved on earlier maps, a lack of relief and hydrological information meant they were often far from ideal.

During the First World War, British map production for the Western Front was piecemeal, at least initially. British troops relied on existing small-scale French and Belgian maps, which were suitable while the troops were on the move. But as the conflict stalled, detailed large-scale maps to support accurate artillery and trench warfare became essential. One of these, a 1:10,000 map, shows details including trenches, barbed wire and machine gun and artillery positions. Crucially, the First World War saw the extensive use of aerial photography. Since Napoleonic times, military leaders had been seeking the advantage by sending observers up in hot air balloons to survey the enemy before battle. But it wasn't until the First World War that

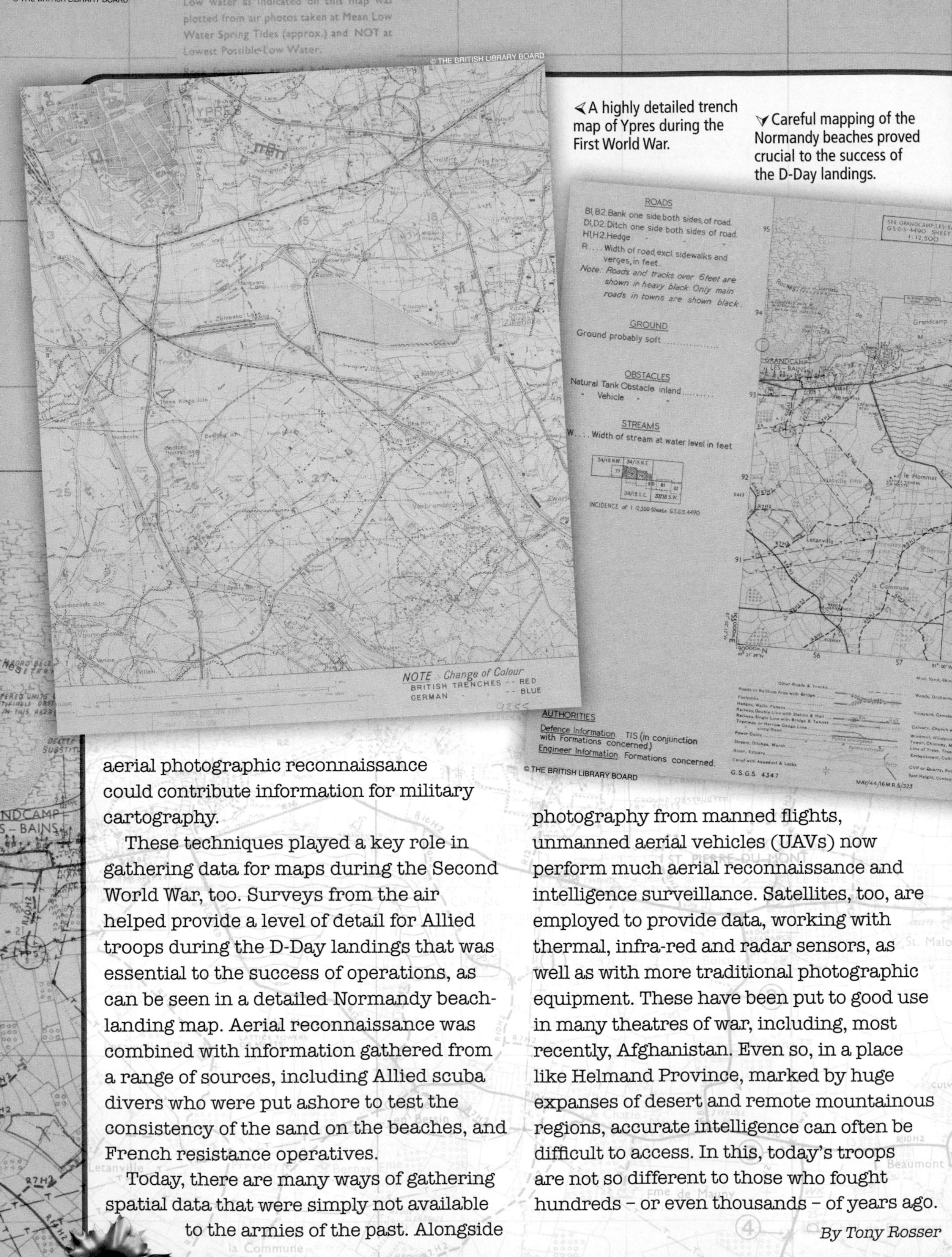

A highly detailed trench map of Ypres during the First World War.

Careful mapping of the Normandy beaches proved crucial to the success of the D-Day landings.

aerial photographic reconnaissance could contribute information for military cartography.

These techniques played a key role in gathering data for maps during the Second World War, too. Surveys from the air helped provide a level of detail for Allied troops during the D-Day landings that was essential to the success of operations, as can be seen in a detailed Normandy beach-landing map. Aerial reconnaissance was combined with information gathered from a range of sources, including Allied scuba divers who were put ashore to test the consistency of the sand on the beaches, and French resistance operatives.

Today, there are many ways of gathering spatial data that were simply not available to the armies of the past. Alongside photography from manned flights, unmanned aerial vehicles (UAVs) now perform much aerial reconnaissance and intelligence surveillance. Satellites, too, are employed to provide data, working with thermal, infra-red and radar sensors, as well as with more traditional photographic equipment. These have been put to good use in many theatres of war, including, most recently, Afghanistan. Even so, in a place like Helmand Province, marked by huge expanses of desert and remote mountainous regions, accurate intelligence can often be difficult to access. In this, today's troops are not so different to those who fought hundreds – or even thousands – of years ago.

By Tony Rosser

MILITARY MAPPING

NATO militaries use a geo-co-ordinate standard called the Military Grid Reference System (MGRS) to map locations. This sophisticated grid system covers the entire Earth and can provide a reference to within one metre, allowing for astonishing accuracy.

MGRS co-ordinates, or grid references, consist of three parts:

- a *grid zone designation* composed of a number and a letter, which identifies an area covering 6° East–West, and 8° North–South
- a *100,000-metre square identification* made up of two letters
- and a *numerical location* represented by up to ten digits, split down the middle into two readings. The first five digits give the easting in metres, measured left-to-right from the east edge of the square, and the last five digits give the northing in metres, measured bottom-up from the south edge of the square.

If ten digits are used in the numerical location, the co-ordinates are precise to a single metre. If a resolution of ten metres is enough, the final digit of the easting and northing can be dropped, so that only 4 + 4 digits are used. For a one-hundred-metre resolution, 3 + 3 digits are used; for one kilometre, 2 + 2 digits, and for ten kilometre, only 1 + 1 digits. The NATO standard is ten-metre resolution.

Take as an example Buckingham Palace, whose geographic co-ordinates are 51°29'59" N and 0°8'09" W. This translates to an MGRS coordinate of **30UXC9879209288**, which would be read as follows:

- **30U** indicates a *grid zone designation* that covers most of Great Britain
- **XC** locates an *100,000-metre square* covering London and the surrounding area
- **98792** is the easting and **09288** is the northing, which together give a precise location to within one metre.

In addition to the topographic symbols used to represent the natural and manmade features on maps, military personnel need to be able to indicate the identity, size, location and movement of soldiers (theirs and the enemy's), as well as military activities and installations. A system of codified symbols – known as military symbols – has been developed to communicate this information. These symbols are not normally printed on maps because the features and units that they represent are constantly moving or changing; military security is also a consideration. Instead, these are often drawn on or marked on an overlay. In NATO, friendly forces are in blue or black, while enemy forces are in red.

Here are some of the basic military mapping symbols:

•	Firearm or small squad / section of 4–10 soldiers commanded by a Corporal or Sergeant
• •	Larger squads / sections, commanded by a Sergeant or Staff Sergeant
• • •	Platoon (infantry) / troop (armoured or cavalry) of 30–40 soldiers commanded by a Lieutenant
I	Company (infantry) / squadron (armoured or cavalry) / battery of 150–200 soldiers commanded by a Captain or Major
I I	Battalion (infantry) / regiment (armoured, cavalry or artillery) of 500–800 soldiers commanded by a Major or Lieutenant Colonel
I I I	Regiment of 1,000–3,000 soldiers under a Lieutenant Colonel or Colonel
XX	Division of 10,000–18,000 soldiers commanded by a Major General
XXX	Corps of 50,000–80,000 soldiers commanded by a Lieutenant General
XXXX	Army of 350,000+ soldiers under a General or a Colonel General

40

You can convert the latitude and longitude of your location to MGRS coordinates here **http://bit.ly/bCgSqP** or by using your smartphone to scan this code:

SGT MICK LOCKETT

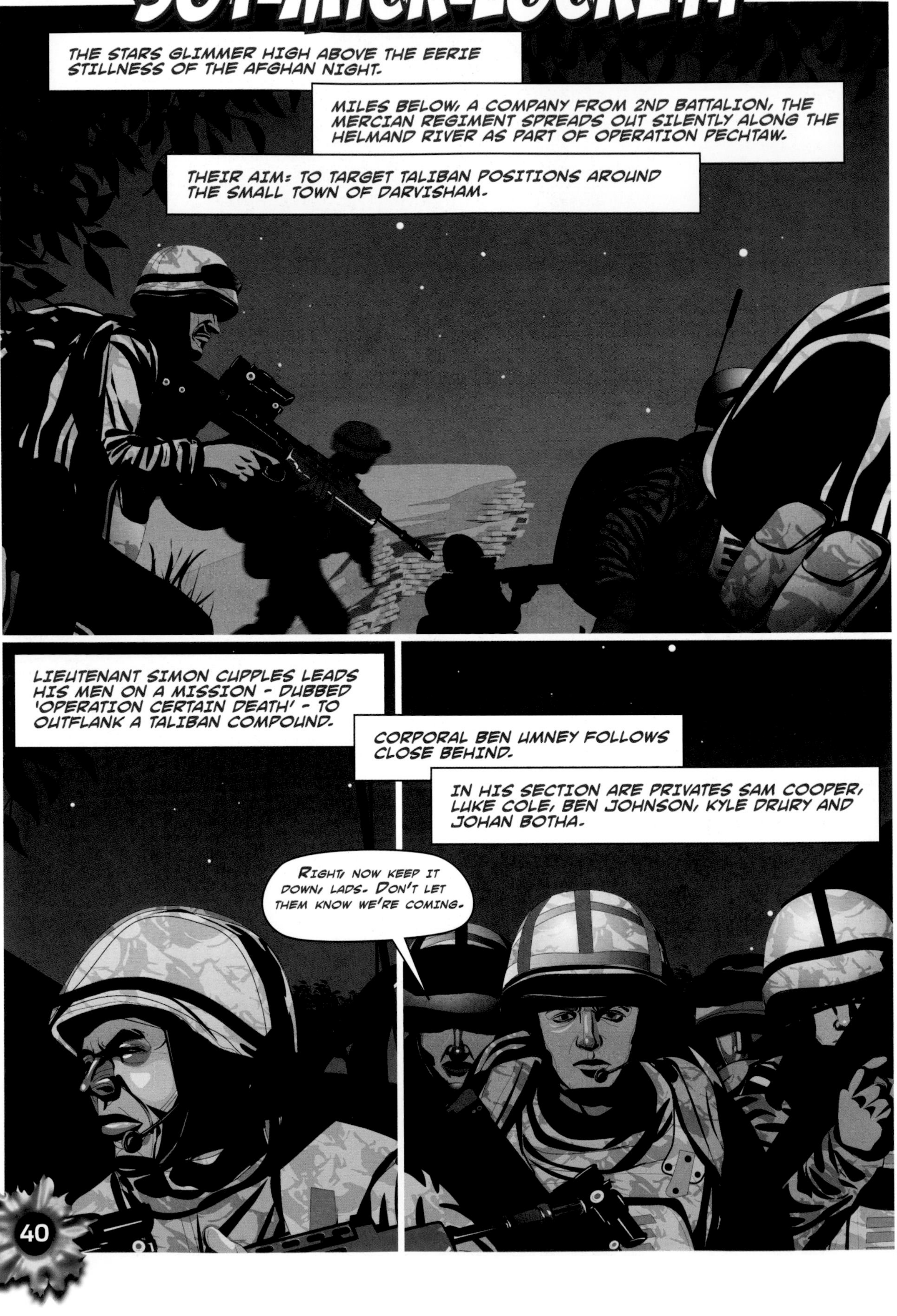

LIEUTENANT SIMON CUPPLES LEADS HIS MEN ON A MISSION - DUBBED 'OPERATION CERTAIN DEATH' - TO OUTFLANK A TALIBAN COMPOUND.

CORPORAL BEN UMNEY FOLLOWS CLOSE BEHIND.

IN HIS SECTION ARE PRIVATES SAM COOPER, LUKE COLE, BEN JOHNSON, KYLE DRURY AND JOHAN BOTHA.

RIGHT, NOW KEEP IT DOWN, LADS. DON'T LET THEM KNOW WE'RE COMING.

BUT THE ENEMY DO KNOW THEY'RE COMING...
...AND HEAVY FIRE RAINS DOWN ON THE STARTLED MEN.
AMBUSH! GET THE HELL DOWN!
RETURN FIRE! RETURN FIRE!
THE MEN ARE PINNED DOWN.
WITH NO WAY OUT FOR THE AMBUSHED TROOPS, LIEUTENANTS RUPERT BOWERS AND CUPPLES QUICKLY LEAD THEIR MEN FORWARD TO BOLSTER THEIR NUMBERS.
KEEP YOUR HEADS DOWN!
BUT ALREADY SOME HAVE FALLEN IN THE BLISTERING ONSLAUGHT...
BUT LOCKETT, CUPPLES AND THE OTHERS ARE DETERMINED TO RETRIEVE THEM.
NO MAN GETS LEFT BEHIND. I GAVE THE BLOKES MY WORD AND I MEANT IT.
I PROMISED THE MEN I'D BRING ALL THEM BACK. IF NOT ALIVE, THEN THEIR BODIES WOULD COME HOME.
IF IT MEANT GOING BACK INTO THE FACE OF ENEMY FIRE, I DIDN'T CARE.
I WANTED MY MEN BACK.
LOCKETT

THE RESCUE TEAM WADES ONCE MORE INTO THE THICK OF THE ACTION. THE FALLEN MEN LIE TANTALIZINGLY CLOSE....
OVER THE CLAMOUR OF BATTLE, LOCKETT HEARS INJURED PRIVATE LUKE COLE CALLING.
LOCKY, COME AND GET ME... COME GET ME.
LOCKETT, CUPPLES AND A BAND OF COURAGEOUS VOLUNTEERS RUN BACK INTO THE KILLING ZONE AN ASTONISHING THREE TIMES, UNDER HEAVY FIRE, IN AN ATTEMPT TO RECOVER THEIR WOUNDED MATES.
HELP ME... SOMEONE, PLEASE!
WE'RE GOING TO GET YOU OUT OF HERE! HANG ON!
AMIDST THE CHAOS, THEY SPOT PRIVATE COLE.
BUT NO SOONER HAVE THEY REACHED HIM THAN THE TALIBAN CRAWL FORWARD IN A BID TO GRAB PRIVATE JOHAN BOTHA.
JESUS, THEY'RE GOING FOR BOTHA! THEY'RE GRABBING THE BIG MAN!

IN A STAGGERING ACT OF BRAVERY, WOUNDED COLE BLAZES AWAY WITH HIS RIFLE TO STOP THE TALIBAN CAPTURING HIS MATE.
You b*****ds! Get off him!!
BRAAAP! BRRAAAAP!
I kept telling Private Cole to keep firing. He was in bloody agony, but he was doing it! And doing it brilliantly.
LOCKETT

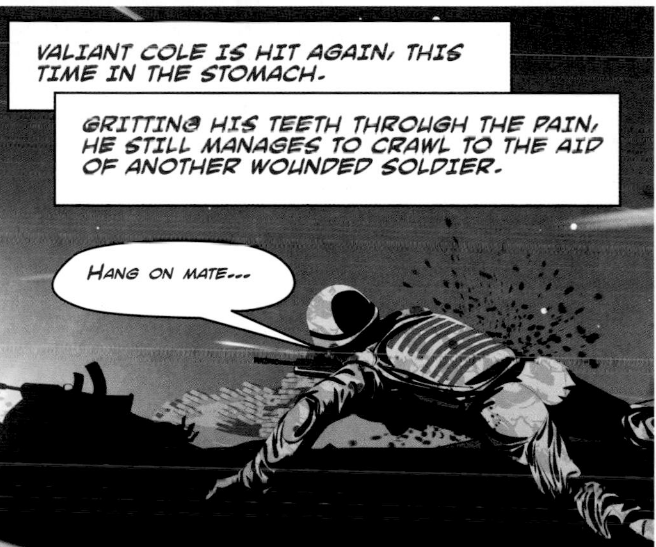
VALIANT COLE IS HIT AGAIN, THIS TIME IN THE STOMACH.
GRITTING HIS TEETH THROUGH THE PAIN, HE STILL MANAGES TO CRAWL TO THE AID OF ANOTHER WOUNDED SOLDIER.
Hang on mate...

COLE INJECTS HIS FALLEN COMRADE WITH MORPHINE, THEN SWIFTLY ROLLS AWAY SO HE WON'T COMPROMISE HIS MATE'S POSITION TO THE ENEMY.

AS THE BULLETS FLY, ON ANOTHER PATCH OF THE DARK AND BLOODY BATTLEFIELD BOWERS HAS FOUND ONE OF THE FALLEN MEN.
Got you!

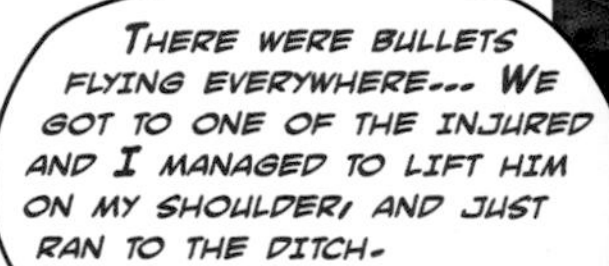

THE RESCUERS FALL BACK UNDER THE RELENTLESS FIRE, AND HELP ARRIVES IN THE FORM OF ANOTHER SECTION OF MERCIANS, LED BY SERGEANT CRAIG BRELSFORD.

AS THE EXHAUSTED TROOPS PLAN THEIR NEXT MOVE, THE COMPANY C.O. GIVES THE ORDER TO REGROUP. THE MEN ARE TOLD TO PULL BACK BEFORE AN ARMOURED VEHICLE ASSAULT ON THE INSURGENTS.
FALL BACK! FALL BACK!
I WAS HAVING NONE OF IT! I ASKED FOR MORE VOLUNTEERS TO GO AND GET BOTHA BACK. EVERY HAND WENT UP, NO HESITATION.
LOCKETT
THE ORDER TO RETURN TO BASE IS REPEATED.
LOCKETT, GODDAMMIT, FALL BACK!
LOCKETT
I REFUSED. I WAS NOT LEAVING MY MAN ON THE GROUND. IT WAS BREAKING MY F****** HEART.
BUT LOCKETT'S DUTY IS TO HIS MEN - ALL HIS MEN - AND DEEP DOWN HE KNOWS THAT FOR EVERYONE'S SAKE THEY NEED TO REGROUP, REBOMB AND COME UP WITH A NEW PLAN.
RELUCTANTLY, HE RETURNS TO BASE.
BUT AS DAWN BREAKS, THIS BRAVE BAND OF WARRIORS IS STILL DETERMINED TO RECOVER THEIR FALLEN PAL.
I KNEW WE HAD TO GET HIM BACK. IMAGINE TELLING HIS FAMILY YOU DON'T KNOW WHERE HE IS OR WHAT HAPPENED TO HIM? THAT WAS SIMPLY NOT AN OPTION. THE REASON THE BLOKES FIGHT SO HARD IS BECAUSE THEY KNOW WE ALL DO EVERYTHING TO HELP EACH OTHER.
CUPPLES
IN THE COLD LIGHT OF DAWN, THEY FIND JOHAN BOTHA'S BODY CLOSE TO VACATED TALIBAN TRENCHES.
THEY WILL BRING HIS BODY HOME, WHERE HIS FAMILY AND FRIENDS WILL MOURN HIM.
BUT IT'S SMALL COMFORT FOR THE PAIN OF LOSING A BROTHER IN ARMS.

THE HEROIC EFFORTS OF THIS BAND OF BROTHERS WAS TO BECOME ONE OF THE BEST-DOCUMENTED EXAMPLES OF THE BRAVERY OF BRITISH TROOPS.

THE MEN'S COURAGE RESULTED IN AN ASTONISHING CLUTCH OF GALLANTRY MEDALS, INCLUDING A CONSPICUOUS GALLANTRY CROSS, THREE MILITARY CROSSES - ONE OF THEM AWARDED TO SERGEANT MICK LOCKETT - AND TWO MENTIONS IN DISPATCHES, AS WELL AS FIVE JOINT COMMANDERS' COMMENDATIONS.

TRAGICALLY, MICK LOCKETT, A VETERAN OF NORTHERN IRELAND AND BOSNIA, WAS KILLED IN SEPTEMBER 2009 BY A ROADSIDE BOMB WHILE ON FOOT PATROL IN THE TOWN OF GERESHK, HELMAND.

HE DIED ONLY DAYS BEFORE HE WAS DUE TO END HIS SECOND OPERATIONAL TOUR TO AFGHANISTAN.

'And there's still a job to do. There's always a job to do.'

Sergeant Mick Lockett, 1980-2009

47

PRIVATE ADAM WAKENSHAW

Young miner Adam Wakenshaw went down in history as one of the bravest of the brave during World War II after single-handedly turning an anti-tank gun on the enemy to save his comrades, even after one of his arms was blown off.

The courageous twenty-eight-year-old private from Newcastle was the last survivor of an anti-tank unit in the Durham Light Infantry when he was caught in a life and death battle with German soldiers in North Africa.

His battalion was caught up in rearguard action in June 1942 as Rommel raced towards Egypt. After seeing an enemy vehicle stray into the sights of their 2-Pounder, Wakenshaw and his crew opened fire, destroying the vehicle. But a second armoured vehicle came into view and unleashed a devastating barrage, killing or seriously wounding all the members of the crew manning the 2-Pounder. Wakenshaw's left arm was blown clean off in the barrage. Despite his agonising injuries and the intense German fire, the brave miner crawled back to the 2-Pounder and loaded it with one arm.

He fired five rounds into the Germans, setting their vehicle on fire and damaging their gun. Tragically, a direct hit to his ammunition finally defeated him and destroyed his gun.

His valour in the face of withering fire and horrific injuries prevented the German advance from using their guns on an infantry company just 200 yards away.

British troops make their way across rough country in the Western Desert, May 1941.

Wakenshaw's VC citation read: 'It was through the self-sacrifice and courageous devotion to duty of this infantry anti-tank gunner that the company was enabled to withdraw and to embus in safety.'

By David Willetts

Due to its rarity, the VC is highly prized and the medal can reach over £400,000 at auction. There are a number of public and private collections devoted to the Victoria Cross. Lord Ashcroft, whose collection contains over one-tenth of the total VCs awarded, announced in July 2008 a donation to the Imperial War Museum, allowing his collection to be displayed there in a new gallery which opened in 2010.

THE LATEST GUNS

SHARPSHOOTER L129A1

The British Army has been in Afghanistan since 2001 and, as time has passed, the weapons and vehicles used by soldiers in the region have developed considerably. In early 2010 the first new rifle for twenty years was introduced to troops – the Sharpshooter L129A1.

The weapon is currently being used by members of the Royal Marines from 40 Commando. Its considerable range takes it into sniper territory but it requires far less training than traditional sniper rifles. Sharpshooters have a 'kill range' of up to 800 metres, a marked improvement on the Army's standard issue SA80A2 assault rifle, which has a 'kill range' of 275 metres.

A corporal from 40 Commando Royal Marines takes aim with a L129A1 rifle.

SHARPSHOOTER STATS

Calibre: 7.62 mm

Weight: 5 kg

Length: 945 mm

Effective range: 800 m

The Sharpshooter rifle is a gas-operated weapon. Its features include:

- an Advanced Combat Optical Gunsight (ACOG) scope that magnifies its target by up to six times
- a 20-round magazine which enables the weapon to fire 20 rounds in 20 seconds at up to 800 metres
- four Picatinny Rails for night vision, thermal and image-intensifying optics.

SNIPER RIFLES

A sniper rifle is a type of gun used to ensure a much more accurate placement of bullets at long range than other small arms.

In order to achieve this, sniper rifles are fitted with telescopic sights; this is their single most important feature, distinguishing them from most other assault rifles. The telescopic sights on sniper rifles provide huge magnification – up to forty times – allowing snipers to spot their targets with ease.

A range of sniper rifles are used by the British Armed Forces today.

L96A1 STATS

Calibre: 7.62 mm

Weight: 6.5 kg

Length: (adjustable) 1124-1194 mm

Muzzle velocity: 838 m/s

Feed: 10-round box

Effective range: 900 m, harassing fire 1100 m

The L96A1, produced by firearm manufacturer Accuracy International, is the sniper rifle of choice. It is designed to achieve first-round hit at 600 m and has recently been upgraded with a new telescopic sight and spotting scope.

A Royal Marine sniper aims his L96A1 at a Taliban target in Sangin.

L115A3 STATS

Calibre: 7.62 mm

Weight: 6.5 kg

Length: (adjustable) 1124–1194 mm

Muzzle velocity: 838 m/s

Feed: 10-round box

Effective range: 900 m, harassing fire 1100 m

The L115A3 Long Range Rifle is referred to as the 'Silent Assassin' by British Army snipers. This gun fires an 8.59 mm bullet, heavier than the 7.62 mm round of the L96, and less likely to be deflected over extremely long ranges.

This particular sniper rifle, also produced by Accuracy International, has been obtained by the British Army at a cost of approximately £4 million. Each of these rifles costs £23,000 and they have been deemed the Army's most powerful sniper weapon.

A Royal Marine sniper using a powerful L115A3 rifle looks for targets.

LIEUTENANT ARAN SANDIFORD

Age	22
Hometown	Exeter
Unit	45 Commando, RM

What is your job and what do you do?
I am a troop commander in 45 Commando, the Royal Marines. I am responsible for the training and welfare of around thirty Royal Marines, living and working at RM Condor in Arbroath, Scotland.

What was your best day?
My best day in the job was on a recent deployment to Canada. The troop took part in a live field firing company attack involving around eighty men and using live ammunition. Seeing the men perform as well as they did was fantastic and gave me much confidence in their ability.

What was your hardest day?
My hardest day so far would probably be the day I passed the infamous thirty-miler on Dartmoor.

What is your favourite bit of kit and why?
My favourite bit of kit is my jack flask, because it is always full of morale (i.e. hot tea or coffee) when I'm in the field.

Please list the last 3 books/magazines you read.
1. Extreme Measures *by Vince Flynn*
2. In the Service of the Sultan *by Ian Gardiner*
3. Front Magazine.

Please list the last 3 films/TV programmes you watched.
1. Commando
2. The Dark Knight
3. The Inbetweeners.

What do you miss most when away from home?
My family and friends and, if I'm in the field, my music.

What is the best thing about being in the military?
A varied lifestyle, job security and the calibre of people I work with in the Royal Marines.

Who do you most admire/who is your hero?
Eric Cantona – he changed the face of English football, what a legend!

THE THIRTY-MILE YOMP

The thirty-mile yomp is the final part of the Royal Marine's Commando test. It is the last task that recruits must complete to win the coveted green beret. The term 'yomp' is Royal Marines slang for a long-distance march in full kit.

The thirty-miler takes place across upland Dartmoor. Recruits must wear full fighting order, as well as carrying safety equipment in their day sacks. Recruits have eight hours to complete the march; Royal Marine officers have seven hours to do so. Officers must also navigate the route themselves, whilst recruits are permitted to follow a DS (a trained Royal Marine). The yomp is the ultimate endurance test, a challenge that Royal Marines never forget.

Marines prepare to receive operational Afghanistan medals at RM Condor in Arbroath.

A DIFFERENT KIND OF MEDICINE

Wounded soldiers can be medically treated in all sorts of ways. Some methods still used today hark back to the First World War and even earlier, whilst other techniques are much more recent and cutting edge. Flesh-eating maggots and bloodsucking leeches might sound more medieval than modern, but if you want a wound treated with maximum efficiency, few therapies can compete with 200 million years of evolution.

MAGGOTS

Maggots are the legless, soft-bodied larvae of flies that eat dead tissue. They've been used for healing wounds by Indians and Aboriginal tribes for hundreds of years, as well as more recently during the Renaissance. They were popular right up to the 1900s and were used in the First World War. The rise of antibiotics meant they fell out of fashion.

Today, maggots are once again being used in high-tech healthcare. When left to graze on broken skin or soft wounds, they clean injuries highly effectively, secreting enzymes which break down dead tissue. A study by a team of British scientists found that maggots can clean wounds that are failing to heal in fourteen days – compared with seventy-two days with the water-based gel treatment normally used to clean them.

LEECHES

Leeches are bloodsuckers. Segmented worms, related to the earthworm, they are particularly useful when it comes to surgery. When a body part is reattached after an injury, it is often impossible to reconnect all the broken veins, which in turn can lead to excessive bleeding. Leeches are able to consume five times their weight in a single session, making them ideal for draining away the excess blood.

Medical use of leeches was first recorded in 200 BC. George Washington is said to have died when too much blood was drained by leeches during an illness. The leech can feed for six hours or more, sucking up enough blood to last it for as long as two years. Leech saliva contains chemicals that prevents blood clotting, so unless carefully monitored a wound might bleed for hours after the leech is removed.

A medic uses an applicator to insert Celox into a wound.

CASE STUDY: CELOX

Celox is a medical product that has been available since 2006. It is a blood-clotting agent, and one of its main ingredients is a polymer – chitosan – that is extracted from crab and shrimp shells.

Discovery

The discovery behind Celox occurred on a beach in the USA when a scientist noticed a number of crabs missing their legs. Despite their wounds, the crabs were alive and the scientist wondered why they hadn't bled to death. The reason: the chitosan in their shells stopped them from bleeding.

How does Celox work?

Celox bonds to the surface of red blood cells and platelets within the blood, forming a clot. It comes in the form of granules which are poured into the wound, stopping it bleeding within minutes. It can even stop bleeding from a severed artery. Once Celox has been poured in, the wound should be packed and pressure should then be applied. The Celox should remain in the wound until it can be seen to by a doctor, who will be able to remove most of it by hand and with water or saline (a sterile salt-water solution) if necessary. Unlike other blood-clotting products, Celox works in extremely cold conditions and it has helped save the lives of many wounded soldiers in Afghanistan.

References: www.celoxmedical.com

CROCODILES AND ALLIGATORS

A new generation of antibiotics could be developed from crocodile and alligator blood. This contains a mixture of proteins which attacks bacteria, viruses and fungi. It even kills the HIV virus and the lethal stomach bug *E. coli*. Now American scientists have taken blood samples from the reptiles and are isolating the disease-fighting white blood cells. They hope this will enable them to develop artificial proteins that could be injected into humans to fight infections.

SPIDERS

A spider's web may look delicate but the silk it is spun from is stronger than steel and lighter than plastic. Now scientists have created artificial spider silk, called BioSteel, by using genetic engineering to breed goats with spider genes in them. The goats produce web proteins in their milk. BioSteel could be made into artificial joints and limbs and be used as ultra-fine stitches to repair wounds.

© ANDREW BAILEY

SNAKES

The bite of the deadly Malaysian pit viper is being tested on victims of strokes and deep vein thrombosis. When the snake bites its victim, it releases an anti-coagulant, a chemical that stops blood clotting. Scientists have used this to create the anti-clotting drug Ancrod, which lowers levels of fibrinogen, a chemical in the blood that instigates potential stroke-causing clots.

© RENEE MORRIS

BEES

Apitherapy – using the bee sting as a medical treatment – goes back thousands of years. Medieval doctors used bee stings for arthritis, reasoning that the pain would make patients forget their aching joints. This may sound barbaric but in fact they weren't too far off the mark. Today, scientists believe that a compound in the bees' poison could actually help combat arthritis. There is some evidence that the bee venom component mellitin makes the body release cortisol, a natural stress-fighting and anti-inflammatory hormone.

© DON FARRALL

SCORPIONS

The venom that Israeli yellow scorpions use to paralyse prey is being used to treat brain-cancer patients. It contains chlorotoxin, a protein that only attacks tumour cells in the brain, which often can't be treated with surgery, chemotherapy or radiotherapy.

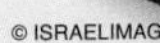
© ISRAELIMAGES

© ANDRZEJ TOKARSKI / FOTOLIA

FROGS

A tiny tree frog in the Amazon, the *epipedobates tricolour* – a species of poison dart frog – could provide a painkiller 200 times stronger than morphine. The amphibian produces a deadly toxin called epibatidine that Amazon Indians use to tip their spears. Scientists have used this to create ABT-594, a painkiller with a similar chemical structure but without the deadly side effects. Trials are being carried out on chronically ill patients.

With thanks to Sam Lister and Henry Biggs

BRAVEST OF THE BRAVE

CAPTAIN HAROLD ERVINE-ANDREWS

At Dunkirk in 1940, the Allies were in a race against time to evacuate back to the safety of Britain's shores as Hitler's marauding army of henchmen tried to chase them down.

Fighting raged mercilessly as British Forces retreated, fighting running battles with the advancing enemy.

Many acted with extreme bravery, with some individuals going beyond the call of duty to slow the enemy and speed up the escape for their fellow soldiers.

Captain Harold Ervine-Andrews of the East Lancashire Regiment was one of those brave men.

WWII hero Captain Harold Ervine-Andrews and his wife in the garden of their Cambridge home.

Thousands of Allied Troops are pictured on the sands of Dunkirk Beach as they wait to evacuate.

The gallant Irishman was awarded the Victoria Cross when he was twenty-eight years old for dealing a hammer blow to the enemy that saved the lives of his comrades.

During the night of 31 May 1940, near Dunkirk, France, Captain Ervine-Andrews' company was heavily outnumbered and under intense German fire.

At dawn, the Germans attacked in a bid to snuff out the captain and his men so they could race on in pursuit of the retreating Allied Forces. But Ervine-Andrews refused to be beaten.

British, Belgian and French troops arrive at a British port after the evacuation of troops from Dunkirk.

He selected a squad of volunteers and advanced to an abandoned barn before climbing up to the roof. Once there, he became the scourge of the advancing enemy, shooting eleven of their number dead with his rifle and many more with a Bren machine gun.

He held up the Nazi advance for hours, buying valuable time for the retreat. When the barn was ablaze and close to collapse, he sent his wounded to the rear before leading his remaining eight men to safety.

Wading for over a mile in water up to their chins, they made it back to the beach and were evacuated back to Britain along with 330,000 other brave Allied warriors.

Ervine-Andrews later achieved the rank of lieutenant-colonel. He died on 30 March 1995, aged eighty-three.

By David Willetts

Members of the British Expeditionary Force arrive at an English port on their return from Northern France.

The Victoria Cross was awarded 182 times to 181 recipients for action in the Second World War. At the time of going to press, only three World War II VC holders are still living: John Alexander Cruickshank, an RAF pilot who sank a German U-boat in 1944 despite his plane being hit by enemy fire in 72 places; Tul Bahadur Pun, a Ghurkha serving in the Indian Army in Burma, who in 1944 single-handedly stormed an enemy position after his entire section was wiped out; and Lachhiman Gurung, also a Ghurkha serving in the Indian Army in Burma, who in 1945 killed 31 Japanese attackers while he held his position, firing left-handed due to horrendous injuries to his right arm.

FIGHTING FOOD

‘An army marches on its stomach,’ Napoleon Bonaparte is said to have observed. And it is as true today as when it first was uttered, almost two hundred years ago.

Good food – or, at least, decent food – is a vital requirement for troops, whether they’re on active duty at established camps where fresh provisions can be sourced; surviving in the Spartan conditions that exist on Forward Operating Bases (FOBs); or on the move in patrols that can last many hours.

The new 24-hour multi-climate ration pack. The contents are tested and evaluated before they are introduced to the front line.

The contents of a 24-hour ration pack in 2004.

Away from camp, servicemen and women may need to survive for as many as fifty days on rations that are delivered to FOBs in shoebox-sized cardboard boxes. Boredom, lack of appetite and the risk of malnutrition are all real dangers when soldiers’ success depends on their being well-fed and fighting fit.

Until recently, troops in Afghanistan subsisted on ration packs that hadn’t changed since the Cold War. The menu consisted of ten meals, which included mostly heavy fare like Lancashire hot pot and corned beef hash, ‘biscuits brown’, dense treacle pudding and chocolate bars that routinely melted in Afghanistan’s fierce heat. Hardly the kind of grub to tempt overheated soldiers, their appetites shrunk in the high temperatures of Helmand. More often than not, troops chucked away the unpalatable fare, unintentionally depriving themselves of vital nutrients.

A change was needed. So, in late 2009, new Operational Ration Packs were introduced for the first time in over twenty years. Now, troops can choose from among thirty-eight individual ration packs, which cater to the varied tastes of the modern

Tucking into the new ration pack.

soldier. Thai curry, vegetable korma, chicken tikka masala, chili con carne, chicken arrabiata, lamb tagine, stroganoff, paella and vegetarian and halal options now sit alongside some of the old favourites such as bacon, sausage and beans.

Breakfasts are now healthier, with porridge or muesli on offer. Nuts, cranberry cereal bars, dried fruits, ginger biscuits, Oreos and Jammy Dodgers have all been added, while teabags have replaced the powdered version.

The new rations menu was based largely on feedback from serving soldiers, though logistical concerns were also taken into

NOW AND THEN

During the Napoleonic Wars, men were entitled to rations of: 1lb of bread, 1lb of beef, 1oz of butter or cheese, 1lb of pease (yellow split peas cooked alongside a ham hock) and 4oz of rice. Breakfast consisted of bread and 'small beer' which, despite its name, was barely alcoholic; the brewing process was undertaken mainly to make water safe. The main meal of the day was at midday, and soldiers were expected to cook this themselves in large copper pans, which made for many repetitive and unappetising meals of boiled meat. It was not until 1840 that a 'tea meal' later in the day was also introduced, though this was often frugal.

In World War I, the reserve ration – which the soldier carried for use when regular food was unavailable – included a 1lb can of meat (often corned beef), two 8oz tins of hard bread, 2.4oz of sugar, 1.12oz of ground coffee, and 0.16oz of salt. This equated to about 3,300 calories in total – enough to keep a soldier going – but the packaging in cylindrical cans was deeply impractical. Nevertheless, by the end of the war, about 2,000,000 rations had been shipped to troops in France.

British soldiers during World War II particularly prized American K rations when they could get them. These were generous by comparison with British rations of the time. They provided three meals – breakfast, lunch and supper – and a caloric intake of about 3,000 calories. Although they were designed to be used for no more than fifteen meals, soldiers on the front lines often found themselves eating the same rations day in, day out, for months. Many suffered from malnutrition as a result – not to mention boredom.

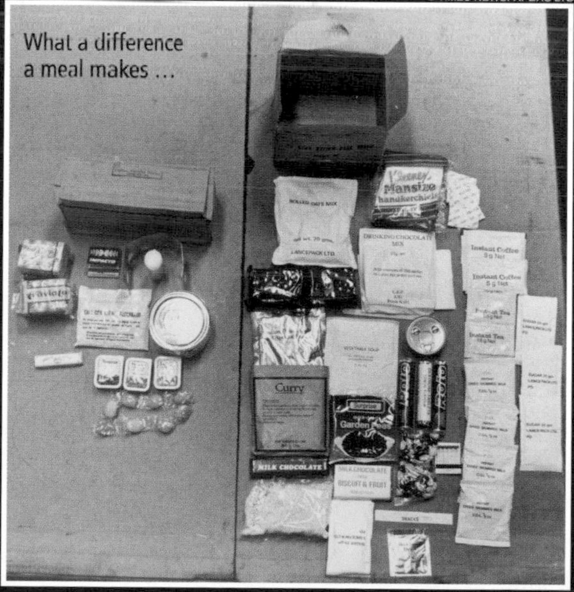

What a difference a meal makes …

This striking image illustrates the disparity in the rations available to the two sides fighting the Falklands War, with Argentinean rations on the left and British on the right. In a cold, rough terrain, a hearty meal can make a vital difference to troops' energy and morale.

account. Shelf life, for instance: when it can take months for rations to get to FOBs, it is essential that foods do not spoil. Ingredients also need to be able to survive being hermetically sealed and sterilised without turning into tasteless mush. And rations must be adaptable to circumstances: when a fire could attract unwanted enemy attention, cooked meals are impossible and so rations must be edible cold as well as hot.

'Biscuits brown, biscuits fruit, pâté, corned beef hash ... this is not what an eighteen-year-old wants to eat for breakfast,' says Lieutenant Commander Neil Horwood, who oversaw the menu overhaul. 'Today's eighteen-year-old eats Chinese, Indian, Thai, Jamaican jerk.'

Hygiene is an issue too. Troops camped out in the desert have little or no access to washing facilities for themselves, let alone for their cooking kit. Foods that leave sticky, gunky residue on mugs and utensils are to be avoided. Boil-in-the-bag soups; disposable, biodegradable spoons; dental cleaning gum and alcohol-free hand wipes that don't cause the skin to crack in extreme temperatures have all been included in ration packs, with the modern soldier serving in Afghanistan in mind.

There are nutritional considerations that need to be taken into account as well. In the furnace-like temperatures of Afghanistan, troops drink dozens of litres of water to avoid heat exhaustion. When bottled supplies run out, this means swallowing the foul-tasting purified version. Ration packs now include drink powders to make this concoction more palatable and to encourage soldiers to consume enough liquids. Many of the new meals also include one of the recommended 'five-a-day', so troops don't miss out on key nutrients and vitamins.

The MOD is also trialling special, lightweight patrol rations for troops in the field. These weigh less than 1kg, compared with a 24-hour ration pack that weighs around 3kg – a welcome relief for soldiers who regularly carry bergens of kit weighing about 30kg.

There are psychological factors at play, too. Familiarity can boost morale amongst troops who find themselves one day in Salisbury and the next in Helmand. A well-known brand or remembered flavour can provide a sense of consistency – as well as a welcome taste of home.

Trooper Chris Forbes of the Kings Royal Hussars eats his ration pack while sat in the rear of a Warrior fighting vehicle.

Number of rations produced each year: **3,000,000**

Weight of one-man ration pack, in kg: **3**

Shelf-life of rations, in years: **4**

Recommended caloric intake per day for a soldier in combat: **4,000**

Recommended caloric intake per day for a civilian: **1,940** (women), **2,550** (men)

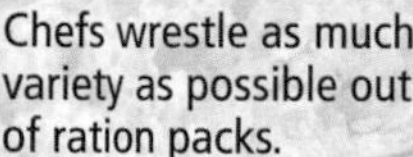

Chefs wrestle as much variety as possible out of ration packs.

There are two main types of ration packs available to the modern British serviceman or woman:

The **Ten-Man Ration Pack** is a one-stop pack for groups, designed to provide ten active adults with a balanced and nutritional diet for twenty-four hours. With five different menus, the Ten-Man Ration Packs provide a number of possible meals. Recently, the MOD issued a cookbook for Armed Service chefs whose job it is to whip up tasty meals for hundreds of hungry men and women every day.

'Producing variety in such a f*ing dangerous environment is undoubtedly daunting ... I salute the work you do on a daily basis to ensure the British servicemen and women eat a balanced and nutritional diet wherever they are in the world. You are without doubt the unsung heroes. Well done and keep up the good work!' Gordon Ramsay**

SAMPLE DISH

PLEASANT PORRIDGE DELIGHT

Ingredients:

- Porridge oats
- 4 x chocolate bar
- Granulated sugar
- Dried fruit mix
- Sliced pineapple

Method:

1. Make the porridge up as per instructions.
2. Add chocolate, sugar and dried fruit
3. Mix to soften.
4. Add the pineapple then serve.

SAMPLE TEN-MAN RATION PACK (MENU E):

1 x porridge oats
2 x baked beans in tomato sauce
1 x sausage
1 x bacon grill
2 x mushroom soup (1.2 l)
10 x noodles
2 x cheese, cheddar-flavoured, in cans
2 x canned ham
1 x canned margarine
1 x chicken in juice
1 x soya mince (textured vegetable protein)
1 x potato flakes
1 x rice, long grain, easy cook
1 x dried onions
3 x sliced mushrooms
2 x whole carrots
1 x yeast
1 x teabag
1 x coffee, freeze-dried
1 x milk powder, semi-skimmed
1 x drink powder, orange
1 x drink powder, tropical
1 x raspberry jam
2 x instant custard
2 x pineapple slices in juice
1 x noodle seasoning, BBQ beef flavour
1 x mixed herbs
1 x garlic powder
1 x seasoning, jerk flavour
1 x salt
1 x pepper
1 x tomato powder
1 x snack bar, castus strawberry
10 x milk chocolate bar
1 x drinking chocolate
1 x bicarbonate of soda
1 x sugar
2 x egg substitute
1 x strong white flour
2 x refuse sack
1 x menu sheet

Total weight 23.83kg
Total kilocalories 13,457
Total protein 429.67g
Total carbohydrate 2,099.64g
Total fat 342.45g

A Hero's Meal

Bryn Parry is co-founder and chief executive of Help for Heroes, and a former soldier.

'Put on your body armour, pull up a sandbag and get that lantern swinging, this is one for all the old dinosaurs like me.

'South Armagh, 1981: The helicopter brings you back to Bessbrook after a five-day operation in "bandit country"; you are cold, wet and very hungry. You unload, dump your bergen and squelch down to the cookhouse. You stir five sugars into a mug of hot tea and make an egg banjo ... Suddenly the world starts to look a whole lot better.'

Egg and Chip Banjo

Ingredients:

2 pieces soft white bread (or a nice soft bap)
1 big scoop of chips
2 eggs
red or brown sauce

Method:

1. Butter the bread/roll.
2. Cook the chips in a hot fryer until crispy, about 5–10 minutes.
3. Shallow fry the eggs.
4. Place one egg onto the bread, top with chips, and add another egg.
5. Then add the sauce of your choice.
6. Top with bread.
7. See if you can eat it without getting egg running down your fingers!

The Egg and Chip Banjo has been a staple diet of all three services for years, traditionally served at the end of operations and exercises. It is so named due to the method used when eating it: take hold of the Banjo in both hands and take a huge bite. The eggs will burst and squirt out in all directions; while lifting the Banjo to the side with one hand, you will make a frantic brushing motion with your spare hand to wipe the mess off the front of your shirt ... looking just like George Formby playing the banjo.

Extracted from 'The Help for Heroes Cookbook'

The **Multi-Climate Ration Pack** was recently designed to fully sustain one person for twenty-four hours. It contains high-energy food, electrolyte drinks and three main meals. There are thirty-eight menus available: twenty General, six Sikh/Hindu, six Vegetarian and six Halal.

A Jackal gunner attached to the 1st The Queens Dragoon Guards, has a ration pack breakfast to keep warm after spending a night in pouring rain.

SAMPLE MULTI-CLIMATE RATION PACK (MENU 2):

1 x oat breakfast
1 x chicken & veg soup
1 x E exotic
1 x O berry
1 x raspberry water flavour
1 x lemon sponge pudding
1 x strawberry/banana/apple
1 x chicken tikka
1 x pilau rice
1 x tabasco green
1 x just fruit
1 x snack bar, castus fruit mix
1 x fruity oatie
1 x mint hot chocolate
1 x tissues, 10-pack
1 x boiled sweets
1 x re-useable poly bag
4 x sugar sticks
4 x beverage whitener
2 x coffee sticks
2 x teabags
1 x matches
1 x steri tabs (blister 6-pack)
2 x wet wipes
1 x chewing gum spearmint
1 x chewing gum peppermint
1 x chewing gum menthol
1 x spoon

Where possible fresh produce is sourced locally – like this Christmas turkey.

64

You can find more ration recipes here **http://bit.ly/ayMp0x** or by using your smartphone to scan this code:

WAYNE OWERS

IMPROVISED EXPLOSIVE DEVICES - DEVASTATING HOME-MADE BOMBS - ARE THE NO.1 DANGER FOR FORCES OPERATING IN AFGHANISTAN. SO AFTER 20 YEARS OF SERVICE, ARMY CAPTAIN WAYNE OWERS DIDN'T HAVE TO VOLUNTEER FOR BOMB DISPOSAL...

BUT WHEN DUTY CALLED, HE ANSWERED.

MARCH 2009. CAPTAIN OWERS' FIRST DAY BACK IN THE FIELD.

A TEAM OF ROYAL ENGINEERS AND MEMBERS OF THE ROYAL LOGISTIC CORPS IS INSIDE THEIR MASTIFF ARMOURED VEHICLE. IT IS HOT, AND THE MEN ARE TENSE.

THEY HAVE BEEN DISPATCHED TO DEAL WITH A POTENTIALLY DEADLY IED, DUG INTO A DUSTY UNPAVED ROAD.
THE SEARCH TEAM MAKE THE AREA SAFE.

WE'RE BLOODY LUCKY IT HASN'T GONE OFF. WE FOUND IT BECAUSE SOME POOR SOD STEPPED ON IT.

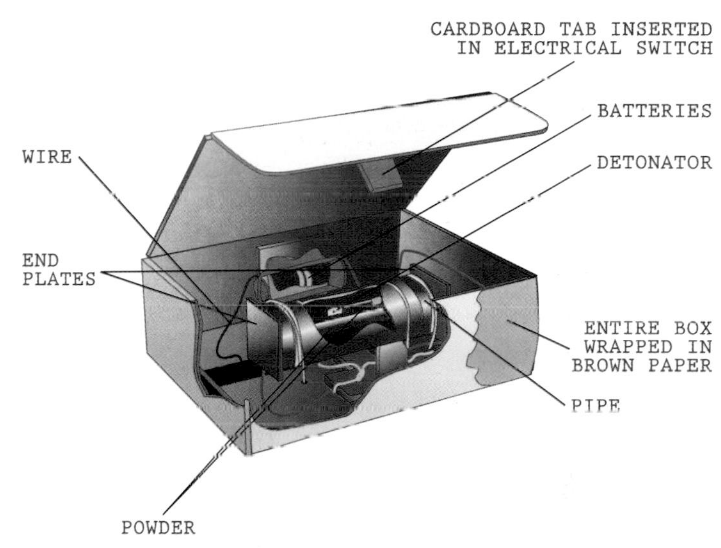
OWERS KNOWS WHAT'S PROBABLY WAITING FOR HIM...
CARDBOARD TAB INSERTED IN ELECTRICAL SWITCH
BATTERIES
WIRE
DETONATOR
END PLATES
ENTIRE BOX WRAPPED IN BROWN PAPER
PIPE
POWDER

AS LOCALS RETREAT TO SAFETY AND THE TEAM KEEP GUARD, OWERS MAKES THE LONG WALK.
JUST GET THERE, LIE DOWN, DEAL WITH THE BOMB.
IT'S NEAR 50°C - TOO HOT TO WEAR THE EXPLOSIVE ORDINANCE DISPOSAL SUIT THAT MIGHT SAVE HIS LIFE IF THE IED BLOWS.

I love you, my girls...

...and I'll come back to you, I swear.

As civilians look on, concerned...

...Wayne gets on with his job.
Eaassy does it. Just breathe. Breathe.

BUT OVER THE NEXT SIX MONTHS, THE DANGER GROWS.

THEN ONE DAY IN JULY OWERS AND FOUR MATES FROM THE ARMY'S EXPLOSIVE ORDNANCE DISPOSAL TEAM 5 - 'THE FAMOUS FIVE' - ARE CALLED OUT TO FIND ANOTHER SUSPECTED DEVICE IN SANGIN.

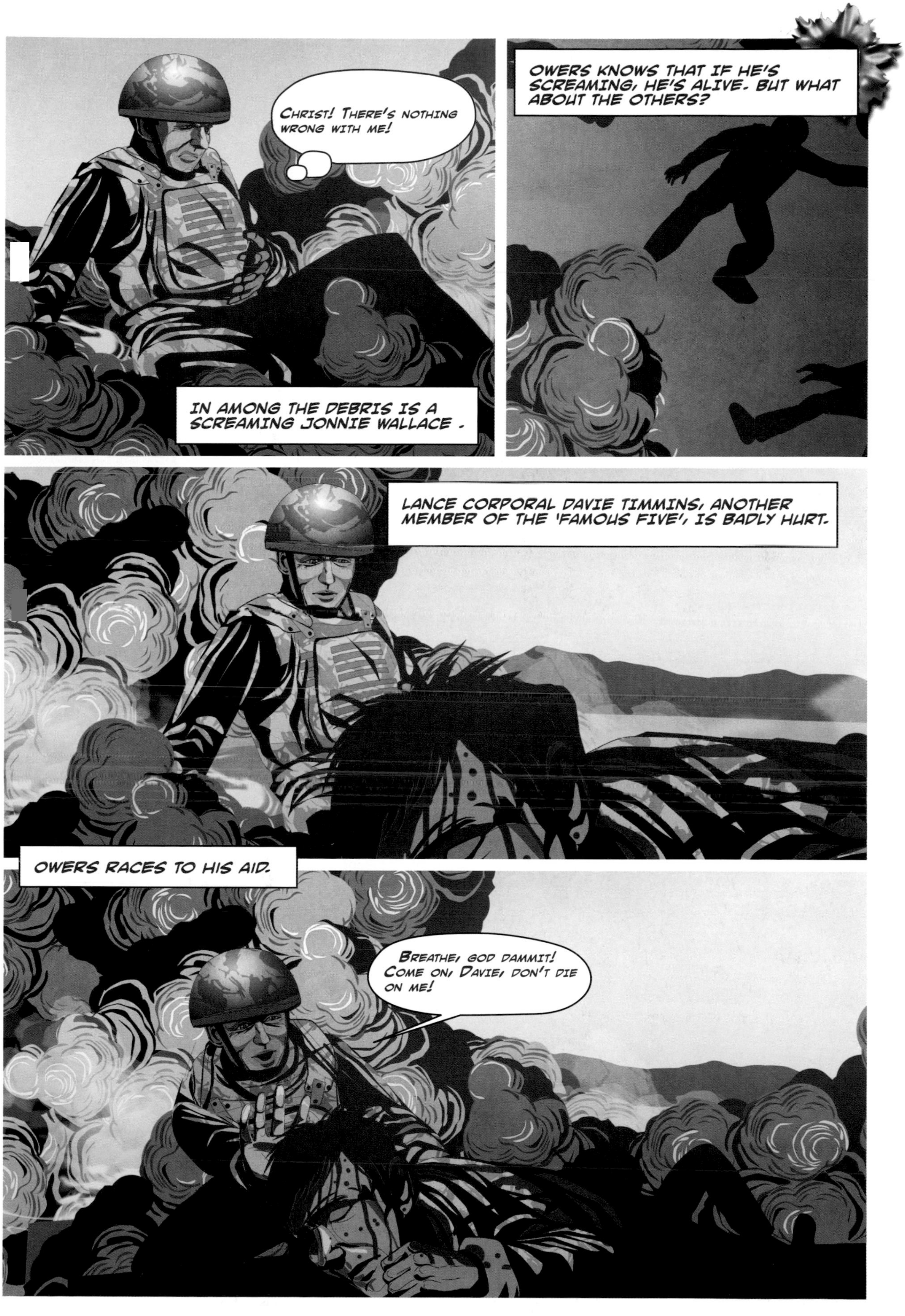

LANCE CORPORAL DAVIE TIMMINS, ANOTHER MEMBER OF THE 'FAMOUS FIVE', IS BADLY HURT.

OWERS RACES TO HIS AID.

BREATHE, GOD DAMMIT! COME ON, DAVIE, DON'T DIE ON ME!

THE MEDICAL EMERGENCY RESPONSE TEAM ARRIVES.
WE'VE GOT HIM! WE'LL DO EVERYTHING WE CAN.

WHAT THE HELL JUST HAPPENED? MY WHOLE TEAM...
BACK AT BASE, THE MEDICS UNLOAD THE WOUNDED.

WAYNE IS DEBRIEFED BY A SENIOR OFFICER.
SIR, I'VE HAD TWO TRAUMATIC EXPERIENCES RECENTLY. I DON'T KNOW IF I CAN TAKE A THIRD...

DURING A SIX-MONTH TOUR IN AFGHANISTAN, OWERS DISMANTLED A RECORD-BREAKING 93 IEDS, SAVING COUNTLESS LIVES AND MAKING HIM THE MOST PROLIFIC BOMB DESTROYER IN THE HISTORY OF THE ARMY TO DATE.

'People say, "Wow, 93 bombs". The number is not important but it has significance. My view is that the more times you walk down to that bomb, the more times you carry that personal risk - and it is a massive risk - the closer you are to something going wrong. People ask me how I managed to get up every day and do that job, but it's different when you're actually out in Afghanistan and in that situation. You just have to get on with it and be as confident as possible. We all just had to knuckle down.'

Captain Wayne Owers

'We don't get to see each other side-by-side as we were on the front line regularly now we're back home, but it's important to me to see all the lads back on the straight and narrow, getting on with life. These guys will be my mates forever. You can't go through what we've been through without becoming close.'

Lance Corporal Davie Timmins

MAJOR NIK CAVILL

Age 35
Hometown Jersey
Unit 45 Commando, RM

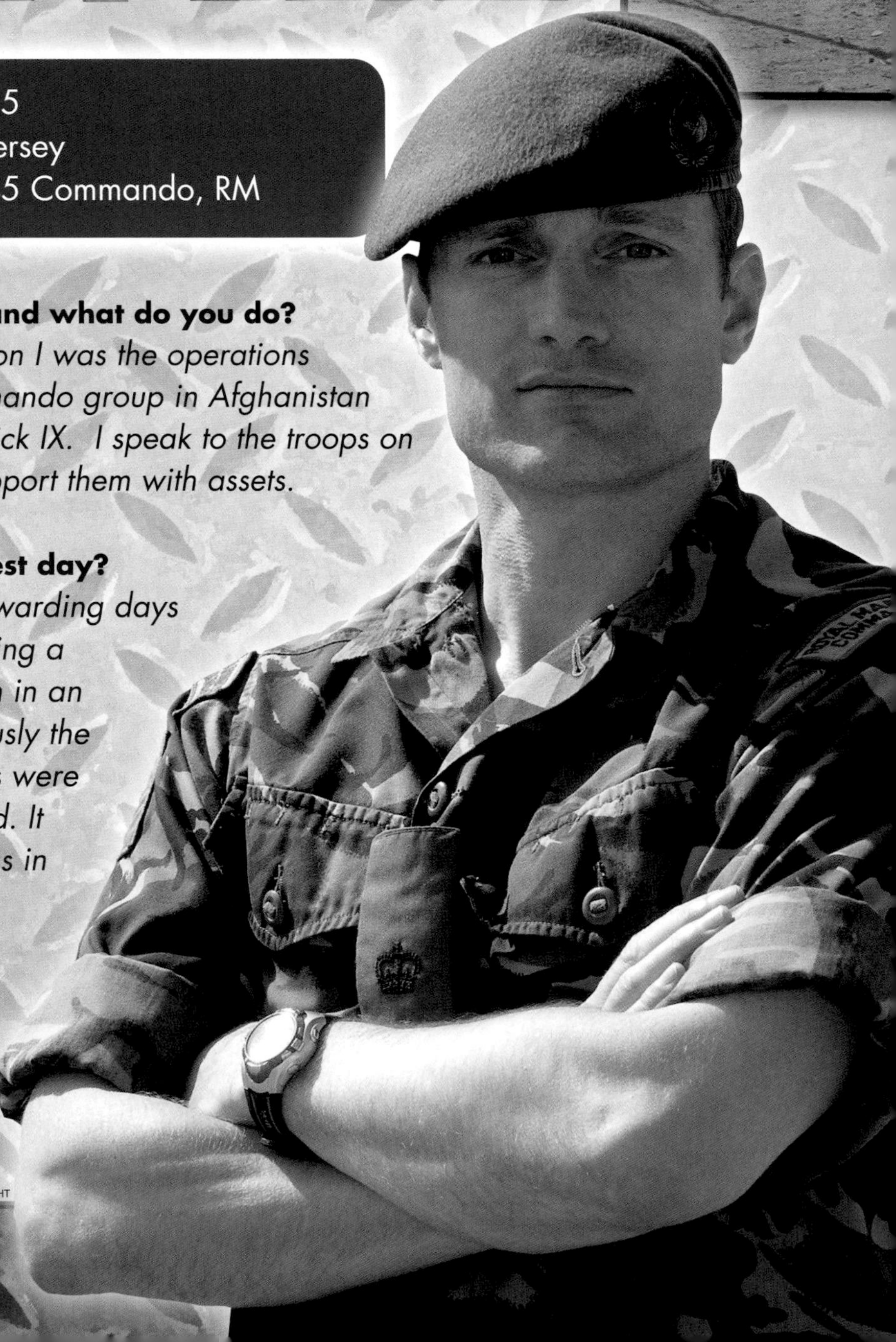

What is your job and what do you do?
On the last operation I was the operations officer of 45 Commando group in Afghanistan for Operation Herrick IX. I speak to the troops on the ground and support them with assets.

What was your best day?
One of the most rewarding days of the tour was seeing a girls' school reopen in an area where previously the teachers and pupils were too scared to attend. It symbolised progress in so many ways.

Second-grade girls sit in the remains of their classroom, which was burned down by suspected Taliban.

What was your hardest day?
12 December 2009 when we lost four men in one day to IEDs and a child suicide bomber.

What is your favourite bit of kit and why?
My bed – it's the only place I can switch off.

What do you miss most when away from home?
My family. My dog. My motorbike.

What is the best thing about being in the military?
It's the ordinary man's way of escaping the ordinary.

Who do you most admire/who is your hero?
My wife – who has a much harder job than me.

GIRLS' SCHOOLS IN AFGHANISTAN

Afghanistan has one of the world's poorest rates of education. When the Taliban came to power in 1996, the *madrasa* (mosque school) became the country's main educational establishment and female education was banned entirely. Girls' schools were closed and female teachers were prevented from working. In the face of the ban, some girls attended underground schools, whilst others were educated secretly at home by their parents.

After the Taliban were overthrown in 2001, Afghanistan received a substantial amount of international aid to restore the country's education system. Girls were welcomed back into schools and by 2003 some 7,000 schools were operating in 20 of the country's 34 provinces, with 27,000 teachers teaching 4.2 million children (including 1.2 million girls).

There are now approximately 2.5 million girls in schools in Afghanistan. Compared to the numbers earlier this decade, this figure marks a significant rise and several hundred girls have taken entrance exams for the University of Kabul. However, Afghanis still face a number of obstacles to education. The country still lacks funding, a shortage of teachers remains, Taliban intimidation remains a real concern, and a 2007 survey showed that 60 per cent of schoolchildren were studying in unprotected structures, including tents. Many parents worry that these conditions are not safe enough and forbid their daughters from attending.

Ferishta, 10, now has a chance at a real education.

GUARDSMAN HOPPY

BY SCOTT BLANEY

© NEWS GROUP NEWSPAPERS LTD / PHOTO BY ARTHUR EDWARDS

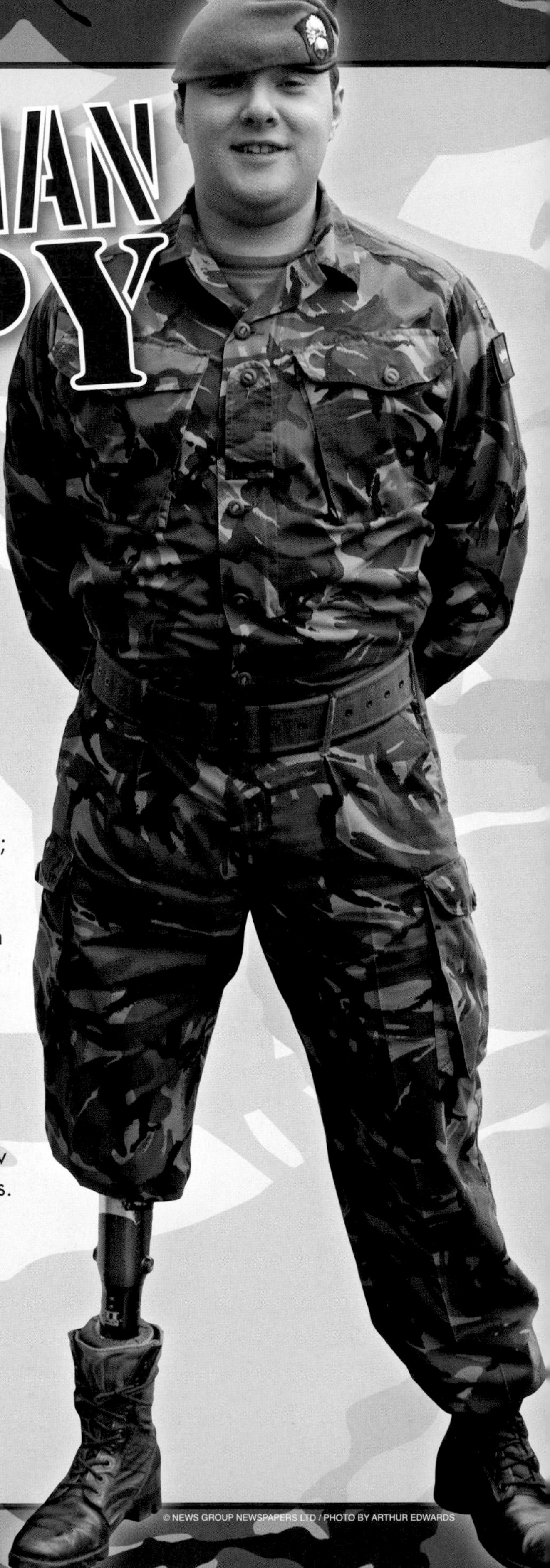

It's only pain.

At 11 a.m. on Monday, 15 February 2009, I became the first amputee to stand on the Queen's Guard at the Tower of London. I stood for two hours and it was great to get back to work again. I hadn't worked for more than a year and hadn't gone on guard in about three. I nearly slipped when I was marching out but nobody noticed.

Some of the tourists can be quite annoying; others try to make you laugh. None of them know about my disability. My mates look past it; they don't really see it as a disability, they just get on with it. They'll nick my leg and hide it.

If it hurts when I stand I just close out the pain – it's only pain. It makes you feel human.

I was injured on 26 May 2007, in Helmand Province, Afghanistan, while on a foot patrol. We got fired on and as we got down they operated a remote device that injured me and three others and killed one of my comrades. I was dragged down and when I looked up I saw that my right leg had been blown to smithereens.

I was in so much pain I could have passed out, but my lads were fantastic. They got to me straight away, calmed me down, stopped me screaming, put morphine into me, got the casevac into action. I was transported to the field hospital and had the rest of my leg amputated. They were going to amputate my right arm too: shrapnel wounds blew it to bits as well. But I've still got it.

When I came round, I felt a bit emotional but I didn't want it to faze me, because I'd already decided not to let this get me down. I was already making goals in my head. The strong squaddie mentality got me through it, as well as my mates. Yeah, I'm disabled, but I'm going to prove to people that I'm not as disabled as they think I am.

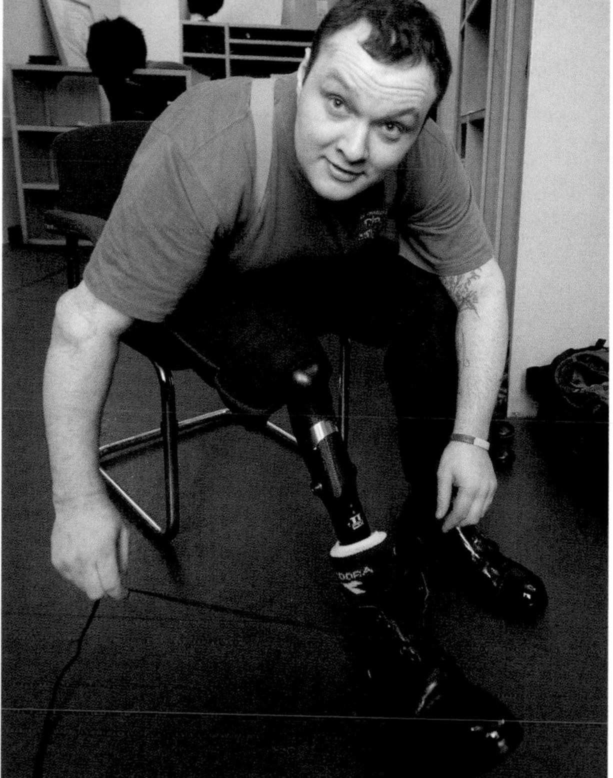
© PAUL EDWARDS

◂Scott laces up his boots before he starts his guard duty.

▾Grenadier Guardsman Scott Blaney, 22, stands guard at the Tower of London.

I was in hospital in the UK for seven weeks, then in and out for about three or four weeks at a time, then at home in Nuneaton, Warwickshire. My new leg feels great now – I can run, ride a bike, all sorts. There's a few things I can't do, like go upstairs properly, but it's not that bad really.

My dad reacted worse to the injury than I did. I just told him to get over it and stop crying. I don't regret a single day of my career; I've loved it. I've been places I'd never have been otherwise. It's always been an up. Even getting injured is kind of an up: look at me now.

The only rough times have been the nightmares about what I experienced, seeing my mates get killed. I miss everyone; they're my family, my brothers. The bloke who died when I was injured, I spoke to his family, visited his grave.

Afghanistan was hot and rough, combat-wise. If you move, you're covered in sweat. When I first heard I was going I felt excited. The thought that I might be injured was in the back of my mind, but I wasn't frightened. I miss active service badly but I can't go back out there. I might go out and do a different job, but I'll not be on the front line again.

I'll be a squaddie forever, though.

Damn right I will.

© PAUL EDWARDS

YOU ARE THE APACHE PILOT

By Ed Macy, MC

The fearsome Apache helicopter is one of the British Armed Forces' most effective – and most feared – weapons. This twin-engined, four-bladed attack helicopter is armed to the teeth with 16 Hellfire missiles, 76 rockets, 1,200 30mm rounds of cannon fire and 4 air-to-air missiles. It carries a crew of two, a pilot and gunner. Frequently summoned to support troops on the ground, the Apache has seen some blistering action in Afghanistan. Each contact presents its own dangers, challenges and nightmare dilemmas that few of us will ever have to face.

With £46 million of weaponry at your fingertips and lives at risk on the ground and in the air, what would *you* do if you were in the cockpit?

Here is just a sample of the dilemmas an Apache pilot might face on the front line. Read through each question, decide how you would react, then check the answers at the bottom of the page to find out how Ed Macy, a pilot with 23 years' service, advises handling each situation.

© ED MACY

Q1. A patrol is driving along a track in the middle of nowhere and you spot what you think is an Improvised Explosive Device (IED) buried ahead of them. You get on the radio and halt the convoy. They know that either side of the track is a minefield and are reluctant to get out of their vehicles. On your thermal camera you confirm that there is a metal object buried in the road. What can you do to assist the convoy?

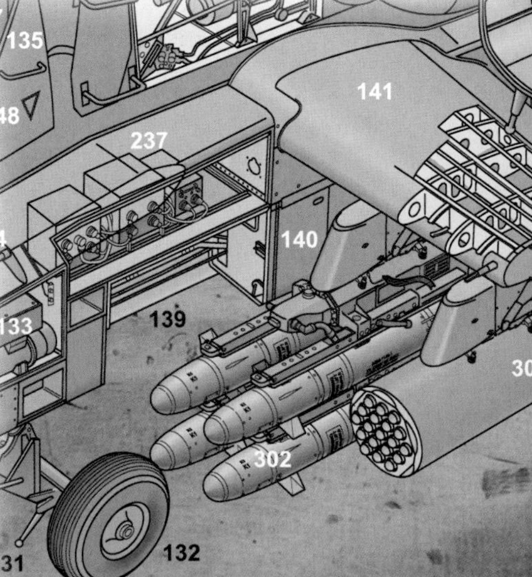

© EPA

Q2. Whilst engaging Taliban combatants who have a British patrol surrounded, you are targeted by Taliban fighter with a Surface to Air Missile (SAM). The missile streaks upwards but your flares pump off the aircraft, directing the missile away at the last second. It explodes high above you. You know the SAM operator is going to re-arm and fire again. What do you do?

Q3. A Taliban SAM has just exploded into your starboard engine. You have hit the fire extinguisher button and the fire is out. The troops you are supporting are surrounded by Taliban and the Apache is shaking badly. The troops are crying out for help but every alarm in the cockpit is blaring at you and every warning lamp glowing bright red for danger. You're barely staying airborne and the Apache warning system is telling you to make an emergency landing. You look out of the right window to see a stream of smoke from the right engine. Do you try to fight the Taliban and risk crashing, make an emergency landing close to your own troops, or limp back to base?

A1. You can offer to engage and blow up the mine using one of the Apache's weapon systems. This will ensure that none of the troops have to go near the mine or enter the minefield.

A2. Ignore the man trying to kill you and get on with the job of protecting the troops on the ground. The Apache will look after itself and you need to look after them. Only when the troops are safe should you turn your attention to engaging the SAM operator.

A3. The Apache's warning system looks after the aircraft first every time: self-preservation. You should ignore the smoke from the engine – you know the fire there is extinguished – and get on with the job. If the fire reignites, the Apache will tell you and you can use the second extinguisher bottle on it. The Apache is designed to withstand damage so that you can protect the troops until they are safe, and only then limp back to base. If the Apache sustains further damage, reappraise your situation.

Q4. You are the leader of a pair of Apaches. Your mission is to destroy a Taliban hideout deep in the Afghan mountains. En route, your wingman reports a fuel leak – he won't be able to make it there and back. Do you abort the mission or continue on your own?

Q5. An army vehicle has been blown up by a bomb and the men it was carrying are caught in an ambush. You get a shout in mid-flight to assist but your wingman is too low on fuel to make it to the site of the contact and get back to base again. You have loads of fuel but are under orders not to leave your wingman as your orders are to fly in pairs or bigger groups. What do you do?

A4. The Taliban don't know you're coming, so you abort and try again later or on another day. Always fly in a pair or in a group, unless absolutely necessary. This way you have someone to watch your back when you turn off-target. Equally, if something goes wrong and you have to make an emergency landing or if you get shot down, you have an Apache hovering above to protect and rescue you.

A5. You send your wingman back for fuel and head directly to the ambush to assist the troops. No orders or procedures are more important than saving a life, and the men on the ground are in grave danger. If things go wrong, then that's tough luck. First, save lives.

Q6. You've been shot down in the Green Zone, an area of lush, green orchards, threaded with irrigation ditches. If you stay with your Apache, the Taliban will get to you before your mates find you, so you escape into a deep-wooded area. You know the British patrol you were supporting is less than a mile away. Your radio isn't working. What do you do?

Q7. You have crash-landed in the Afghan mountains and are on the run from the Taliban. You were the leader of a pair of Apaches and your wingman has run out of fuel and returned to base. It's going to be some time before another aircraft is on station to protect you. Your pilot is badly hurt and is slowing you down. You are out of ammunition and there is an escape route ahead of you. Do you stay together with no ammunition and wait for the Taliban, or do you leave the pilot and make a break for it?

A6. Observe the enemy and your own troops. Look for an escape route to your own troops, or look for an escape route to a safer place. Don't spook your own troops – they might kill you, thinking you are the Taliban. When you get closer to your own troops, try to signal to them without giving yourself away to the enemy. If that fails, stay low and out of sight of the Taliban and creep closer to your own troops, until they see you and you link up.

A7. There is no right or wrong answer for this question. It's every crew's worst scenario and one they discuss as a team. In my crew, we agreed to make a break for it and leave the injured one behind. The reason was simple. There's no way the Taliban would ever trade an Apache pilot and therefore it almost certain that death faces whoever gets caught. Better that one should survive than that all should die. And the main reason I always kept one bullet for myself!

PATROL & PROTECT

As part of the British Armed Forces' joint operations in Afghanistan, the Royal Navy plays a vital role across the region with Royal Marines on the ground at the front line and navy aircraft carriers and warships actively deployed in the Gulf of Aden and the Arabian Sea.

But, away from the front line, another war is being waged – this one on the high seas – and the Navy is deployed to patrol and protect – and keep the seas out of the hands of terrorists.

The RFA *Largs Bay*.

MURKY WATERS

The might of the Royal Navy is deployed in a deadly game of cat and mouse which takes place every day in the Gulf of Aden. Over 23,000 ships pass through this busy shipping route each year – all at risk from the modern-day, cut-throat pirates that haunt these waters.

Piracy on the high seas has boomed in the last few years, and the Gulf is a particular hotspot. Hundreds of pirates, mostly Somali, operate in this region, and in 2009 there was a record number of attacks and hijackings, estimated to have netted around $100 million.

Determined to bring this rampage to a close, various nations have begun patrolling the Gulf. When Britain first sent HMS *Northumberland* in 2009, as part of Operation Atalanta (the European anti-piracy initiative), it was the first Royal Navy warship tasked to fight piracy since 1816.

On board these warships are elite troops specifically trained in 'non-compliant' boarding – in Britain's case, the Fleet Protection Group Royal Marines. They are on short-notice standby, ready to react immediately to a ship's distress call, or to chase suspected pirates using rigid-hulled inflatable boats (RIBs). They can also scramble helicopters carrying Royal Marine snipers, which arrive quickly on the scene.

But it's a complicated situation. The pirates' hunting grounds are vast – over one million square miles – and they can be difficult to identify. Like the many fishermen in these waters, they operate from dhows, towing faster and more agile skiffs behind them. Armed with AK-47s and RPGs which are easily concealed, they shadow vulnerable ships and can lie low until a patrolling warship has moved on.

THE ROYAL NAVY IN ACTION SINCE 1982

1. Falklands, 1982: 2 carriers, 23 destroyers/frigates, 6 submarines, 13 other ships, 22 Royal Fleet Auxiliary (RFA) support vessels, 171 Sea Harriers/helicopters. 13,000 Royal Navy personnel, 3,700 Royal Marines, 2,000 RFAs.

2. Iraq, 1990–91: 8 destroyers/frigates, 2 submarines, 12 support ships (RN and RFA), helicopters from three squadrons and Royal Marine detachments.

3. Bosnia, 1992–96: 1 carrier, 2 destroyers/frigates, 1 submarine, 4 RFA vessels, aircraft/helicopters, Royal Marine detachment.

4. East Timor, 1999: 1 destroyer.

5. Kosovo, 1999–2001: 1 carrier, 2 submarines, 6 destroyers/frigates, 3 other RN ships, 4 RFA, seven Sea Harriers, 6 helicopters, HQ 3 Commando Brigade.

6. Sierra Leone, 2000: 1 carrier, 1 helicopter carrier, 1 frigate, 4 RFA, 42 Commando Royal Marines, Sea Harriers and helicopters.

7. Afghanistan, 2001 onwards: 1 carrier, 2 submarines, 1 destroyer/frigate, 1 amphibious ship, 6 RFA, 7 Harrier GR7s/9s, 3 Commando Brigade on six-month tours, plus 2,400 personnel from the Royal Navy.

8. Iraq, 2003–09: 1 carrier, 1 helicopter carrier, 5 destroyers/ frigates, 2 submarines, 5 other Royal Navy ships, 13 RFA, 3 Commando Brigade on six-month tours, 45 helicopters.

9. Armilla Patrol in Gulf, 1980 onwards: 2 destroyers/ frigates, 3 RFA, 4 minesweepers, 1 support ship.

10. Counter-piracy, 2008 onwards: 1 destroyer/ frigate, 1 RFA Type 45 Daring class destroyer.

Royal Marines on board a rigid inflatable boat checking out dhows in the Gulf of Aden.

MARITIME CONTRIBUTIONS TO JOINT OPERATIONS

Manoeuvre: The Royal Navy (RN) is inherently mobile and is able to act and react quickly, unpredictably, overtly and covertly.

Fire Support: The RN can provide a fire support role through the use of GR7 aircraft, attack helicopters, ship and submarine-launched missiles (TLAM) and shore bombardment guns.

Protection: The RN is capable of protecting forces ashore from the air using GR7 aircraft. Additionally, the RN can extend its protection by its ability to withdraw forces quickly if they come under serious threat.

Electromagnetic Spectrum: The electronic support measures fitted on RN ships, submarines and aircraft can contribute greatly to the control of the electromagnetic spectrum and help deny the enemy the use of it.

Command and Control: The RN's aircraft carriers can provide facilities for a Joint Taskforce Headquarters (Afloat) providing mobility, security and a full command and control suite.

Information and Intelligence: The RN has access to sophisticated high-speed satellite communications allowing secure access to shore-based information networks and intelligence databases.

Deployment: An RN task group is able to move significant quantities of troops and equipment quickly and effectively.

Sustainability: An RN task group is able to sustain forces ashore during all stages of a campaign and likewise remain self-sufficient for long periods of time.

HMS *Northumberland* patrols off the Gulf of Aden.

Attacks can take a crew completely by surprise, as pirates draw alongside in the half-light of dawn or dusk, and use ladders to scale the ship's hull. Heavily armed, they can overwhelm ships in minutes, leaving very little time for a warship to reach the scene and repel an attack. Hostages have so far remained unharmed by the pirates, so troops will not board and attack if a ship has been overpowered, as the crew's lives could be endangered. Once pirated, ships are usually steered for the lawless Somali coast, where the ship and crew are held for ransom.

Despite this, patrols in the Gulf of Aden have begun to improve safety in the area – incidents fell 18 per cent in the first half of 2010 from a year ago, as the presence of several navies make pirates think twice about attacking unarmed ships.

COMBAT ON THE SEAS

When patrolling in the Gulf of Aden as part of the multi-nation anti-piracy operation Standing NATO Maritime Group 2 (SNMG2), vital to the ongoing fight against terrorism, the Royal Navy Type 22 frigate HMS *Cumberland* became involved in a dramatic shoot-out, the like of which has never before been seen by the Royal Navy on the high seas.

The confrontation took place sixty miles south of the Yemeni coast, where HMS *Cumberland*, whose motto is '*Justitia Tenax*' – Tenacious of Justice – detected a dhow in the waters and identified it as a stolen Yemeni fishing vessel which had been involved in an attack on the Danish-registered MV *Powerful*

STANDING DEPLOYMENTS

As well as patrolling the Gulf of Aden, the Royal Navy is deployed across the world in various roles.

Haiti: After the small Caribbean island of Haiti was hit by a devastating earthquake in January 2010, its people left destitute and homeless amongst the shattered remains, the Royal Navy reacted quickly, dispatching a Royal Fleet Auxiliary supply ship carrying vital aid. The RFA Largs Bay transported relief supplies including shelter material for the people of Haiti, equipment to help in rebuilding the port in Port-au-Prince and forty Land Rovers to help charity workers traverse the island. In addition, the Royal Navy deployed a twelve-man operational liaison team to assess what further military specialist requirements were needed.

Falkland Islands Patrol Force: Since the Falklands War, in which the Navy played a key role, the Royal Navy has maintained a constant presence in the Falkland Islands, patrolling and protecting the waters around the UK Overseas Territory. HMS *Clyde* is permanently stationed in the waters of the South Atlantic.

Fishery Protection Squadron: Stationed off the coast of the UK, the Fishery Protection Squadron, the oldest front-line squadron in the Royal Navy, protects the fishing interests of the UK, ensuring the waters are clear and safe for fishermen. Operating from the River Class Offshore Patrol Vessels, British Sea Fisheries Officers (BSFO) also undertake routine inspections at sea of fishing vessels both by day and night.

when pirates had opened fire on the cargo boat with assault rifles.

Commandos from HMS *Cumberland* were dispatched from the frigate and sped towards the pirates' dhow, circling the boat in an effort to detain them. As they approached, several of the pirates, a mixed crew of Somalis and Yemenis, opened fire. The Royal Marines returned fire in self-defence, killing two pirates, and then boarded the dhow where they found a stash of guns and other weaponry.

The battle signalled a new policy of maximum robustness for the Royal Navy on the high seas. Captain Mike Davis-Marks, a senior spokesman for the Navy, said: 'This is bound to have an impact on pirates who for the last two years have been getting away with seizing vessels and receiving large ransoms. Now suddenly there's the threat of death and this may force them to think again, but they are determined people, so we'll have to see.'

An abandoned Yemeni fishing skiff believed to be involved in the pirating of the MV *Saldhana* gets destroyed by gun fire from the HMS *Northumberland*'s heavy weapons.

LIEUTENANT-COLONEL HERBERT JONES

Lieutentant-Colonel Herbert Jones.

Lieutenant-Colonel Herbert Jones became a legend when he stormed an Argentine machine-gun nest and turned the tide of the Falklands War.

On 28 May 1982, Jones was in command of 2 Para and he faced the fight of his life.

The remote Falkland Islands had been overrun by Argentine Forces and its British population put under foreign rule.

A taskforce was despatched by then prime minister Margaret Thatcher to recapture the islands and dispel the invaders.

The first battle was vital: the towns of Darwin and Goose Green had been overrun by enemy forces and the scared inhabitants placed under lock and key in the social club. They were surrounded by hostile troops which greatly outnumbered Britain's tough band of men from 2 Para. It was down to their leader Jones to engage the Argentine Forces, break the enemy's will and force a surrender which would pave the way for victory.

The enemy, however, were dug in and had no intention of going quietly.

With his troops pinned down by heavy, accurate fire for over an hour, Jones could feel victory slipping through his fingers.

Sensing imminent defeat and the loss of morale amongst his troops, Jones realised that only drastic action and inspirational leadership could turn the tide of the battle.

He clambered through heavy artillery fire to the front of his battalion.

Grasping a sub-machine gun, the forty-two-year-old officer gathered his men at his side, and charged the enemy position with complete disregard for his own personal safety.

This action exposed him to fire from a number of trenches – but he continued to fight on.

Spurred on by his gallantry, the loyal troops of 2 Para pursued Jones as he stormed the steep slope towards the Argentine bunker, even after

A Royal Marine mortar team dug in and ready for action on the wet and windy slopes of the Falklands.

The first children to be liberated when Britain's troops stormed ashore at San Carlos lay flowers at Jones's grave.

being wounded by a glancing bullet which knocked him to the floor.

As he charged up a short slope at the enemy position he was seen to fall and roll backwards downhill.

He immediately picked himself up and again charged the enemy trench, firing his sub-machine gun and seemingly oblivious to the intense fire directed at him.

He was hit by fire from another trench which he outflanked, and fell, dying only a few feet from the enemy he had assaulted.

It was his gallant dashing run which galvanized his men's resolve and broke the will of the Argentine invaders.

The men regrouped and attacked the Argentine Forces again, eventually forcing their surrender.

Goose Green and Darwin were liberated, and the battle was won.

By David Willetts

The Victoria Cross is a bronze cross pattée, 41 mm high, 36 mm wide, bearing the crown of Saint Edward surmounted by a lion, and the inscription FOR VALOUR. This was originally to have been FOR THE BRAVE, until it was changed on the recommendation of Queen Victoria, as it implied that not all men in battle were brave. On the reverse of the medal is a circular panel on which the date of the act for which it was awarded is engraved in the centre.

By Richard Holmes, CBE

FIGHTING TALK

Warfare and war zones may have changed hugely in some respects over the centuries – the weaponry, the technology, even the very nature of the front line – but one thing has remained constant: the man in uniform fighting his enemy for his country. Here, top military historian and brigadier in the Terrestrial Army, Richard Holmes, brings some of those soldiers' tales back to life in extracts from his favourite war accounts written by serving soldiers through the ages.

I spend much of my life reading about war, and, believe me, there is no shortage of books on the subject. But I want to share with you my favourite honest personal narratives, written by British soldiers who have experienced combat firsthand.

In all my reading, I have realised that the earlier the date, the harder it is to look into the cannon's mouth. Listen to Royalist Captain Richard Atkyns describing the 1643 Battle of Lansdown in Peter Young's edition of *The Vindication of Richard Atkyns:*

A Lee-Enfield rifle from the time of the Boer War.

French cuirassiers charging a British square during the Battle of Waterloo.

When I came to the top of the hill, I saw Sir Bevill Grinvill's stand of pikes, which certainly preserved our army from a total rout, with the loss of his most precious life: they stood as upon the eaves of a house for steepness, but as unmovable as a rock ...

We can see Britain's war in the Iberian peninsula through the eyes of officers, like Captain John Kincaid, who wrote *Random Shots from a Rifleman* and *Adventures in the Rifle Brigade*.

15 March: We overtook the enemy a little before dark this afternoon. They were drawn up behind the Ceira, at Fez D'Aronce,[1] with their rear-guard, under Marshal Ney[2], imprudently posted on our side of the river, a circumstance which Lord Wellington took immediate advantage of; and, by a furious attack, dislodged them, in such confusion that they blew up the bridge before half of their own people had time to get over. Those who were thereby left behind, not choosing to put themselves to the pain of being shot, took to the river, which received them so hospitably that few of them ever quitted it.

By and large it was not until the Napoleonic Wars (1802–15) that private soldiers and non-commissioned officers began to put their experiences into print and our 'epaulette history' is counterpointed by views from the ranks. Benjamin Harris's *The Recollections of Rifleman Harris* (edited by Christopher Hibbert) gives us a view from the man on the ground:

1. The River Ceira carves its way through the northern half of the Gois region in central Portugal.
2. Marshal Michel Ney, 1st Duc d'Elchingen, 1st Prince de la Moskowa (1769–1815), was a French soldier and military commander during the Napoleonic Wars. He was known as *Le Rougeaud* ('red faced') by his men and nicknamed *le Brave des Braves* ('the bravest of the brave') by Napoleon.

The Duke of Wellington (1769–1852).

I myself was very soon so hotly engaged, loading and firing away, enveloped in the smoke I created, and the cloud which hung about me from the continued fire of my comrades, that I could see nothing for a few minutes but the red flash of my own piece amongst the white vapour clinging to my very clothes. This has often seemed to me the greatest drawback upon our present system of fighting; for whilst in such state, on a calm day, until some friendly breeze of wind clears the space around, a soldier knows no more of his position and what is about to happen in his front, or what has happened (even amongst his own companions) than the very dead lying around.

Antony Brett-James's edition of *Edward Costello: The Peninsula and Waterloo* is also

Charge of the Light Brigade, Balaclava, 25 October,1854 by Richard Woodville.

a good example of battle writing from the front line around the same time. Do not be misled by the title of *A Hawk at War: The Peninsular Reminiscences of General Sir Thomas Brotherton* (edited by Bryan Perrett). Though Brotherton died a general, he was a captain of light dragoons during the period he describes. And I cannot resist breaking my own rule to include a Frenchman. Baron Marcellin de Marbot, for whom the adjective swashbuckling could very well have been invented, might literally have crossed swords with Brotherton, and his memoirs are available in English. This extract describes a tense scene on the Russian front as Napoleonic forces swelled in advance of battle:

> The French army was now massed around and before Brunn. The Russian advance-guard occupied Austerlitz, while the bulk of their army was positioned round the town of Olmutz, where were also the Emperor Alexander of Russia and the Emperor of Austria. A battle seemed inevitable, but both sides being well aware that the outcome would have an immense bearing on the destiny of Europe, each hesitated to make a decisive move. Napoleon, usually so swift to act, waited for eleven days at Brunn before launching a major attack. It is, however, true that every day of waiting increased his forces by the arrival of great numbers of soldiers who had lagged behind because of illness or fatigue, and who having now recovered, hastened to rejoin their units.

Sergeant Major George Loy Smith charged with the Light Brigade in the Crimean War (1853–56), and his *A Victorian RSM: From India to the Crimea* is worth reading alongside the Marquess of Anglesey's edition of *Little Hodge; being extracts from the letters and diaries of Colonel Edward Cooper Hodge written during the Crimean War*. For the infantry's experience of the same conflict, look at Timothy Gowing's *A Voice From the Ranks*:

> At one time victory trembled in the balance – some of our guns were in the hands of the enemy, and the gunners had been shot or cut down. But the boys of the Emerald Isle were close by. The 88th Connaught Rangers

Ships dock at Cossack Bay, Balaclava, in present-day Ukraine, during the Crimean War.

and the 49th went at them and recaptured the guns. The advance of our Guards at the Sandbag (or Two-Gun) Battery was grand, and surely it could be said of them, 'Nothing could stop that astonishing infantry'. No sudden burst of undisciplined valour, no nervous enthusiasm, weakened their order; their flashing eyes were bent upon the dark masses in their front; their measured tread shook the ground; their ringing cheer startled the infuriated columns of the enemy as their bayonets were brought down to the charge; and, led by the grandson of a king, in they went, shoulder to shoulder, and the enemy, with all their boasted strength, were driven down the hill.

One of the best accounts of the Boer War (1899–1902) is *Commando* by Deneys Reitz, who joined the Boer forces at the age of seventeen. He was ultimately reconciled to the war's outcome and served as a British lieutenant colonel in the First World War but here he writes of seeing the English enemy massing before him:

We could see nothing, but heavy fighting had started close by, for the roar of the guns increased and at times we heard the rattle of small arms and Maxims. None of the fire, however, was directed at us, and so far as we were concerned nothing happened, and we fretted at the thought of standing passively by when others were striking the first blow of the war. After perhaps an hour the sound died down, indicating, although we did not know it at the time, that the English had driven the Vryheidmen from Talana Hill with heavy losses.[3] Towards midday the weather cleared somewhat, and while it still continued misty, patches of sunshine began to splash the plain behind us, across which we had approached the mountain overnight. And then, far down, into one of these sunlit spaces rode a troop of English horsemen about 300 strong. This was our first sight of the enemy, and we followed their course with close attention … Now, for the first time in my life, I heard the sharp hiss of rifle-bullets about my ears, and for the first time I experienced the thrill of riding into action.

---

3. Vryheid is a coal-mining and cattle-ranching town in KwaZulu-Natal, South Africa. '*Vryheid*' is Afrikaans for 'freedom' or 'liberty'.

◀ British soldiers manhandle a 9.2m Howitzer over muddy ground near Ypres during World War I.

▼ Troops shelter in the trenches near Ypres in October 1917.

Though the British would eventually win the war, the outcome that day favoured the Boers. Reitz records the British surrender and his first sobering glimpse of casualties:

> I saw a white flag go up…so I hastened to be present at the surrender. By the time I got there the soldiers had thrown down their arms and were falling in under their offices. Their leader, Colonel Moller, stood on the stoep[4] looking pretty crestfallen, but the private soldiers seemed to take the turn of events more cheerfully. Officers and men were dressed in drab khaki uniforms, instead of the scarlet I had seen in England, and this somewhat disappointed me as it seemed to detract from the glamour of war; but worse still was the sight of the dead soldiers. These were the first men I had seen killed in anger, and their ashen faces and staring eyeballs came as a great shock, for I had pictured the dignity of death in battle, but I now saw that it was horrible to look upon.

---

4. Veranda or porch.

The British Army of the First World War was bigger than it ever had been before or ever would be again, and amongst the tens of thousands of men swept into its ranks were many who, in the normal way of things, would never have thought of becoming soldiers. Captain JC Dunn was medical officer of the 2nd Royal Welch Fusiliers, and his anthology *The War the Infantry Knew* tells the story of the battalion in the words of some of its surviving officers. Amongst them were the poets Siegfried Sassoon and Robert Graves, both of whom were to write accounts of their service. In the same battalion was the eternally unpromoted Frank Richards, whose *Old Soldiers Never Die* adds the authentic – and so rarely heard – regular private's voice.

Most of the ordinary soldiers (a contradiction in terms for this extraordinary generation) who wrote about the First World War were hostilities-only men. For instance, John Jackson joined the Cameron Highlanders in August 1914, won a Military Medal at Passchendaele and, in *Private 12768: Memoir of a Tommy*, tells us how loyalty to good mates and a fine battalion could help a man through. Fred Hodges was a conscript, though by no means an unwilling one, and his *Men of 18 in 1918* tells us much about that last few months on the Western Front when this army, half of its soldiers only eighteen years old, won a victory too easily forgotten. In sharp contrast, Ronald Skirth was an intelligent volunteer whose zeal was corroded, as he tells us in *The Reluctant Tommy,* by callous and incompetent officers. For the story of one officer who was neither, read Charles Carrington's *Soldier from the Wars Returning*. I often complain about the fact that too many of us come to the First World War as history rather than as literature, but for all that there is something about David Jones's prose-poem *In Parenthesis* that never fails to move me.

Although the Second World War did not engender writing on quite the same scale as the First, there are many excellent accounts. Alex Bowlby, a public schoolboy who served as a private in the infantry in North Africa and Italy, called his memoir *The Recollections of Rifleman Bowlby* as an echo of Benjamin Harris's Peninsular War memoir, for both served in the Rifle Brigade. You cannot

▲War in Africa. The crews of a British Army tank regiment photographed in cheerful mood after fighting continuously in the desert for a month during World War II.

◄A German tank crew surrenders to British infantry in North Africa, October 1942.

beat Bowlby's eye for his comrades, those 'Cockney Arabs' who moved 'with the relaxed assurance of successful poachers'. Although I have long been a fan of George MacDonald Fraser's character Flashman, I think the best thing Fraser ever wrote was *Quartered Safe Out Here*, an account of his service in the ranks of the Border Regiment in Burma. He understood, perhaps better than most, the power of written accounts to capture, in vivid detail, the essence of battle:

It is satisfying, and at the same time slightly eerie, to read in an official military history of an action in which you took part, even as a very minor and bewildered participant. A coloured picture of men and guns and violent movement comes between the eye and the printed page; smells return to the nostrils, of dusty heat and oil and cordite smoke, and you hear again the rattle of small arms and crash of explosions, the startled oaths and the yells of command.

Falklands' hero General Sir Hew Pike.

I could fill a page or two with accounts of post-1945 conflicts, but must keep my list short. Ken Lukowiak's *A Soldier's Song* caused a stir when it first appeared, and still provides one of the best sharp-end commentaries on the 1982 Falklands War. My choice for Iraq would be Dan Mills's *Sniper One*, telling the story of that lethal but unkempt band

Soldiers on air defence duty at Bluff Cove on the Falkland Islands, ready for Argentine air attack.

Marines 'debus' a Chinook helicopter after landing at Sangin Platoon House in Helmand, Afghanistan.

of brothers, the sniper platoon of 1st Battalion, The Princess of Wales's Royal Regiment in Al Amarah.

Although the men and women now fighting in Afghanistan look very different to Captain Atkyns spurring his way up Lansdown Hill in 1643, there are strong threads of continuity linking soldiers and soldiering across the years. Hew Pike's *From the Front Line* is a masterly anthology, taking us, by way of the words of eight family members (two were killed and three became generals), through South Africa, two world wars, Korea, Aden, the Falklands and Afghanistan. It tells us a good deal about the qualities of courage, comradeship, loyalty and duty that run like a golden filament through so many of these accounts. The closer we come to the cannon's mouth, the more big issues fade away and the stronger the bonds of mateship become.

Writer of the book *Sniper One*, Dan Mills.

THE TROJAN

© ANDY BUSH / THE SUN

© CROWN COPYRIGHT

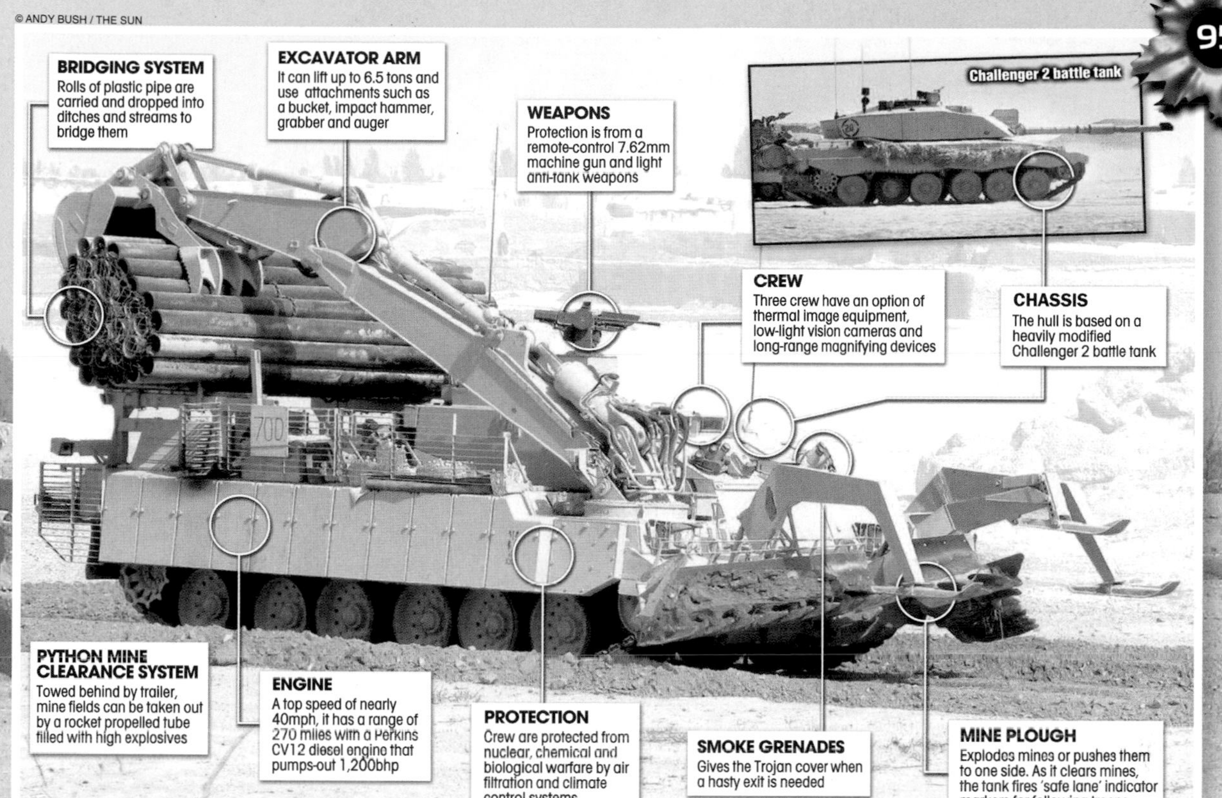

TROJAN ARMOURED ENGINEER VEHICLE

Crewed by three personnel, the Trojan is a modern armoured engineer vehicle which offers high-speed cross-country mobility.

The Trojan is capable of carrying out a wide range of roles. With its enormously capable excavator arm, mine plough and dozer blade, it is easy to move around the battlefield to perform complex obstacle clearance tasks without the crew having to leave the protection of the tank.

Its excavator arm can dig ditches and trenches and clear or smash its way through all sorts of obstructions, such as abandoned vehicles, rubble, fallen trees and buildings. The Trojan can be fitted with a front-mounted, hydraulically controlled dozer blade that can excavate ditches, push heavy obstacles aside and construct protection for troops and vehicles.

It can also be fitted with a technically advanced mine plough which can clear a safe path through a minefield and simultaneously fire 'safe lane' indicator markers into the ground to mark safe routes for friendly forces.

Additionally, for mine clearance operations, Trojan can fire the Python, which is a rocket-propelled explosive mine clearance system. Python is essentially a long hose filled with over a ton of high explosives, which can blast a clear route through a minefield.

Trojan can also drop fascines – bundles of very strong plastic pipes – into ditches and streams so that other vehicles may traverse them.

Whilst the Trojan is primarily an engineer vehicle, it is fitted with a remote-control machine gun and smoke grenade discharger, which enable the vehicle commander to provide covering fire and smoke to support extractions from enemy contact.

IMPROVISED EXPLOSIVE DEVICES

A WMIK after hitting a mine in Goreshk, Afghanistan.

In the two years from 2007 to 2009, the number of improvised explosive devices planted in Afghanistan is estimated to have more than doubled. Last year, 75 per cent of UK casualties in Afghanistan were a result of IEDs. And soldiers aren't the only ones getting injured – the United Nations estimates that 200,000 people in Afghanistan have been disabled by landmines and the explosive remnants of war. The problem doesn't stop there, either – worldwide, about 87 per cent of all terrorist attacks involve IEDs.

'There is no single solution, there is no panacea,' said Colonel Robert Herring, Assistant Head of Joint Explosive Ordnance Disposal and Search. 'There is no equipment solution, no technological solution or particular way of operating that will solve the problem. It is a multi-faceted approach to solving the problem. The insurgents are extremely mobile, agile and adaptive, and they know they can't defeat us man-to-man, firefight-to-firefight, so they use what we call asymmetric tactics to engage us and their weapon of choice is the improvised explosive device.'

In accordance with NATO strategy, three lines of operation have been adopted:

- **attack the system**: target the insurgents' finances, intelligence systems and IED-making capability
- **defeat the device**: employ specialist counter-IED searchers, bomb disposal experts and the equipment they use to carry out such operations, and mitigate the effects of devices if they do go off
- **prepare the force**: provide all service personnel with training and education to be aware of the threat and how best to counter it.

But what exactly *is* an IED? And what can we do to stop them and to prepare the men and women who must do battle with this deadliest of foes on a daily basis?

Afghan policemen inspect the site of a car bomb near the Indian Embassy in Kabul.

© ASSOCIATED PRESS / ANJUM NAVEED

A Pakistan Army official flips through a book about making explosives, recovered from a militants' hideout.

ATF	Vehicle Description	Maximum Explosive Capacity	Lethal Air Blast Range	Minimum Evacuation Distance	Falling Glass Hazard
	Compact Sedan	500 pounds 227 kilos (in trunk)	100 feet 30 meters	1,500 feet 457 meters	1,250 feet 381 meters
	Full Size Sedan	1,000 pounds 455 kilos (in trunk)	125 feet 38 meters	1,750 feet 534 meters	1,750 feet 534 meters
	Passenger Van or Cargo Van	4,000 pounds 1,818 kilos	200 feet 61 meters	2,750 feet 838 meters	2,750 feet 838 meters
	Small Box Van (14 ft. box)	10,000 pounds 4,545 kilos	300 feet 91 meters	3,750 feet 1,143 meters	3,750 feet 1,143 meters
	Box Van or Water/Fuel Truck	30,000 pounds 13,636 kilos	450 feet 137 meters	6,500 feet 1,982 meters	6,500 feet 1,982 meters
	Semi-Trailer	60,000 pounds 27,273 kilos	600 feet 183 meters	7,000 feet 2,134 meters	7,000 feet 2,134 meters

WHAT IS AN IED?

An IED is a 'homemade' explosive device that can be composed of almost anything. IEDs can be any size, packed in any number of containers, and delivered by multiple means. Because they are essentially 'handmade', using whatever materials are available, each IED is unique – which raises unique challenges for the men and women who need to identify them, either to avoid them or to dismantle them. Broadly speaking, however, IEDs fall into three categories:

- **Package-type IEDs** are usually military munitions such as concealed mortar or artillery projectiles. These are often placed along known routes or in potholes, they may be time-delay triggered or remotely detonated, and are even sometimes thrown in front of vehicles.
- **Vehicle-borne IEDs** are devices that use a vehicle as the 'package'. The bomb can be loaded into anything from a donkey cart to a large cargo truck – or even an ambulance. In some cases, multiple vehicles are involved, with a lead vehicle operating as a 'decoy' to lure victims in closer and maximise casualties. Larger vehicles can pack a bigger payload, as this graph from the US Bureau of Alcohol, Tobacco and Firearms demonstrates.
- **Suicide bombs** often incorporating fragmentation – or shrapnel – are contained in specially modified vests, belts or clothing. The bombs are often detonated by hand, using a switch or button. The aim of the suicide bomber is not to commit suicide, per se, but to kill or injure as many of his or her victims as possible.

Though they can vary widely in shape and form, IEDs share a common set of components. These are:

- an initiation system or fuse
- explosive fill
- a detonator
- a power supply for the detonator
- a container.

Once these basic components are assembled, IEDs can be triggered in a number of ways:

- A **command-wire improvised explosive device** uses electrical firing cable, which gives the bomber control over the device right up until the moment of detonation.
- **Radio-controlled improvised explosive devices** (RCIED) are triggered by radio link. The receiver is connected to an electrical firing circuit, while the transmitter is operated by the bomber from a safe distance away. A signal from the transmitter causes the receiver to trigger a firing pulse, which operates the detonator switch. An RCIED can be triggered from any number of different mechanisms, including car alarms, wireless doorbells, mobile phones, pagers and encrypted radios.
- **Victim-operated improvised explosive devices** (VOIED) – also known as booby traps – explode upon contact with a victim. VOIED switches are usually well hidden. These can include tripwires, pressure mats or spring-loaded releases. Common forms of VOIED include the under-vehicle IED and improvised landmines.

It's not just the type of IEDs that troops in Afghanistan have to worry about, but also how they've been deployed. There are multiple ways of combining and enhancing IEDs for maximum misery.

Staff Sgt Colin Hill of the Royal Engineers Bomb Disposal handling a booby trap.

- Some IEDs are **coupled**, or linked, usually with detonating cord. When the first IED detonates, it sets off the linked IED.
- **Rolled** IEDs are coupled in a more complex fashion in order to create maximum mayhem. With rolled IEDs, pressure on the first, unfused device detonates the second device. This then sets off the first device.
- Buried IEDs can be **boosted**, or stacked on top of one another. In this case, only the most deeply buried device is fused, which helps to hide the IED from metal detectors and increases the force of the blast.
- Some IEDs are created by **sensitising anti-tank mines**. This is when the pressure plate on an anti-tank mine is adjusted so that less weight is needed to detonate the mine.
- **Daisy chains** are networks of mines, linked together with tripwire or detonating cord. When one mine is detonated, the others also blow, creating large, lethal engagement areas.

The Joint Forces Explosive Ordnance Disposal teams are one of the busiest call signs in Helmand Province.

99

COUNTER-IED

Against these dreadful innovations, makers of defensive equipment are always working to improve counter-IED measures and equipment, and to find new and better ways to protect the troops on the ground.

In the UK, the newest military response to the IED problem is known as **Talisman**. This is composed of five elements:

- two enormous armoured vehicles
- a JCB digger
- a bomb disposal robot
- an unmanned aerial vehicle (UAV).

The Talisman system is currently being used by Royal Engineers to clear and build safe routes around Helmand Province in Afghanistan.

A **Mastiff** armoured vehicle and its crew act as Talisman's eyes, with video screens inside the rear compartment of the truck displaying aerial video footage gathered by a Honeywell T-Hawk UAV. This heavily-armoured, 6x6-wheel drive, protected patrol vehicle can carry eight people, plus two crew. With a maximum speed of 55mph, the newer model, **Mastiff 2**, is armed with the latest weapon systems, including a 7.62mm general-purpose machine gun, 12.7mm heavy machine gun or 40mm automatic grenade launcher. Its hull is V-shaped, as opposed to flat, which pushes the force of any explosion outwards, making it a safer ride along mine-strewn roads.

The indirect vision system is another safety measure of the Mastiff, which allows it to be driven at night-time without using any lights. Cameras at the front, back and sides of the vehicle use infra-red to see in the dark and the driver uses a small TV screen to watch where he is going. The new Mastiff 2 vehicles have improved axles and suspension to cope with the harsh terrain; better thermal imaging for the drivers; explosive-attenuating seats – providing better protection to the soldier on impact; improved armour; and greater crew capacity.

Another armoured vehicle, known as the **Buffalo**, has a remote-controlled, extendable, pronged 30-foot arm attached to the front, which is used to comb or 'rummage' the ground, detecting signs of IEDs. This six-wheeled vehicle combines ballistic and blast protection with technology to detect the presence of dangerous ordnance.

The **JCB digger** is used to fill in ditches or potholes that might prevent soldiers or vehicles from moving forward.

The **Talon** remote-controlled robot then allows troops to say out of harm's way once devices have been found. The smallest and one

© AFP

Soldiers stand alongside a MRAP (Mine Resistant Ambush Protected) Mastiff with mine roller attachments.

100

To find out more about what to do in case of a mine encounter visit **www.thesun.co.uk/realheroes** or use your smartphone to scan this code:

© TIMES NEWSPAPERS LTD

The Dragon Runner robot with Captain Judith Gallagher from 11 EOD Regiment RLC.

of the newest members of Talon family of robots is the **Dragon Runner** (20cm wide x 7.5cm tall x 23cm long), a rugged Small Unmanned Ground Vehicle (SUGV) that weighs 10–20kg. It can be easily carried by a soldier in a backpack and can travel at speeds of around 5mph, move over rough terrain, as well as climb stairs and open doors. It is equipped with a manipulator arm to assist with the disarming of IEDs, and can also be configured for a variety of other reconnaissance and surveillance operations. The Dragon Runner is also able to operate in sewers, drainpipes, caves and courtyards. Day and night pan/tilt/zoom cameras, motion detectors and a listening capability allow the all-seeing, all-listening robot to send video footage back to its operator, enabling troops to assess a situation prior to moving forward. The Dragon Runner is particularly suited to operational environments similar to those experienced in Afghanistan, where the road system has been ravaged by almost continuous fighting since the late 1970s and where many troop movements are conducted either on foot or by helicopter.

The unmanned **Micro Air Vehicle** (MAV), otherwise known as the 'Flying Robot' or 'T-Hawk', has two cameras which feed information back to a laptop so that the commander has all the information needed to make decisions. At 20lb, the T-Hawk is small enough to fit in a backpack and be operated by a single user. It can travel at speeds of up to 80mph, can reach heights of 10,500 feet, and has an endurance of 40 minutes.

OTHER CUTTING EDGE EQUIPMENT SAVING LIVES ON THE FRONT LINES ...

The **Vallon Minehound VMH3** state-of-the-art metal detector is lightweight (only 2.5kg), waterproof, and can operate in a range of temperatures. Hypersensitive, the radar will detect buried objects in almost all soil

© CROWN COPYRIGHT

Soldiers operate an MAV.

conditions. Audio and visual signals warn the user of any potential threats. The adjustable handle allows the operators to shorten the device for use in a kneeling position.

The **Python rocket** is a trailer-mounted, rocket-propelled mine clearing system pulled behind the indestructible Trojan tank – an armoured vehicle that boasts a dozer blade, mineplough and excavator arm. Once launched, the rocket 'whip' fires a string of high explosives that reaches up to one-third of mile. The explosives are then detonated, triggering any mines or IEDs that are lying within or close to its path.

In inhabited areas where the Python's mighty blast would be too dangerous, or in situations too complex for the Dragon Runner, it falls to the bomb disposal expert on the ground to dismantle the device. These brave men and women run grave risks and must be given every advantage possible in training, support and equipment in order to do their job safely.

Explosive Ordnance Disposal suits and helmets provide bomb disposal experts with protection against blast, fragmentation, impact, heat and flame. The suit consists of trousers, a separate groin plate, a jacket and a helmet. Breakaway zips on the suit legs allow access to the lower limbs in case of injury. Bomb disposal experts in Afghanistan frequently operate in temperatures of up to 50°C, so to counteract dehydration, EOD suits include a hands-free hydration system. This is worn like a backpack in the jacket's insulated rear centre pocket and has a clip-on, non-drip mouthpiece.

EOD helmets include directional searchlights, a de-fogger, ventilation fans and a filter to keep dust out. These helmets also have an automatic decibel control that cuts out detonation blast noise, protecting the wearer's hearing.

Without the specialist equipment which is available to the troops on the ground, the front line would be an even tougher place than it already is. Technology is always evolving and every new innovation could mean a life on the ground saved.

A bomb disposal officer from the British Army's 321 Explosive Ordnance Disposal Squadron RLC.

3 Squadron RAF Regiment use Vallon mine detectors on patrol in the desert near camp Bastion in Afghanistan.

CAMO[U]

A VITAL WEAPON

When out on patrol, blending into the landscape is of extreme importance if a soldier is to avoid being targeted by enemy combatants. And so the role of camouflage on the front line cannot be underestimated. But in a place like Afghanistan, where the terrain varies from the dry dusty landscape of the desert to the lush green fields of the Green Zone, camouflage has to work even harder in order to be effective.

So, in April 2010, British soldiers in Afghanistan began wearing the first new camouflage design in forty years. The multi-terrain pattern (MTP) camouflage was developed to help British troops blend into Afghanistan's varied terrain better than the standard army woodland or desert camouflage disruptive pattern material (DPM), which had been in active combat use since 1968.

The colours and textures of the new MTP camo are designed to keep troops hidden for longer during ambush operations or while on patrol in Helmand Province. It will protect soldiers in a large range of environments including compounds, grassland, crops and woodland.

To develop the new camo, scientists looked at existing aerial photography of Afghanistan to gauge the colour palette of the landscape. In addition, they sent cameras to Helmand for soldiers to take specific scientific photographs of the various backgrounds and landscapes they operate in. The colour properties for

Left to Right (if you can spot them!): Woodland Camouflage, MTP, MTP and (far right) Desert Camouflage.

A Royal Marine in the old camouflage pattern patrols the Green Zone in Sangin.

FLAGE

each image were then measured, and seven major background types identified. Scientific trials of the new MTP were then run in areas of the UK that provided a good colour match for the Afghan landscape.

It may seem lo-tech in comparison to the range of weapons available to today's Armed Forces, but these small changes in camouflage will have a huge impact for the men and women on the ground.

The final camouflage has a pattern that is similar to the current woodland DPM, as it allows for easy identification between soldiers.

The old-style uniform (left) compared to the new style.

ARTISTS AND PHOTOGRAPHERS ON THE BATTLEFIELD

BY MICHAEL UPCHURCH

In the twenty-first century, the age of rolling news, we have become used to seeing pictures from war zones on our screens. Video footage on news channels and photographs in newspapers and magazines allow us to get a real sense of what it is like to be in the thick of the action and the awful suffering caused by conflict. Before television footage became as widespread as it is today, the public relied on photographers and artists to show them the reality of war. And even now, despite the advances in technology, photography and art are still vital tools used to illustrate modern warfare.

WAR ARTISTS

Portraying the truth of war, the physicality of battle and emotions of conflict is extremely difficult, but that is the aim of the many talented artists who go to war. The British military has a commendable history of allowing soldiers armed with pencils and paints to express themselves freely. Indeed, it is symbolic of the fact that, throughout much of modern warfare, Britain has been fighting in order to defend individual expression and personal liberty.

In many ways, the artists' visual interpretations complement the journalists' and historians' accounts of warfare; they are painting history.

'Wounded Under Ground – A Highland Officer', by Sir Muirhead Bone – the first appointed British war artist, 1916.

Sometimes art is used for propaganda purposes, commissioned by governments, but a vast amount of art created under fire depicts the harsher elements of war that are often difficult to describe in words.

There are various types of war artist. They include:

- Official war artists, usually appointed by governments for information purposes, to record events on the battlefield.
- Combatants who are artists and illustrate their own experiences.
- Non-combatants who are observing war.
- Prisoners of war who may be recording their conditions for personal reasons, or have been instructed to do so by a senior officer.

THE ARTISTS RIFLES

This is a volunteer regiment of the British Army. It began in 1859 and is still active today, serving in the Army Air Corps as the 21st Special Air Service Regiment (Artists) (Reserve). It consists of painters, sculptors, engravers, musicians, architects and actors. Although the regiment saw active service during the Boer Wars and World War I, it did not serve outside Britain during World War II and its current role is quite small.

Scottish artist, Peter Howson at work in his Glasgow studio on a project resulting from being in Kosovo as a war artist.

There are many famous British war artists, going back as far as the Napoleonic Wars. Some are known simply for their war art while others were already established artists before they embarked upon warfare as a subject. The first officially appointed British war artist was Sir Muirhead Bone, but he was soon followed by a host of others.

English war artist Paul Nash.

The waste land: 'Totes Meer' (Dead Sea) by Paul Nash in which wrecked warplanes stretch across the landscape.

Paul Nash (1889–1946) is widely regarded as one of the most important English artists of the first half of the twentieth century. He enlisted into the British Army in 1914, at the outbreak of the Great War, volunteering for the Artists Rifles. In 1917, Nash was injured and sent home to London, where he exhibited a series of drawings of the front line, working from sketches he had made in the trenches. Shortly afterwards, Nash was recruited as an official war artist and sent back to the Western Front. This time he turned his drawings into oil paintings and used the opportunity to bring home the full horrors of the war. His paintings are some of the most lasting images of the First World War.

Henry Moore (1898–1986) is most famous for his abstract sculptures, but during the Second World War he was commissioned to produce drawings of Londoners sleeping in the London Underground whilst sheltering from the Blitz. Moore himself was a victim of the German bombing campaign, as his house was hit by bomb shrapnel in 1940.

Ronald Searle (born 1920) is a celebrated artist and cartoonist, best known as the creator of *St Trinian's*. He enlisted in the Royal Engineers at the beginning of the Second World War, and in 1942 he was captured by the Japanese when the British surrendered in Singapore. He spent the rest of the war as a prisoner, initially in Changi prison in Singapore, then working on the notorious Siam-Burma Railway, where so many prisoners were worked and starved to death (it is estimated one man died for every sleeper laid). Searle recorded the conditions around

One of Searle's sketches from his time as a POW.

Ronald Searle, the artist and cartoonist.

War artist Arabella Dorman in her Studio in Chelsea, London. She has just returned from working in Afghanistan with the British forces.

You can find examples of Arabella Dorman's work from Iraq here **http://bit.ly/aQPVEx** or by using your smartphone to scan this code:

him each morning before work. Paper wasn't easy to come by and in one instance he used a Japanese document as the canvas for a portrait of two guards. To keep his drawings hidden from the guards, Searle would hide them under the bodies of prisoners dying of cholera. His collection of 300 drawings was donated to the Imperial War Museum.

Matthew Cook (born 1964) was appointed War Artist for *The Times* in 2003, at the beginning of the war in Iraq. Three years later, he found himself in Afghanistan, accompanying the 1st Battalion, the Royal Gloucestershire, Berkshire and Wilshire Light Infantry. His watercolours combine artistry and reportage to paint a vivid and accessible portrait of day-to-day life on the front line.

Arabella Dorman (born 1976) is a portrait artist who, after painting Iraq war veterans, was inspired to spend some time with regiments on the front line in Iraq and Afghanistan. She drew very quick charcoal portraits at the scene of the men she encountered, then once back in England the sketches helped her to use art to 'evoke the emotions and psychological impact of war'.

The Times war artist, Matthew Cook, at work drawing a Tornado GR4 at ali Al Salem air base, in the northern Kuwaiti desert.

You can hear Matthew Cook talk about his work and see more of his paintings here **http://bbc.in/3ktU8M** or by using your smartphone to scan this code:

© TIMES NEWSPAPERS LTD

◄Soldiers during the Crimean War, north of the Black Sea.

▼Robert Capa's striking image of the first wave of American troops to land at Ohama Beach on 6 June 1944.

© ROBERT CAPA / MAGNUM PHOTOS

WAR PHOTOGRAPHERS

Unlike paintings or drawings, photographs are not easily altered (although the camera may not always show the whole picture) and so offer a unique insight into war. War photography dates as far back as the Crimean War (1853–55), though in the early days of photography, cameras were extremely bulky and it was far more difficult (and dangerous) for the photographer to carry heavy equipment, rather than pen and paper, into the battlefield. Early photographers were also unable to capture images of moving targets, a subject had to be still for several minutes. As a result, many action scenes at the time were 'staged' after the event to be photographed properly.

As their equipment became lighter, more mobile and easier to use, it allowed the photographers to get closer to the action. In the twentieth century, increasingly, iconic shots of conflict seemed to place the viewer right at the heart of the action. Celebrated war photographer Robert Capa reported on five different wars and captured stunning images of the Normandy invasions of World War II by swimming ashore with the second assault wave on Omaha Beach on D-Day, 6 June 1944. However, in the pursuit of front-line action shots, many photographers were themselves killed. Capa died in 1954 when he stepped on a landmine while reporting on the First Indochina War.

Most experienced photographers in combat zones are photo-journalists. They are protected by international conventions of armed warfare, but unfortunately they are often considered targets. In the recent conflicts in Iraq and Afghanistan, several photographers have been captured and executed by terrorists and insurgents.

◄One of Allan's candid snaps of soldiers at ease.

▼Self-portrait by Captain Alexander Allan.

Nowadays, photography is a tool available to almost everybody. In the Second World War, one photographer may have accompanied a regiment or company, but now most soldiers have their own cameras and choose to record their own varied yet personal experiences of war.

During a tour of Afghanistan, Captain Alexander Allan of 1st Battalion, The Grenadier Guards took photographs with his digital SLR camera. The pictures give a day-to-day soldier's-eye view of what it means to be involved in Britain's operations in Afghanistan.

Captain Allan describes the circumstances in which some of his pictures were taken, from gruelling 'contacts' with Taliban fighters to R & R in a water tank belonging to a friendly farmer. 'Taking photographs was a bit of a hobby. It was almost therapeutic,' he says. 'Taking this self-portrait and pictures like it helped to pass the hours when we had some downtime. I also wanted to try to capture the beauty of the country: some of the landscape is incredible – it feels like a travesty to be fighting in it.' He explained, 'What I saw is only a tiny snapshot of what our soldiers face in Afghanistan every day – often in circumstances many times more challenging.'

Captain Alexander Allan's images of the front line have been collected and published in a book titled* Afghanistan: Tour of Duty*. Profits from sales of the book go to the British Limbless Ex-Service Men's Association.

110

You can find out more about BLESMA and order your copy of Alexander Allan's book on **www.blesma.org**, or by using your smartphone to scan this code:

SERGEANT ROBERT CHESTER

Age	43
Hometown	Hartlepool
Unit	45 Commando, RM

What is your job and what do you do?
I am a troop sergeant, second in command of a troop of thirty men and responsible for the daily admin.

What was your best day?
Passing commando training. The birth of my daughter and son.

What was your hardest day?
It will be when I leave the Royal Marines after twenty-two years' service (very soon).

What is your favourite bit of kit and why?
L96 sniper rifle – the weapon I trained on to become a sniper. It give you an immense sense of pride being able to hit a target at beyond 800 metres with accuracy.

What is your favourite sport/and or sports team?
Fly fishing.

Please list the last 3 books/magazines you read.
1. Crete: the Battle and the Resistance *by Anthony Beevor*
2. One Soldier's War in Chechnya *by Arkady Babchenko*
3. The SS, a history of the 1st Leibstandarte.

Please list the last 3 films you watched.
1. Book of Eli
2. The Road
3. The Hangover.

What do you miss most when away from home?
Family, classic vehicle project and fishing.

What is the best thing about being in the military?
Every day brings a different challenge.

Who do you most admire/who is your hero?
Families of those who have died or been injured, for their display of strength.

© DPL

COMMANDO TRAINING

Becoming a Royal Marine Commando is tough. Marines must undertake a thirty-two week training course to reach Commando level. Split into six modules – foundation, individual skills, advanced skills, operations at war, commando course and King's Squad pass-out week – the course covers a huge range of activities including maths and English tests, weapon training, corps history, map reading, first aid, grenade throwing, troop attacks and ambushes, as well as various assault courses.

At the start of week twenty-six, recruits must complete a six-mile speed march. They have to march the distance carrying full fighting order (weighing thirty-one pounds) in one hour. Later in the course, they have to complete a nine-mile speed march and a thirty-mile march. These tasks require determination and courage. Only once the Commando tests have been passed can successful recruits wear the green beret.

Recruits haul themselves through Peters Pool on the Endurance Course, which is one of the main Commando tests.

© THE DEFENCE PICTURE LIBRARY

BRAVEST OF THE BRAVE

Sepoy Singh, the first Sikh recipient of the VC.

SEPOY ISHAR SINGH

An astonishing display of personal courage by Sepoy Ishar Singh in 1921 helped his company recover from the brink of defeat and made him the first ever Sikh to win the Victoria Cross.

Singh was part of the 28th Punjab Regiment of the Indian Army, battling vicious rebel tribesmen in the lawless badlands of the India-Afghanistan border.

On 10 April 1921, his company was escorting a supply group when they were ambushed by 100 Mahsud tribesmen, who surrounded them on either side.

Before long, all the officers were dead and Singh had taken a vicious shot in the chest and collapsed. The Lewis Gun he was manning was seized by the enemy and escape looked impossible.

But somehow Singh mustered his strength, picked himself up and called to the men to charge.

Still pouring blood from his chest, he wrestled back control of the Lewis Gun and turned it on the attackers, buying his company crucial time to rally their forces.

Relieved by another trooper, Singh was ordered to fall back and get medical attention. Thinking only of his fellow troopers however, Singh instead began helping locate the wounded and carry water to them, making repeated trips to a nearby river and protecting them with suppressing fire.

Soldiers operate a Lewis gun.

At one stage, he even stood with his back to the enemy to protect the medical officer while he treated a wounded man.

It was only after three hours of incredible heroics that he allowed himself to be evacuated, and only then because he was too weak from loss of blood to protest.

His Victoria Cross citation read: 'His gallantry and devotion to duty were beyond praise. His conduct inspired all who saw him.'

By David Willetts

A recommendation for the VC is normally issued by an officer at regimental level, or equivalent, and has to be supported by three witnesses. The recommendation is then passed up the military hierarchy until it reaches the Secretary of State for Defence. The recommendation is then laid before the monarch who approves the award with his or her signature. Victoria Cross awards are always promulgated in the *London Gazette*, with the single exception of the award to the American Unknown Soldier in 1921.

MATTHEW TOMLINSON

THE PATROL STOPS - THEY ARE OPEN TO TALIBAN AMBUSH!

FROOSH!
THE FIRE HITS HOME, TO DEVASTATING EFFECT.
KBOOOOOM-BROOOM

KCHOOOOOMB!
THE ATTACK INTENSIFIES.
AAAAH!!
PTOOOM!
PTOOOM!

*!@! I'VE GOT TO HELP!

HANG ON, LADS, HANG ON...

BLOODY HELL!

THERE'S 50 METRES OF OPEN GROUND TO COVER. AND IT'S FULL OF FLAMES, SMOKE AND ENEMY FIRE...

RIGHT, LADS, YOU KNOW WHAT TO DO. EYES OPEN FOR FURTHER IEDS, AND RETURN FIRE!
SHARPISH!

WITH BARELY A THOUGHT FOR HIS OWN SAFETY, MATT RACES TO HELP THE WOUNDED.
YOU OK, MATE? WHERE ARE YOU? MAKE SOME NOISE!

ALRIGHT, I'VE GOT YOU SON...

HANG IN THERE, MATE, WE'LL GET YOU PATCHED UP. WHERE'S YOUR CONTROLLER?

BUT AS FIRE RAGES THROUGH THE DESTROYED CAB, THE FIERCE HEAT SETS OFF THE AMMUNITION.
FTOOMM!
BLOODY HELL!
COUGH! HACK!

MEANWHILE, THE MARINES BLAST BACK AT THEIR ATTACKERS!
BRAAAK!
BRAAAK!

THE LEAD VIKING'S TURRET HAS BEEN BLOWN RIGHT OFF.
HELL. JASON WAS IN THERE.

INSIDE THE RUINED VIKING...

...MARINE JASON MACKIE HASN'T MADE IT.
A BRAVE YOUNG MAN IS DEAD...

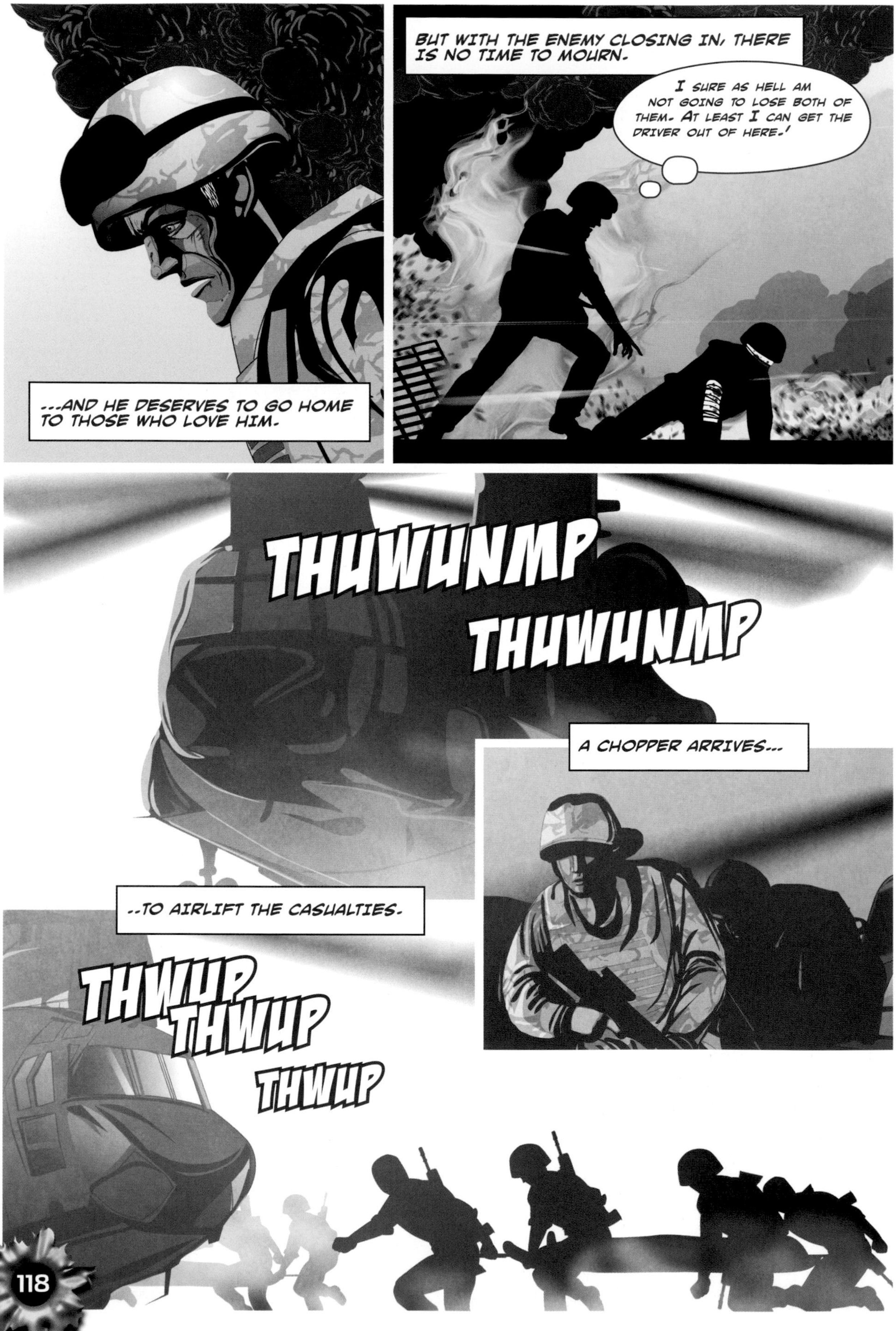

THUWUNMP
THUWUNMP

A CHOPPER ARRIVES...

..TO AIRLIFT THE CASUALTIES.

THWUP
THWUP
THWUP

THERE IS STILL A FALLEN COMRADE TO HONOUR.
SORRY, MATE. I... SORRY.

GIVE HIM SOME ROOM, LADS.

BUT THE MARINES' WORK IS FAR FROM OVER.
WE CAN'T LEAVE THAT GUN FOR THE ENEMY.

NO WAY I'M LETTING THOSE B******S GET THEIR HANDS ON IT.

THROUGH THE SMOKE AND THE INCOMING FIRE, MATT DRAGS THE SMOULDERING WEAPON TO SAFETY.

UNGH!

THE REST OF YOU, GET THE HELL OUT OF HERE! THEY'RE WAITING FOR US AT THE HLS!

PTOOOM!
PTOOOM!
ONCE MORE INTO THE BREACH! MATT TURNS BACK YET AGAIN TO SECURE VITAL EQUIPMENT.

PTOOOM!
PTOOOM!

'I am very proud and feel highly honoured to be recognised with the Military Cross. However, I must say that these were tragic circumstances. Also, I could not have acted with the confidence I did without the assurance that I had a top team behind me. If my Viking had been hit, then I know the lads would have acted in exactly the same way.

'I am still very proud to have served with them. The ranks of the Armoured Support Group are the real heroes.'

Warrant Officer Matthew Tomlinson

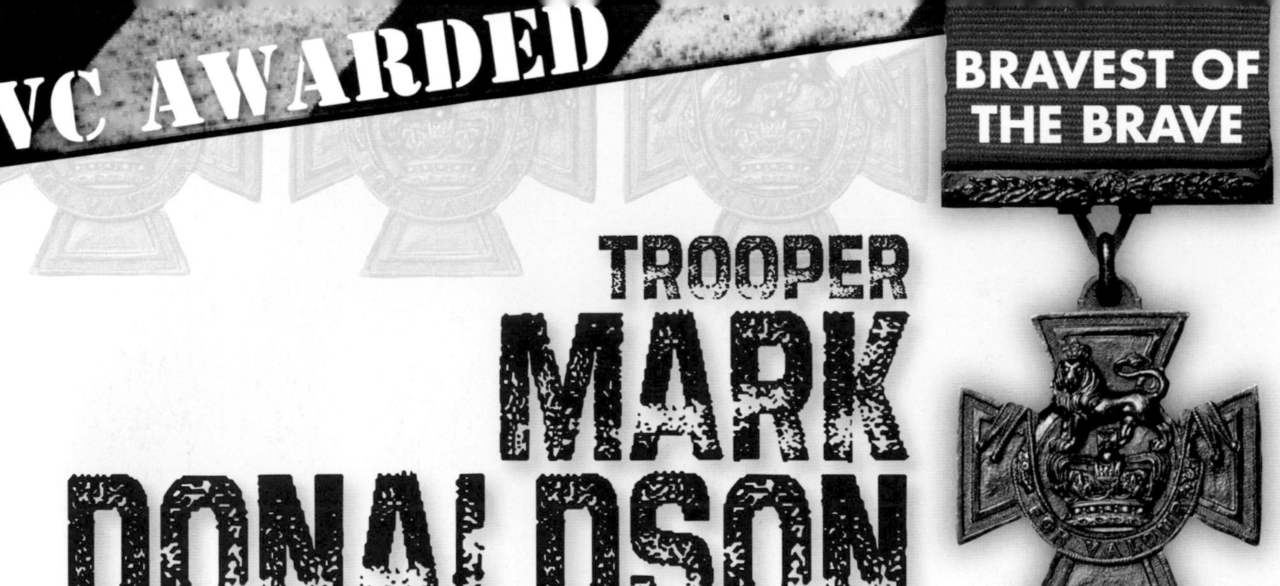

BRAVEST OF THE BRAVE

TROOPER MARK DONALDSON

Trooper Mark Donaldson was responsible for one of the most daring acts of bravery of the Afghan conflict so far – risking all to save a comrade and win the day.

Already a 'Who Dares Wins' SAS soldier, Australian trooper Donaldson had to call on all his elite training when his patrol was ambushed by bloodthirsty Taliban insurgents on 2 September 2008.

Vastly outnumbered and cornered, the American, Afghan and Australian troops were pinned down with zero chance of safe escape.

The Taliban attackers poured in fire from AK-47 machine guns and Rocket-Propelled Grenades (RPGs), wounding many almost instantly.

For two hours the Allied Forces were pinned down, but it was Donaldson's quick thinking that seized back the initiative and turned the tide.

Springing into action, he returned fire with his M4 rifle before deliberately exposing himself to the enemy – turning himself into a human target – to draw fire away from his wounded pals.

The daring diversion worked and the injured men were dragged to safety.

As the firefight raged on, the patrol had to manoeuvre over four

Australian Special Air Service trooper Mark Donaldson.

kilometres of unforgiving terrain in Oruzgan Province to safety, still under intense fire. With their vehicles full of men cut up by bullets and shrapnel, Donaldson and the remaining un-injured soldiers had to run alongside the armoured vehicles, further exposing themselves to a hail of Taliban fire.

But during the hurried move to get out of the killing zone, a severely wounded Afghan interpreter was accidentally left behind. Showing complete disregard for his own safety, Trooper Donaldson dashed alone across eighty metres of exposed ground to save the lad.

Trooper Mark Donaldson, centre, is congratulated by former Australian Prime Minister Kevin Rudd, left, as Australia Governor-General Quentin Bryce looks on.

During the mad run he was spotted by the Taliban, who concentrated all their efforts on trying to shoot him dead. As the bullets whistled overhead and kicked the dirt at his feet, Donaldson picked up his wounded colleague and carried him back to safety.

He gave him emergency first aid, then carried on the fight.

His Victoria Cross citation read: 'Trooper Donaldson's acts of exceptional gallantry in the face of accurate and sustained enemy fire ultimately saved the life of a coalition force interpreter and ensured the safety of the other members of the combined Afghan, US and Australian Forces.

'Trooper Donaldson's actions on this day displayed exceptional courage in circumstances of great peril.'

Donaldson has since been promoted to the rank of corporal.

By David Willetts

Victoria Cross holders Jonson Beharry (L) and Mark Donaldson (R).

The Victoria Cross is the UK and Commonwealth's highest military decoration, awarded for 'valour in the face of the enemy' to members of the Armed Forces and civilians. It is always the first award to be presented at an investiture, even before knighthoods. It is also the first decoration worn in a row of medals, and it is the first set of post-nominal letters used to indicate any decoration or order.

BEATING THE BOREDOM, Counting the Hours

By Patrick Hennessey, author of *The Junior Officers' Reading Club*

One of the toughest challenges for soldiers out on operations is not fighting the enemy, but the boredom – which is a big part of being deployed. Although life on the front line is busy and tiring, whether out on fighting patrols or on guard duty back in the FOBs, there are often long periods of downtime or waiting time when there's nothing to do and you have to find ways of passing long nights and quiet days while not out on the ground.

Back in Camp Bastion and some of the bigger FOBs, the power supply means that laptops and TVs can be used and DVDs watched and games played. Welfare packages sent from supportive families back home tend to contain lots of comedy; stand-ups with foul mouths and laughs to take your mind off the difficult stuff. Bases shared with Americans tend to benefit from popular movie nights with free popcorn, although it's usually more action and thrillers than romance.

Right out on the front, however, with no power and running low on batteries, good old books and magazines are all that can be relied upon. Welfare packages gratefully received from home burst with lads' magazines and news weeklies to keep people in touch with what's happening in the rest of the world (and to decorate the FOBs with pin-ups). Books are heavy so libraries accumulate – from the vast

© RICHARD POHLE

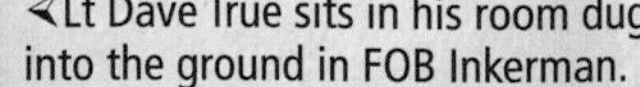

◄ Lt Dave True sits in his room dug into the ground in FOB Inkerman.

and professionally run lending library in Camp Bastion to the dusty cardboard boxes full of leftover paperbacks in patrol bases. When a soldier has eaten and slept and still has nothing to do then the best way to escape is in a book.

◂British Paratroopers receive their mail at a FOB.

▴A member of 16 Air Assault Brigade reads a book on a Hercules transport plane while his comrades around him sleep.

Some choose escapism – *Flashman* adventures or even the odd *Harry Potter*; others read military books – biographies of recent soldiers and historical accounts of bygone wars. The oddest choices crop up (a copy of Herman Hesse's *Siddhartha* found amongst the John le Carrés in Sangin stayed with my team for the whole tour until every man had read it), but the morale boost from a few minutes spent not thinking about yesterday's fight or tomorrow's mission is invaluable. And as for a soldier's favourite read? Easy. Whatever your preference, the best is always a letter from home.

SQUADDIES' LIBRARY

Want to read more about front-line action? Check out these top ten bestselling soldier stories…

- *Sniper One: The Blistering True Story of a British Battle Group Under Siege* by Dan Mills
- *Vulcan 607* by Rowland White
- *Seven Troop* by Andy McNab
- *3 Para* by Patrick Bishop
- *Eight Lives Down* by Chris Hunter
- *Ross Kemp on Afghanistan* by Ross Kemp
- *Apache Dawn* by Damien Lewis
- *3 Commando Brigade* by Ewen Southby-Tailyour
- *The Circuit* by Bob Shepherd
- *Apache* by Ed Macy

To read the first chapter of *Flashman on the March*, visit **www.thesun.co.uk/realheroes**.

MEDICINE AND WAR

Today, soldiers in Afghanistan are surviving wounds that even 20 years ago would have proven fatal. Better armour and enormous advances in battlefield medicine are saving lives that would have been lost in previous conflicts. Combat doctors today move with the infantry and can often stabilise injuries that would otherwise kill within three minutes. Casualty helicopter evacuation crews are able to reach all parts of Helmand within 30 minutes and can deliver sophisticated treatment inside the helicopter. And British medical emergency response teams (MERTs) can reach the battlefield with their equipment in a Chinook helicopter, saving critical time in the so-called 'golden hour' after injury.

And yet with every war, advances in weaponry are made, challenging our doctors and other medical providers to rise to ever greater heights, to perform every more unlikely miracles. As soldiers face new kinds of warfare, they sustain new types of injuries, and medical staff, both on the battlefield and in hospitals, must learn how to treat these wounds. The past century has seen stunning medical breakthroughs, many of them made in response to the injuries received during times of terrible conflict.

▲ Wilfred Owen.

◄ Siegfried Sassoon.

First World War

The carnage of the First World War presented medicine with many challenges. A war fought by mass armies, the sheer number of the wounded reached unprecedented levels, reaching the tens of thousands, then hundreds of thousands. In order to deal with the injuries, advances were made in the fields of blood transfusion, artificial limbs and facial reconstruction, amongst other areas.

Strides were also made in the realm of mental health; thousands fell victim to what is now commonly referred to as Post-Traumatic Stress Disorder (PTSD). By the latter part of the war, a number of leading psychologists recognised the role of emotional disturbance in producing 'shell shock' – named after the exploding shells with which combatants on both

PERCENTAGE OF SOLDIERS DIED OUT OF TOTAL WOUNDED

Afghanistan and Iraq	12
Vietnam	32
World War II	41

From 'Mental Cases' by Wilfred Owen

Who are these? Why sit they here in twilight?
Wherefore rock they, purgatorial shadows,
Drooping tongues from jaws that slob their
relish,
Baring teeth that leer like skulls' teeth
wicked?
Stroke on stroke of pain, – but what slow panic,
Gouged these chasms round their fretted
sockets?
Ever from their hair and through their hands'
palms
Misery swelters. Surely we have perished
Sleeping, and walk hell; but who these hellish?

sides were bombarded – and special units were set aside for patients suffering from psychological illnesses. War poets Wilfred Owen and Siegfried Sassoon both stayed in one of these units.

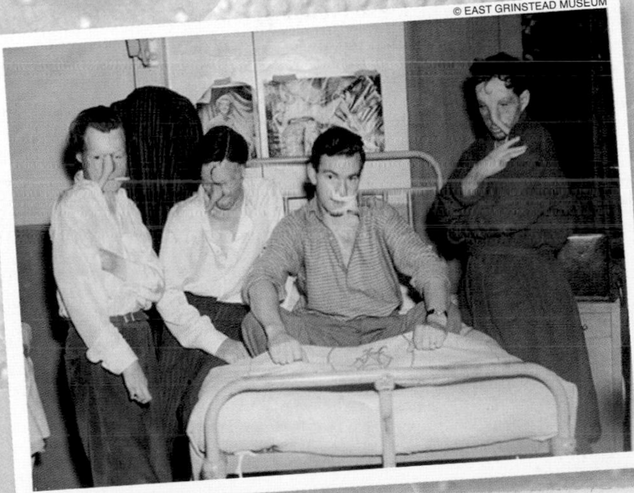

Second World War

The Guinea Pig Club, established during the Second World War, is a famous example of how medicine has developed in response to war. In 1940, when the Battle of Britain began, many pilots and other aircrew suffered from horrendous burns when their aircraft were hit. Their wounds were unlike any that doctors had seen before; the new high-octane fuels used in aircraft that ignited when hit by enemy fire resulted in deep tissue burns. These men were taken to East Grinstead hospital where new medical advances had to be made to deal with these injuries.

The Guinea Pig Club originally started as a drinking club and was set up to ensure that the badly wounded men were not isolated whilst undergoing treatment. Surgeon Sir Archibald McIndoe was the club's president and their emblem was, and remains today, a guinea pig with RAF wings – a self-deprecating joke by the club members who were McIndoe's 'guinea pigs' for new forms of care at a time when burns treatment and plastic surgery were in their infancy.

One of the techniques that McIndoe introduced was saline baths after he noticed that the burns injuries of pilots who had crashed in the sea healed more rapidly. He also took rehabilitation a step further, emphasizing the importance not

The Guinea Pig Club set up by Sir Archibld McIndoe (above, centre) provided badly injured men with the medical treatment – but also the companionship – they badly needed.

'The Guinea Pig Anthem'

We are McIndoe's army,
We are his Guinea Pigs
With dermatomes and pedicles,
Glass eyes, false teeth and wigs.
And when we get our discharge
We'll shout with all our might:
'Per ardua ad astra'[1]
We'd rather drink than fight.

We've had some mad Australians,
Some French, some Czechs, some Poles.
We've even had some Yankees,
God bless their precious souls.
While as for the Canadians
Ah! That's a different thing.
They couldn't stand our accent
And built a separate wing.

We are McIndoe's army,
We are his Guinea Pigs
With dermatomes and pedicles,
Glass eyes, false teeth and wigs.
And when we get our discharge
We'll shout with all our might:
'Per ardua ad astra'
We'd rather drink than fight.

1. 'Through Adversity to the Stars' is the motto of the RAF and other Commonwealth air forces.

only of repairing physical damage, but rejuvenating the mind. At the end of the war, there were 649 Guinea Pigs – 62 per cent of whom were from Britain, 20 per cent from Canada, 6 per cent from Australia, 6 per cent from New Zealand and a further 6 per cent from a number of other countries across the globe.

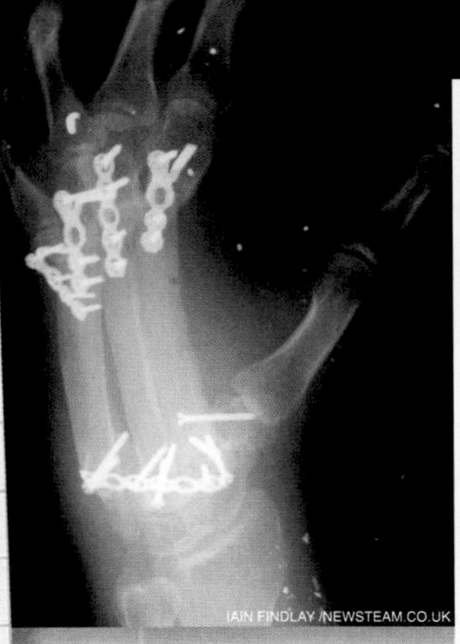

Private Neil McCallion and the silicon rods in his reconstructed left hand

The War in Afghanistan

IEDs and landmines are the signature weapons of the conflict in Afghanistan. Medical staff have learnt to deal with the wounds that these weapons inflict on soldiers – predominantly soft tissue and bone wounds – and, as a result, significant advances in a range of areas have been made. Boundaries are being pushed in the realms of reconstructive surgery, infection control and physiotherapy, amongst others.

In order to maximise the damage done to soldiers, IEDs are often packed with shrapnel, such as steel nuts and nails. This makes it very likely that wounded soldiers will develop infections and, in response to this type of injury, these wounds are now cleaned using a new device – Versajet. This is a high-pressure jet of sterile salt water, which is directed through a small jet nozzle at the end of a handpiece. Versajet is, doctors say, more accurate than a metal scalpel and has greatly improved the way in which wounds are cleansed.

The creation of new dressings to treat wounds more effectively has also made a significant impact on the healing process. Special silver-based dressings are used to prevent infection; they contain anti-microbial properties, inhibiting the growth of bacteria, and army medics are keen that these are taken further into Afghanistan and applied to wounds at an earlier stage.

Dealing with never-before-seen injuries has led to some groundbreaking procedures. Private Neil McCallion's left hand was completely shattered by a shrapnel wound in Afghanistan in 2006. His hand required major reconstruction and was rebuilt using three of his ribs and muscle from the right side of his torso. Surgery of this kind had never been performed on a hand before. Now, after several operations, Private McCallion is able to drive and perform most daily activities.

Great improvements are also being made to the ways in which physiotherapy can help wounded servicemen and women recover. The Defence Medical Rehabilitation Centre in Headley Court recently acquired an anti-gravity treadmill that is changing the way people recover. Patients using the treadmill zip themselves into a waist-high enclosure. Once inflated, air pressure within the enclosure elevates the user's body, counteracting the force of gravity and approximating what it would be like to walk or run on the moon. The NASA-based technology thus allows wounded men and women to run or walk at a fraction of their body weight, and so reduces the impact of exercise on injured muscles and tendons. Truly a space-age treatment!

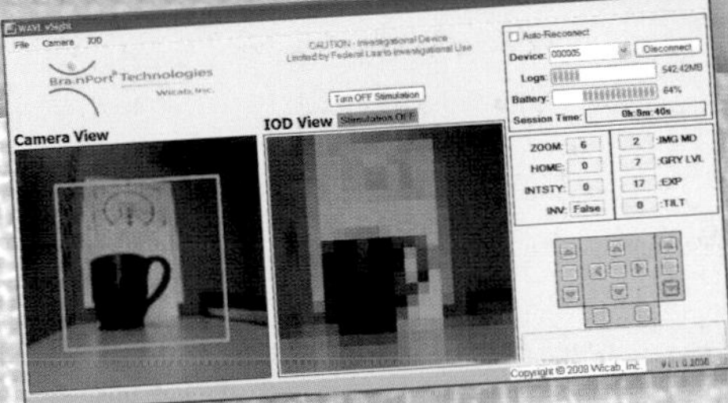

CASE STUDY: BRAINPORT

What is it?

One of the most revolutionary pieces of medical equipment to have been developed recently is the BrainPort vision device. Essentially, BrainPort allows blind people to 'see' through their tongues; sensory information is sent to the brain via a signal from the device, ending in an electrode array which sits on top of the tongue.

How does it work?

To use the BrainPort, the patient wears a pair of glasses which contain a video camera. Images are fed into a lollypop-like device that is held in the mouth and transforms the pictures into electrical impulses that are felt on the tongue. The sensation is a tingling of different intensities that correspond to the relative darkness of the pixels recorded on the camera, allowing the patient to perceive light and dark and negotiate his way around objects.

Is it easy to use?

BrainPort doesn't take long to learn how to use; within an hour of practice, users can generally identify and reach for nearby objects. They can also point to and estimate the distance of objects out of reach. And, with further training, they are able to identify letters and numbers.

BrainPort in action

When soldier Craig Lundberg was hit by a rocket-propelled grenade in Iraq in 2007, his injuries left him completely blind. However, being selected by the MoD to pioneer the new device being developed in the USA – BrainPort – changed everything. Now, Craig is able to reach out and pick up objects straightaway, when previously he would have been fumbling around for them. 'It's only a prototype,' he says, 'but the potential to change my life is massive, it's got a lot of potential to advance things for blind people.'

Lance Corporal Craig Lundberg whose life has been transformed by ground-breaking technology that enables him to 'see' with his tongue.

SERGEANT LIAM VARLEY

Age	32
Hometown	Chester
Unit	1 Mercian

What is your job and what do you do?
I am the platoon sergeant for 10 Platoon, 1st Battalion, The Mercian Regiment. My job is to ensure that the platoon's administration is always up-to-date, ensuring that they have the right kit and equipment, water, rations, ammo, etc. On the ground it's my job to constantly think about casualty evacuation as well as command and control of the troops. To date I have had to personally evacuate five casualties and assisted many more.

For the last two months of the tour I will be the platoon sergeant for the Fire Support Group. The role is to give heavy weapons support for the troops on the ground. As the commander of a Jackal, the platoon commander and I have to share the ground to ensure complete situational awareness is achieved and passed to the patrols whilst simultaneously de-conflicting the battle space so we can engage the enemy without hitting friendly forces. This is the hardest part of the job, as to get it wrong would have horrific consequences.

What has been your best day?
Each day that I return from patrol with all my men, having successfully completed the mission is the best.

What has been your hardest day?
We began a counter-IED patrol into the Green Zone with the aim of clearing a vital route for us and the locals. Almost instantly we came under contact from all directions. Whilst pushing forward to kill the enemy, one of our soldiers was killed by an IED. Once the extraction of his body was complete, I knew we had to continue on task. I had to simultaneously lead the men to a series of compounds vital to the integrity of the cordon whilst holding the platoon together after the tragic incident.

Once in the compounds, we were subject to close-quarter fighting for the next twenty-six hours. The situation was dire, with insurgents moving close enough to throw grenades over the wall both day and night.

Throughout all this I knew we needed to mourn the loss of our soldier, but not until safely back in camp, otherwise we would not have been able to hold the cordon and the operation would have been in vain.

Troops on patrol must be as wary of IEDs as they are of enemy combatants.

What food do you eat and cook?
For the first three months we were on rations but now we have cooked food when in the patrol base. We still have rations when on patrol for anything up to two weeks.

How often do you get to eat?
Cooked food is twice a day but when out on the ground you snack when you remember, but it drops right down your list of priorities.

What are your toilet facilities like? How often do you get to have a proper bath or shower?
For the first three months it was bottles or solar showers but now we have showers in the patrol base. When out on the ground it is in streams or with baby wipes.

What are your sleeping arrangements?
I have a bed space in the patrol base which is a cot bed in a mosquito net dome, but I rarely sleep in it. When on the ground you just sleep where you fall.

How heavy is your equipment and what do you have to carry?
I have to carry body armour, ammunition (plus 10 per cent extra to resupply the platoon), six litres of water, a radio, night sights, spare batteries and other equipment plus my weapon, all of which comprises 60–70 lbs.

ENTERTAINING THE TROOPS

'Every Night Something 'Appens' FLORENCE DESMOND

On 15 November 1939, the little square of Douai in France displayed a large banner saying 'Welcome to Gracie'. Only three weeks before, the adjutant general, Lieutenant General Brownrigg, had met with Lieutenant Basil Dean, the head of ENSA and had rather reluctantly agreed that 'live' shows could go to forward areas where troops were stationed, provided they were all-male shows. *Under no circumstances*, however, should female entertainers be sent to France.

Brownrigg reckoned without Gracie Fields. The 'Lass from Lancashire' fought her way to the front, where her concert was such a success organizers became worried they would be unable to get the entertainers through the blackout in time for her next performance in Arras.

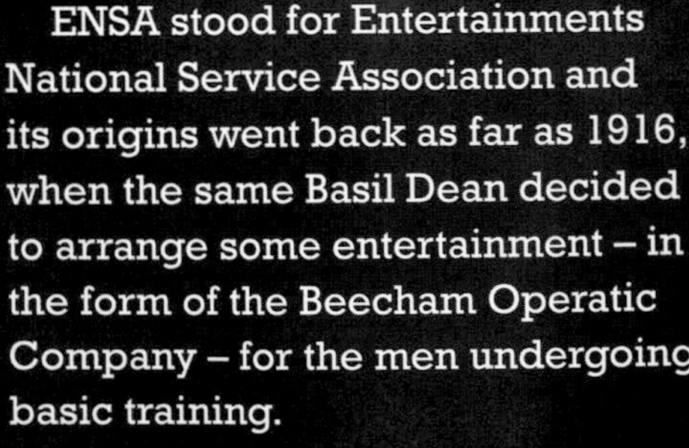

ENSA stood for Entertainments National Service Association and its origins went back as far as 1916, when the same Basil Dean decided to arrange some entertainment – in the form of the Beecham Operatic Company – for the men undergoing basic training.

Over twenty years later, on 10 September 1939, Dean was behind the first ever official ENSA Concert – only a week after war was declared with Germany. Throughout the Second World War, he continued to arrange for the top acts of the time to travel to the front lines, where the men were often in desperate need of a morale boost. Singers, dancers and musicians all made the effort, as well as some of the best actors of the era – John Gielgud, Laurence Olivier, Michael Redgrave, James Mason, Deborah Kerr, Sybil Thorndike and Noel Coward were only a few of the big names involved.

For many of the well-known artists who agreed to entertain the troops, conditions

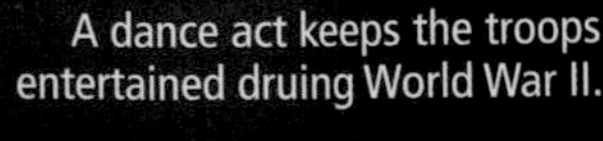

A dance act keeps the troops entertained druing World War II.

Forces Sweetheart Vera Lynn entertains the troops.

could be rather grim. Singer Ann Shelton recalls performing in a sleeveless dress to an audience of gunners on a night in Suffolk so bitterly cold she could see her breath. At the end of each song, she rushed to the wings where she was briefly wrapped in a blanket before going back to sing another ballad. There were logistical problems, too. Six mini pianos sent to West Africa for use by ENSA artists vanished and were not discovered until several weeks later. When they were found, only the ivory keyboard and the metal components remained. The rest had been eaten by white ants!

'You must keep the boys entertained, no matter where they are. It means a lot to them – they feel a little closer to home ... When you're on the front line, you need to know that you are not being forgotten.' DAME VERA LYNN

Colonel Jack Hawkins was responsible for ENSA in the Far East. He discovered that very few artists were prepared to come to India. Vera Lynn was the exception. When she arrived, she had a small holdall with a pink chiffon dress, two sets of khaki and – the most important item – her lipstick. Vera was amused to hear, on visiting a casualty clearing station close to the front line, that the Japanese played her records over their loudspeakers in an attempt to lower the British troops' morale. It failed! Her presence was a real tonic for the men who looked upon themselves as the Forgotten Army.

By 1940, ENSA was putting on 500 shows per week and two years later they were responsible for some 4,000 shows per week. When the invasion of Europe began on 6 June 1944, the race was on to see who would be the first entertainer to perform for the forces in France. The first ENSA show arrived on 24 July 1944 and was led by George Formby. Three weeks later Gertrude Lawrence, Margaret Rutherford and Ivor Novello arrived. The first major show to be

George Formby raises a laugh on the front line.

Over the years acts from Frankie Howerd to Ozzy Osbourne (left) have done their bit for serving men and women.

staged by ENSA took place in Paris on 15 November, five years to the day after Gracie Fields sang at Douai. This time topping the bill was Noel Coward and the very popular Frances Day, who caused a sensation when she threw her underclothes to the audience.

Gracie Fields continued performing for troops throughout the war. She was singing for a group of servicemen in the Pacific when the local commander stopped the concert to announce the war with Japan was over. He asked Gracie to sing something appropriate; she sang *The Lord's Prayer*.

'Who would have thought that, in a desert far from home, such things could happen? Our thanks go to all the entertainers who perform these shows and live in the same austere conditions of the troops whilst doing so.'
SOLDIER AT CAMP BASTION

From September 1939 to March 1946, the grand total of ENSA performances given to HM Forces and various branches of industry was 2,656,565. ENSA was replaced in the summer of 1946 by the Combined Services Entertainment unit (CSE), whose work continues to this day.

Today, CSE produces shows and arranges celebrity visits for operational troops and the Royal Navy fleet worldwide. With over 500 shows a year, featuring comedians, dancers, musicians, sports personalities and celebrities, CSE reaches upwards of 30,000 troops. As in the old days, entertainers are happy to make do with sometimes spartan conditions and unconventional stages, whether it's a cookhouse or an operating base. In Afghanistan, Cyprus, Oman, the Falkland Islands and on Royal Navy ships worldwide, comedians, dancers, rock bands and celebrities work tirelessly in sometimes

Comedians: Gina Ashere, Paul Tonkinson, Andy Askins, Iestyn Edwards and Rhodri Gilbert visit troops in Iraq.

© COURTESY OF CSE

Sport stars are as popular with the troops as entertainers. David Beckham's visit to Afghanistan in 2010 proved a major hit.

© COURTESY OF CSE

difficult conditions to deliver top quality shows where they're needed most.

In 2009, CSE began providing small-scale comedy shows to forward operating bases in Afghanistan, bringing British entertainers the furthest forward they've been since the Second World War.

In May 2010, CSE took football legend David Beckham to visit troops in Camp Bastion, Afghanistan. He signed over 1,500 autographs in two days and met approximately 2,000 people. As one senior officer put it after the visit, 'Carlsberg don't do visits to Afghanistan, but if they did, it would probably be nearly as good as this weekend's visit!'

By Alan Grace and Angie Avlianos

© CROWN COPYRIGHT

© CROWN COPYRIGHT

A ship's company relax and enjoy a CSE show in Bahrain.

HEROES OF THE SILVER SCREEN

By David Willetts

© AP PHOTO / DREAMWORKS, DAVID JA

For decades, the bravest heroes of war have been immortalised on the big screen, bringing gallant acts of history to jaw-dropping life. War flicks continue to keep the past alive, reminding previous generations of their exploits while educating new ones about the horror and sacrifice of conflict.

From big-budget Hollywood blockbusters to black-and-white classics of the silver screen, films bring to life the most amazing drama of all – the battlefield. Capturing the camaraderie and the brutality perfectly, a handful of movies through the years have gone further than all the others to sum up the essence of war and become hailed as great.

A recent poll set out to discover the top ten war movies of all time and the nation's ultimate war film, and these were the results:

1 *Saving Private Ryan* was named the best war film of all time. Steven Spielberg's multi-Oscar-winning 1998 World War II epic, starring Tom Hanks and Matt Damon, begins with the brutal landing on a French beach as the Allied Forces begin their bloody bid to recapture Europe from Nazi occupation.

Audiences around the world were dazzled and frightened by the intense opening; twenty-seven minutes depicting the assault on Omaha beach on 6 June 1944. After the successful attack, Captain John Miller, played by Hanks, and his band of loyal followers are tasked with finding Private James Ryan – the last surviving brother of three fallen servicemen. They must bring him home safely, but instead become embroiled in a tense battle to secure a vital bridge.

2 *The Great Escape* proved a hit with film fans in 1963 and came in second place, with just over a tenth of the final vote. The film – which features Steve McQueen, James Garner, Richard Attenborough, and Charles Bronson, among other stars – tells the story of an audacious mass jailbreak from a tough World War II POW camp.

3 Spielberg's harrowing account of the Holocaust, *Schindler's List*, claimed third place in the poll. The film earned worldwide acclaim for its portrayal of one businessman's selfless effort to save the lives of over a thousand Polish Jews during World War II.

4 Francis Ford Coppola's notorious 1979 epic, *Apocalypse Now*, came in at fourth place. A modern retelling of Joseph Conrad's *Heart of Darkness*, the film follows a young American captain during the Vietnam War, who must travel up-river to confront a

© WARNER BROS / THE KOBAL COLLECTION

© ALLSTAR / CINETEXT / UNIVERSAL

© ZOETROPE / UNITED ARTISTS / THE KOBAL COLLECTION

renegade colonel who has assumed the role of warlord.

5 The Vietnam War proved a popular conflict in the top ten, with Stanley Kubrick's *Full Metal Jacket* of 1987 in fifth place. The film follows a group of US Marines during their participation in the Tet Offensive.

6 Vietnam also provided the backdrop for the sixth most popular film, *Platoon*, the first instalment of Oliver Stone's napalm-loaded war trilogy.

7 They may have taken lives but they could never take his freedom – Mel Gibson's *Braveheart* was the seventh most popular war film. Gibson's role as William Wallace in the 1995 historical epic about the bloody battles the Scottish waged with England for independence raked in 5 per cent of all votes cast.

8 Modern classic *Black Hawk Down*, about American Delta Force soldiers fighting through claustrophobic streets in the Battle of Mogadishu in Somalia after a chopper was brought down, came eighth in the poll.

9 Director Wolfgang Peterson's *Das Boot* – about a German U-boat and its crew during World War II – brilliantly captures the excitement of battle as well as the tedium of the hunt and claustrophobic submarine conditions. It received 3 per cent of the vote, coming in ninth.

10 With its all-star cast headed by Robert De Niro, *The Deer Hunter*, about a trio of pals sent to fight in Vietnam, claimed tenth place with 1 per cent of the vote.

Modern classics are sure to break into the top ten soon including films like Oscar-winning movie *The Hurt Locker* about US bomb disposal experts in Iraq. And there are many more incredible cinematic tales which missed out but are worth a mention like *A Bridge Too Far* (1977) and *The Dam Busters* (1955).One thing is for sure: as long as gallant men and women risk everything for the cause and their comrades, their heroic actions will always be immortalized in film.

Help for Heroes has produced a limited-edition DVD, drawing on film industry archives to create the definitive collection of the greatest war movies ever made. With excerpts from everything from *Saving Private Ryan* to *The Dam Busters*, this is the perfect film anthology for any war movie buff. The film features the 'best bits' from *Saving Private Ryan, Schindler's List, The Hurt Locker, The Bridge on the River Kwai, Platoon, The Great Escape, Zulu, Dr Strangelove, Lawrence of Arabia, Ice Cold in Alex, Gallipoli* and many more.

SALLY CLARKE

JUNE 2009, AFGHANISTAN. LANCE CORPORAL SALLY CLARKE, A MEDIC, IS ON PATROL WITH 2 BATTALION, THE ROYAL REGIMENT OF FUSILIERS, IN SANGIN, HELMAND PROVINCE. IT IS HOT, DUSTY, AND TENSE.

HOLD UP! I'VE GOT SOMETHING!

AN ANTI-TANK MINE - IT HAS A MASSIVE EXPLOSIVE CHARGE AND IS TRIGGERED BY TANKS AND OTHER ARMOURED FIGHTING VEHICLES.

OUT OF NOWHERE...
...THE TALIBAN RAIN SMALL-ARMS FIRE DOWN ON SALLY'S PATROL.
KR-KR-KR!!
AMBUSH! TAKE COVER!!
KR-KR-KR!!
THE SOLDIERS RACE TO COVER UNDER THE DEVASTATING FIRESTORM.
HNK!
KBOOOOM!!

MACHINE-GUN FIRE AND SHRAPNEL BLAST PAST SALLY.
GAH!
FTOOM!
PRAANG!

DAMN!

SALLY'S BACK IS HURT...

HOT SHRAPNEL HAS LODGED IN HER SHOULDER.

BWRANNG!
PTOOM!
BUT THE FIREFIGHT IS STILL BLAZING...

...AND SALLY'S PATROL MATES ARE IN TROUBLE.

THE DITCH IS FULL OF FILTHY WATER...
BUT ON THE OTHER SIDE THERE'S WORK TO BE DONE.

MY GOD...FIVE... SIX, SEVEN DOWN!!!

FOCUS, CLARKE, FOCUS.

PAUL! IT'S ME, SALLY!

GAH! DAMN THAT HURTS.
HANG ON, PAUL, HANG ON.

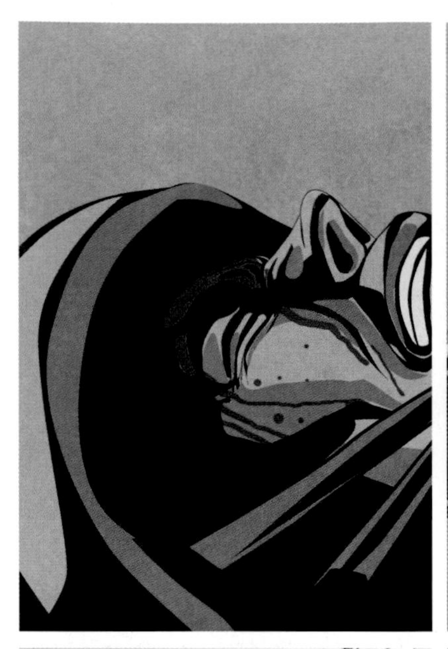

SALLY WORKS FAST...

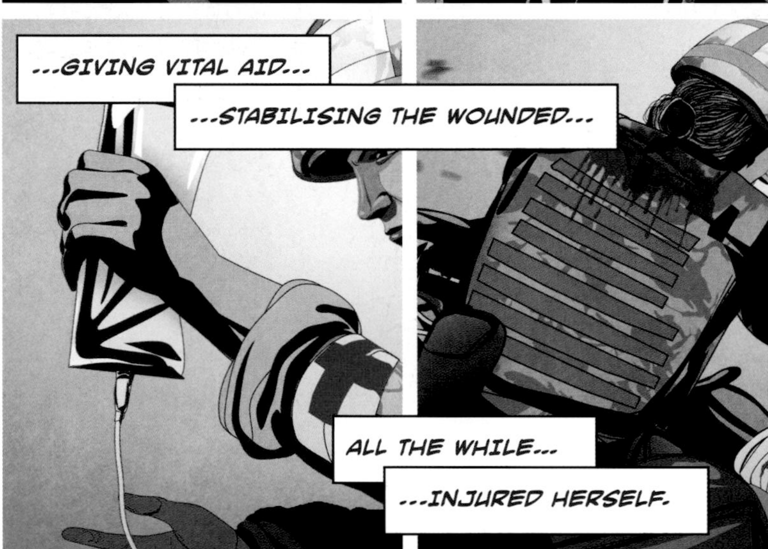
...GIVING VITAL AID...
...STABILISING THE WOUNDED...
ALL THE WHILE...
...INJURED HERSELF.

THWUP
THWUP

COALITION AIR SUPPORT HAS DRIVEN THE TALIBAN OFF...

...AND THE MEDICAL EMERGENCY RESPONSE TEAM CAN LAND.
OVER HERE! MAN DOWN! QUICK!

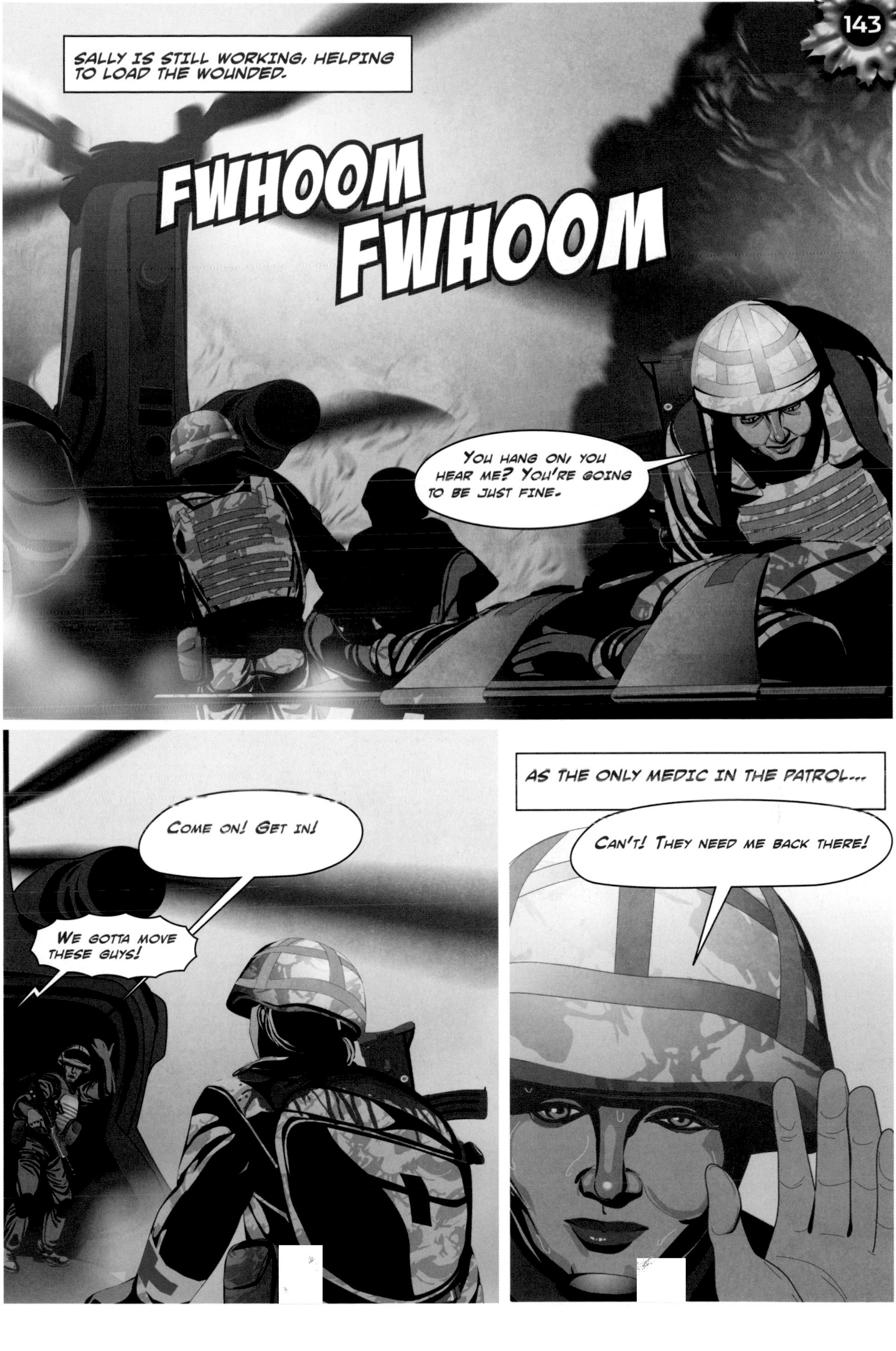

SALLY IS STILL WORKING, HELPING TO LOAD THE WOUNDED.

FWHOOM FWHOOM

YOU HANG ON, YOU HEAR ME? YOU'RE GOING TO BE JUST FINE.

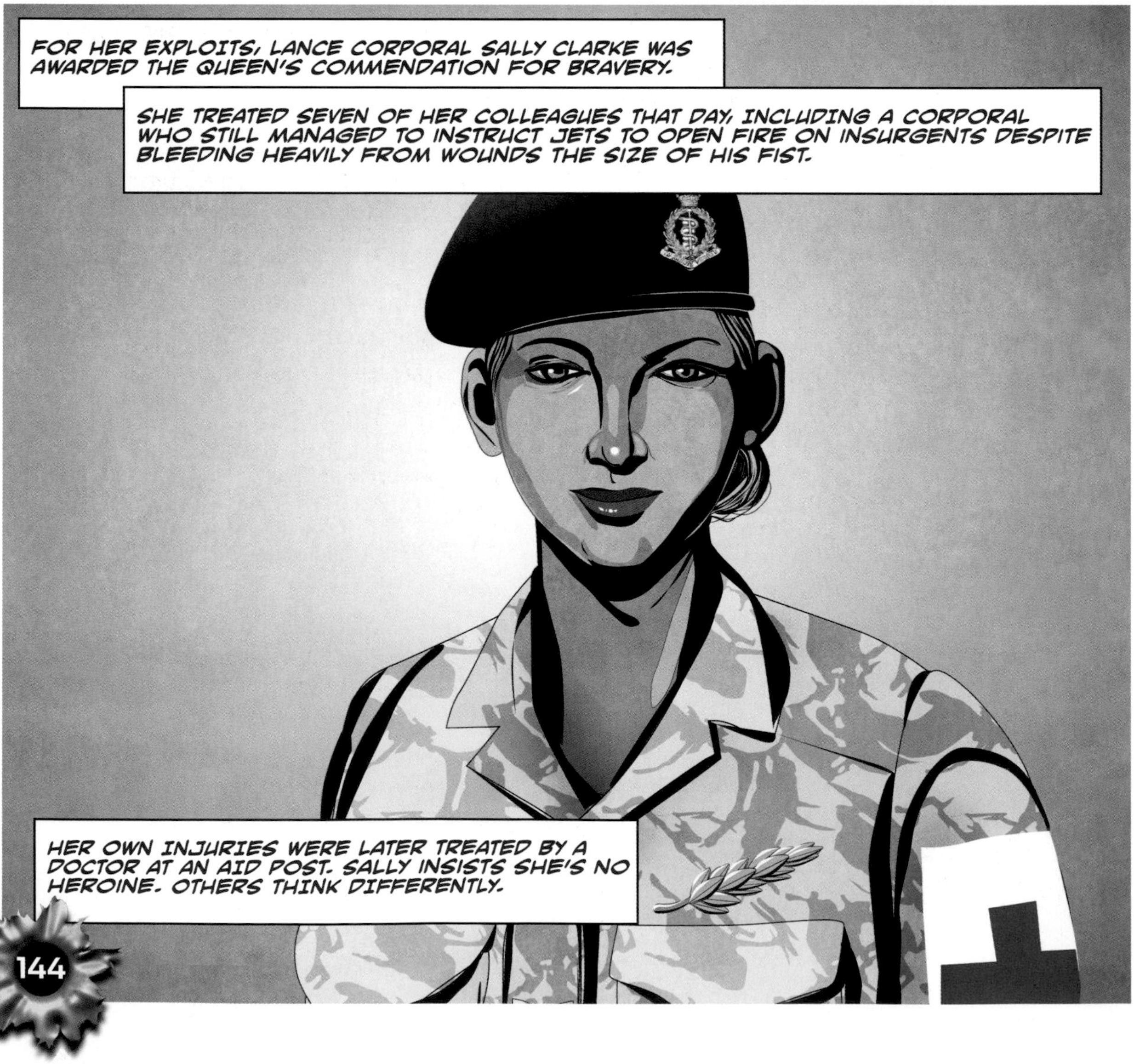

FOR HER EXPLOITS, LANCE CORPORAL SALLY CLARKE WAS AWARDED THE QUEEN'S COMMENDATION FOR BRAVERY.

SHE TREATED SEVEN OF HER COLLEAGUES THAT DAY, INCLUDING A CORPORAL WHO STILL MANAGED TO INSTRUCT JETS TO OPEN FIRE ON INSURGENTS DESPITE BLEEDING HEAVILY FROM WOUNDS THE SIZE OF HIS FIST.

HER OWN INJURIES WERE LATER TREATED BY A DOCTOR AT AN AID POST. SALLY INSISTS SHE'S NO HEROINE. OTHERS THINK DIFFERENTLY.

AN EXCELLENT MESS

One of the earliest attempts to improve the gastronomic lot of the British Tommy came from, of all people, a Frenchman. Alexis Soyer had cooked for some of the top aristocratic names in France when he was forced to flee the country during the 1830 revolution. He washed up in London, becoming chef at the Reform Club where his innovations – including cooking with gas, refrigeration and adjustable ovens – were so famous that his kitchen was open for tours.

As his fame grew, Soyer made use of his status to help those less fortunate. He invented the soup kitchen to feed victims of the Great Irish Famine in 1847, and donated the proceeds of his book, *Soyer's Charitable Cookery*, to the poor. During the Crimean War, Soyer was inspired by reporting in *The Times* to offer his services to the British Army, writing the following to the newspaper's editor:

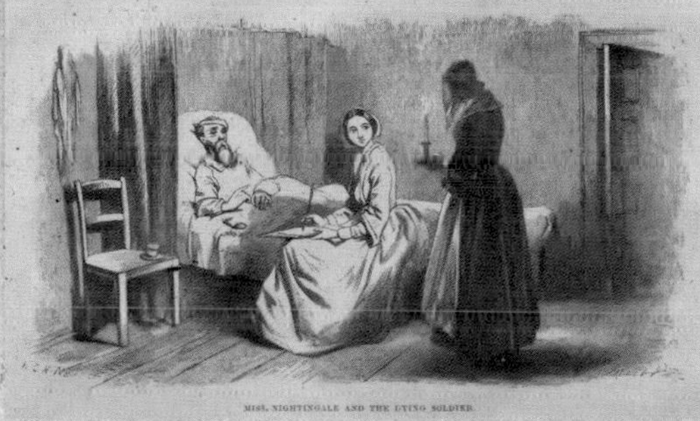

> Sir, – After carefully perusing the letter of your correspondent, dated Scutari, in your impression of Wednesday last, I perceive that, although the kitchen under the superintendence of Miss Nightingale affords so much relief, the system of management at the large one in the barrack-hospital is far from being perfect. I propose offering my services gratuitously, and proceeding direct to Scutari, at my own personal expense, to regulate that important department, if the Government will honour me with their confidence, and grant me the full power of acting according to my knowledge and experience in such matters.
>
> I have the honour to remain, Sir,
> Your obedient servant,
> A. Soyer
> *2 Feb 1855*

Soyer made good on his promise, travelling to the Crimea, reorganising the provisioning of army hospitals, training regimental cooks and even designing a field stove for use on the front lines. A master of self-promotion, he celebrated his own efforts in his *Culinary Campaign*, a wonderfully florid travelogue-cum-cookbook. And while his recipes for boiled salt pork are unlikely to pass muster with today's serving soldier, they shed a fascinating light on battlefield conditions of the time.

SOYER'S FIELD AND BARRACK COOKERY FOR THE ARMY

No 1 – Soyer's Receipt to Cook Salt Meat for Fifty Men
Headquarters, Crimea, 12 May 1856

1. Put 50lbs of meat in the boiler.
2. Fill with water, and let soak all night.
3. Next morning, wash the meat well.
4. Fill with fresh water, and boil gently three hours, and serve.
5. Skim off the fat, which, when cold, is an excellent substitute for butter.

Soyer très heureux.

For salt pork proceed as above, or boil half beef and half pork – the pieces of beef may be smaller than the pork, requiring a little longer time doing.

Dumplings, No 21, may be added to either pork or beef in proportion; and when pork is properly soaked, the liquor will make a very good soup. The large yellow peas as used by the Navy may be introduced; it is important to have them, as they are a great improvement. When properly soaked, French haricot beans and lentils may also be used to advantage. By the addition of 5lbs of split peas, ½lb of brown sugar, two tablespoonfuls of pepper, ten onions; simmer gently till in pulp, remove the fat and serve; broken biscuit may be introduced. This will make an excellent mess.

No 1a – How to Soak and Plain-boil the Rations of Salt Beef and Pork, on Land or at Sea
To each pound of meat allow about a pint of water. Do not have the pieces above 3 or 4lbs in weight. Let it soak for seven or eight hours, or all night if possible. Wash each piece well with your hand in order to extract as much salt as possible. It is then ready for cooking. If less time be allowed, cut the pieces smaller and proceed the same, or parboil the meat for twenty minutes in the above quantity of water, which throw off and add fresh. Meat may be soaked in sea water, but by all means boiled in fresh when possible.

I should advise, at sea, to have a perforated iron box made, large enough to contain half a ton or more of meat, which box will ascend and descend by pulleys; have also a frame made on which the box might rest when lowered overboard, the meat being placed outside the ship on a level with the water, the night before using; the water beating against the meat through the perforations will extract all the salt.

Meat may be soaked in sea water, but by all means washed.

No 2 – Soyer's Army Soup for Fifty Men

Headquarters, 12 May 1856

1. Put in the boiler 60 pints, 7½ gallons, or 5½ camp kettles of water.
2. Add to it 50lbs of meat, either beef or mutton.
3. The rations of preserved or fresh vegetables.
4. Ten small tablespoonfuls of salt.
5. Simmer three hours, and serve.

P.S. When rice is issued put it in when boiling, 3lbs will be sufficient. About 8lbs of fresh vegetables. Or 4 squares from a cake of preserved ditto. A tablespoonful of pepper, if handy. Skim off the fat.

A STORM IN A FRYING-PAN.

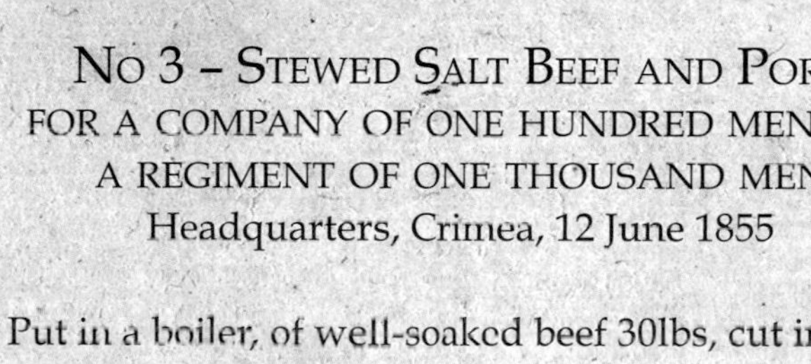

No 3 – Stewed Salt Beef and Pork

FOR A COMPANY OF ONE HUNDRED MEN, OR A REGIMENT OF ONE THOUSAND MEN

Headquarters, Crimea, 12 June 1855

Put in a boiler, of well-soaked beef 30lbs, cut in pieces of ¼lb each.

20lbs of pork.

1½lbs of sugar.

8lbs of onions, sliced

25 quarts of water

4lbs of rice.

Simmer gently for three hours, skim the fat off the top, and serve.

Note – How to soak the meat for the above mess: Put 50lbs of meat in each boiler, having filled them with water, and let soak all night; and prior to using it, wash it and squeeze with your hands, to extract the salt.

In case the meat is still too salty, boil it for twenty minutes, throw away the water, and put fresh to your stew.

By closely following the above receipt you will have an excellent dish.

The full text of Soyer's account on his voyage to the front lines can be found here **http://bit.ly/95y0UC**

FLYING OFFICER ROBIN FOWLER

Age	25
Hometown	Guildford
Unit	3 Squadron RAF Regiment

What is your job and what do you do?
I am a Rifle flight commander on a RAF Regt field squadron. I command and lead thirty RAF Regt Gunners in barracks, on exercise and operations.

What was your best day?
Landing back in the UK with everyone that we deployed with, having suffered no major casualties or deaths.

What was your hardest day?
Leading my flight on a vehicle patrol down a wadi that was a known hotspot for IEDs.

Soldiers line up in front of the new Jackal 2 high mobility vehicle that will be deployed to Afghanistan as an upgrade to the standard Jackal.

What is your favourite bit of kit and why?
The Jackal vehicle because it is very well thought out and soldiers' thoughts and opinions have been acted on.

What is your favourite sport/and or sports team?
Running.

Who do you most admire/ who is your hero?
Douglas Bader.

What is the best thing about being in the military?
The people that you work with.

DOUGLAS BADER

Douglas Bader (1910–1982) was a Group Captain in the Royal Air Force during the Second World War. He joined the RAF in 1928 as an Officer Cadet. Just three years later he was seriously injured in an aircraft accident, in which he lost both his legs. He refused to let his injuries prevent him from being part of the action, however. He undertook refresher training and passed his check flights, but in April 1933 was forced to retire from the RAF.

With the outbreak of the Second World War, things changed. In 1939, Bader re-entered the Armed Forces and requested that he be assigned to the RAF. In January 1940, at age 29 considerably older than his peers, he was posted to No. 19 Squadron, near Cambridge, where he got his first glimpse of a Spitfire. It wasn't long before he was patrolling Dunkirk in his own Spitfire and, in July 1940, he found himself in the thick of the Battle of Britain.

Over the course of the war, Bader shot down twenty-two German aircraft. It was thought by some that his missing legs were instrumental to his astonishing success. Airmen undertaking sharp combat turns often lost consciousness as the pull of gravity caused blood to drain from the brain to other parts of the body – in particular, the legs. As Bader didn't have legs, he was able to remain conscious for longer than his fellow pilots, giving him a crucial advantage in the air.

Bader was honoured with a Distinguished Service Order and Bar and a Distinguished Flying Cross and Bar, and made a Commander of the British Empire.

FIGHTING FIT

Soldiers on the front lines can spend days on patrol in temperatures up to 50°C, carrying kit bags that can weigh up to 60 or 70 kgs. Only the fittest men and women are up to the challenge.

How would you fare under these conditions? Would you have the strength and the stamina it takes?

Below are some of the fitness requirements for joining the Army, Navy and RAF, along with exercises to allow you to test yourself against the best.

ARMY FITNESS REQUIREMENTS

Press-ups: Men must complete 44 press-ups and women must complete 21 press-ups in 2 minutes. Arms should be fully extended with your hands shoulder width apart, legs should be straight and off the ground. Bend your arms and lower your chest to just above the floor then fully extend your arms again.

Sit-ups: All candidates must complete 50 sit-ups in 2 minutes. Using a mat, lie on your back, knees bent at 90°, feet flat on the floor and secured. Your arms should be crossed over your chest with fingertips touching your shoulders. Sit up until your upper body is in a vertical position then, under control, return to the starting position, making sure your shoulder blades touch the mat before you start the next sit-up. You should not flick your hips or bounce off the mat for extra momentum.

Multi-stage fitness test: Candidates must complete a shuttle run conducted over a 20-metre track. The test is progressive – an increasing number of shuttles have to be completed within an ever shorter period of time. A successful pass is roughly comparable to a 1.5-mile run, completed within 10.5 minutes for males and 13 minutes for females.

RAF FITNESS REQUIREMENTS

Run: The basic Pre-Joining Fitness Test (PJFT) for the RAF is a 1.5-mile run on a treadmill. This needs to be completed within 12 minutes 12 seconds by men and 14 minutes 35 seconds by women.

Some candidates may also have to complete a beep test and do as many press-ups and sit-ups as they can in a minute.

RAF Regiment Gunners also have to pass the 3-day Potential Gunner Acquaintance Course at RAF Honington, which includes a shuttle run or beep test for about 10 minutes, followed by at least 10 press-ups, 25 sit-ups and a 50-metre swim. A 3-mile run to be completed in less than 24 minutes.

ROYAL MARINES FITNESS REQUIREMENTS

Run: The PJFT for the Royal Marines is a 1.5-mile run on a treadmill that has to be completed in under 10 minutes.

Potential recruits also need to complete the Pre-Royal Marine Commando Course (PRMC) – a 3-day assessment course held at the Commando Training Centre at Lympstone. This includes a 3-mile run to be completed in 2 parts: a 1.5-mile run to be completed as a squad in 12.5 minutes or under and a 1.5-mile free run to be completed in less than 10.5 minutes.

Stress tests: This sequence of tests runs as follows:

- Press-ups x 60 in 2 minutes
- Rest for 2 minutes
- Sit-ups x 80 in 2 minutes

- Rest for 2 minutes
- A minimum of 6 'heaves to the beam' – full pull-ups with the palms facing away from the body (from 'full hang' to your chest touching the bar)

ROYAL NAVY FITNESS REQUIREMENTS

Run: The PJFT for the Royal Navy consists of a 1.5-mile run on a treadmill, to be completed within the following times according to your age and gender.

Men:	Aged 15–24 – 12 m 20 s
	Aged 25–29 – 12 m 48 s
	Aged 30–34 – 13 m 18 s
	Aged 35–39 – 13 m 49 s
Women:	Aged 15–24 – 14 m 35 s
	Aged 25–29 – 15 m 13 s
	Aged 30–34 – 15 m 55 s
	Aged 35–39 – 16 m 40 s

FIGHTING FIT PROGRAMME

Press-ups: Lie face down on the ground, put the palms of your hands flat on the ground underneath your shoulders, stiffen your back and legs, and raise your body up, pivoting on your toes. Keep your back straight throughout the exercise and repeat slowly and deliberately in sets of 20–40, depending on your fitness level.

Dips: You need 2 parallel bars about 60 cm apart and about 1.2 m off the ground, though the backs of 2 sturdy chairs would do just as well. Stand between the bars, grip one with each hand and lift yourself off the ground until your arms lock straight. Cross your legs and raise your feet to keep them out of the way. Now, lower yourself until your upper arms are parallel with the bars, then raise yourself up and lock your arms straight again – try to do 20 of these (they are very difficult at first).

Hyperextensions: Lie face down on the floor with your hands behind your head, then raise your chest and shoulders as far as you can off the floor and lower them again – you should be able to do sets of at least 30 of these. Avoid hooking your feet under any stationary objects as you will end up training your legs more than your back.

Tricep dips: You need 2 stable benches (or a sofa and a chair) about 1.2 m apart. Adopt a sitting position with your feet on one bench and your bum on the other. Take your weight on your hands and slide your body forwards so your bottom is clear to drop below the level of the bench. Lower yourself until your upper arms are parallel to the ground, then straighten them. Repeat in sets of 20.

Crunches: Lie on your back with your legs bent, your feet flat on the floor and your hands behind your head. Raise your upper body as if trying to touch your knees with your elbows. When you have 'crunched' up as far as you can, pause before lowering your body down. The movement is not as l arge as for a traditional sit-up but is far better for you.

Leg raises: Lie flat on your back with your hands under your bum. Keeping your legs straight and pointing your toes, raise your feet 15 cm off the ground. This is the start position. Now raise your feet from 15 to about 45 cm off the ground, then back to 15 cm again. Keep your feet off the ground throughout the exercise and do 30 in a set.

V-crunches: Lie on your back with your hands behind your head and your knees slightly bent. Crunch your upper body as for normal crunches, but bring your knees up as well and touch your knees to your elbows. Do sets of 25.

Crossover crunches: These are performed as for v-crunches, but alternatively touching your right elbow to your left knee and vice versa. Do them in sets of 20.

AGAINST ALL ODDS

Britain's soldiers are renowned for their physical prowess – not just on the battlefield, but on the playing field as well. For many servicemen and women, a love of physical activity goes hand in hand with the stamina needed to undertake demanding tasks on the front line. So what happens when these very active men and women find themselves facing physical challenges that most people find it difficult to even imagine? The fighting spirit of these two men has helped them to survive injuries that might crush lesser men, and has led to dreams of sporting glory ...

Craig Lundberg works as a volunteer helping blind and disabled children with Daisy UK and Liverpool Actionnaires.

CRAIG LUNDBERG

At the age of just twenty-one, soldier Craig Lundberg's world was plunged into darkness.

One day, while out on duty in Basra, a rocket fired by an Iraqi insurgent hit him in the chest. The blast gave off so much heat it even warped the metal in his assault rifle – and blinded him forever.

For many it would have been the end. For Craig it marked a new beginning.

He now teaches partially sighted and blind youngsters to play football, changing their lives as they discover they don't have to be excluded from the sport.

But modest Craig, now twenty-four, insists, 'It's me that's grateful to the kids. They've taught me far more than I've passed on to them.'

For the uninitiated, blind football is a five-a-side game played with a ball containing rattling beads. Only the goalie is sighted. The coaches shout instructions from the sidelines and from behind the goal. Players must also shout before they tackle.

Craig, from Liverpool, is such an inspiration that he was nominated for a *News of the World* Children's Champions trophy in the sports category by SAS legend and bestselling author Andy McNab, a longtime fan of the awards.

'I met Craig two years ago and he astonished me,' said Andy. 'Within three months of losing his sight he was volunteering to work with children because he couldn't bear having so much time on his hands.' It was while he was recovering at home that lifelong soccer fan Craig met the man who would help give new direction to his life – Dave Kelly of the charity DaisyUK, a group that promotes equal opportunities for disabled youngsters through sport.

For Craig, coaching the great game to blind children was an ideal opportunity. 'He was an instant hit with the kids,' said Dave. 'He's this inspirational lad, like a big brother who they can all look up to.' Taking up the story, Craig added, 'I soon realised I had twenty-one years of vision to draw experience from, yet most of these kids have been blind or partially sighted since birth. Some have lost their sight through accident, and for some their blindness is a secondary symptom of another condition, like cerebral palsy.'

THE PARALYMPICS

The Paralympic Games take place once every four years (with a Winter Games two years after each summer edition of the Games), in the same city and year as the Olympic Games. The next Paralympic Games will take place in London in late August and early September 2012.

There are twenty sports in the Paralympic programme for London 2012. These are:

- Archery
- Athletics
- Boccia
- Cycling – Road
- Cycling – Track
- Equestrian
- Football five-a-side
- Football seven-a-side
- Goalball
- Judo
- Powerlifting
- Rowing
- Sailing
- Shooting
- Swimming
- Table Tennis
- Volleyball
- Basketball
- Fencing
- Rugby
- Tennis

At the last Paralympics, in Beijing, Team Great Britain comprised 206 athletes across 18 of the 20 Paralympic sports – one of ParalympicsGB's biggest teams of all time. Britain won a total of 42 gold, 29 silver and 31 bronze medals at the Beijing 2008 Paralympic Games, finishing second in the medal table.

Soon Craig started playing competitively. He did so well he is now a member of the England visually impaired and blind football team, and spends three days a week at the blind football academy at the Royal National College for the Blind in Hereford. Next year the town hosts the Blind World Cup.

But between training sessions and coaching kids, he still finds time to travel the UK as an ambassador for the RNC, encouraging thousands of blind children to chase their dreams.

One confirmed fan is thirteen-year-old Jack Cullen, who beamed, 'Craig is amazing. I'd come every day if I could.'

Jack's dad, forty-eight-year-old John Cullen, was also delighted to nominate Craig for the award. 'I enjoy coming to these sessions as much as my lad because it's rewarding to see what the kids get out of it,' he said. 'Some of the lads wear glasses but their vision is still very poor. In some cases they can barely see at all. But you have to make the most of your sight, even if it hardly exists.'

Craig's life has been changed forever by the attack in Basra. But his determination and spirit have meant that this is the beginning of a whole new life for him.

By Paul McNamara

DEREK DERENALAGI

Comrades inching through the dust towards the broken body of Private Derek Derenalagi had every reason to think he was dead and were ready to put his bloodied remains in a body bag.

The thirty-four-year-old had been manning a machine gun in the back of an army Land Rover which hit a buried Taliban anti-tank mine. The explosion threw Derek thirty metres into the air. Both his legs were blown off and his spine and collarbone were shattered. Yet he somehow clung to life.

Derek Derenalagi before the incident.

Flown by helicopter to a field hospital where surgeons amputated what was left of his ragged lower limbs, Derek fell into a coma and his regiment, 2 Mercians, was mistakenly told he had died.

Nine days after Fiji-born Derek was flown to Britain, he woke up in Selly Oak Hospital in Birmingham with his thirty-four-year-old wife, Anna, crying at his bedside. It was then that he learned he had lost his legs. Derek recalls, 'That was the lowest point of my life. Anna was in a terrible state and we didn't know if we would be able to cope.'

His distraught daughter, also called Anna, went to stay with relatives in Fiji and Derek, from Watford,

Herts, left hospital with his life in turmoil.

He says, 'I was in tears when I came back from hospital and had to bum-shuffle around the house. I used to play rugby for Staines and for my regiment and I couldn't do even simple things anymore. But as I started my rehabilitation I was standing within weeks and I realised I was still breathing. I was injured doing something I loved. At least I'm alive and I'm grateful for that.'

Today, Derek has his heart set on wearing a medal or two — but in the 2012 Paralympics rather than on the battlefield. He runs on futuristic prosthetic metal blades and throws the shot put and discus well enough to represent Britain at the highest level. He is ranked seventh in the UK for disabled athletics, having twice broken the national shot put record. He also takes an active role in helping other amputee soldiers at the Headley Court medical rehabilitation centre in Surrey.

He says, 'I am a Fijian but I am also British. I joined the Army because I wanted to fight for Britain. That's where my loyalties lie.'

And his loyalties look set to do Britain proud.

By Martin Phillips

Derek Derenalagi with Lawrence Dallaglio at Twickenham.

HRH Prince Harry with Derek and Anna Derenalagi at *The Sun* Millies awards for bravery.

WO2 MATTHEW CAMPBELL HENRY

Age 36
Hometown Stockport
Unit 1 Mercian

What is your job and what do you do?
I am the Company Sergeant Major (CSM) for A Company. I also command the Quick Reaction Force (QRF).

What has been your best day?
I get a good feeling when my Casevac (Casualty Evacuation) plan has worked well and I have got the casualties back in double-quick time to the FOB and to a doctor.

The most difficult – but also most successful – day was recovering one of my sergeants who was a Cat A (the highest casualty level) after a Rocket Propelled Grenade was thrown at him. My team and I had to blast through four compound walls with bar mines to get to him. It was hard work putting the rest of the wall through with a sledge hammer after the bar mine had gone off, but very satisfying to know that my Casevac plan was a success. We got the casualty back to the FOB safely and in pretty quick time. He is now recovering well and back in the FOB following treatment at the hospital in Camp Bastion.

What has been your hardest day?
As QRF Commander there have been quite a few hard days.

I assisted with a downed Pedro (medical helicopter) at an FOB – that was a long hard and very sad day. I casevac-ed three ANA (Afghan National Army) soldiers on a joint patrol after an IED went off. Two were seriously injured and the third was walking wounded. As I got them back to the FOB, one of our soldiers was shot so I crashed out to get him. Two of the ANA soldiers later died.

Last week I Casevac-ed two injured troops and one fatality after an IED; again a very sad, hard and long day.

What is your favourite bit of kit and why?
The quad bike is great fun to ride and an excellent bit of kit to assist with casualty evacuation.

What do you miss most when away from home?
My wife and kids.

What is the best thing about being in the military?
A rewarding job, representing your country, friendship, teamwork and the banter.

Who do you most admire/who is your hero?
All soldiers. I have nothing but admiration and respect for what they do out the front gate on a daily basis.

Casevac units must be ready to scramble at a moment's notice.

CASEVAC (CASUALTY EVACUATION)

Casualty Evacuation is a term used to denote the emergency evacuation of injured persons from a combat zone. Casevacs can be done by ground and air – the latter are almost exclusively done by helicopter, a practice that started in World War II. The main role of the Casevac vehicle is to transport casualties to a safe location where they can be treated by professional medical staff.

Casevacs are different from Medevacs (medical evacuations), which use medically equipped vehicles that provide the wounded with en route care. Casevacs use non-standardized vehicles, when there is no time to wait for a Medevac, or when a Medevac is unable to get to the casualty at hand.

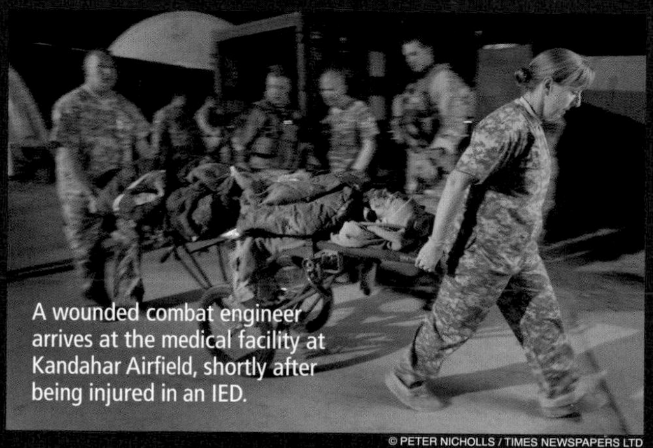

A wounded combat engineer arrives at the medical facility at Kandahar Airfield, shortly after being injured in an IED.

MY HEROES

BY FERGAL KEANE

© PRESS ASSOCIATION

Kate Peyton

Near the town of Bayeux in Normandy there is a garden of stone which I try to visit at least once every year. Compared to the vast cemeteries of the dead from World War II, it is a small place. Yet for me it is one of the most moving memorials to the grief of war that I know.

My reasons are personal. The Bayeux Memorial Garden commemorates journalists who have been killed while covering conflicts around the world. As I walk from one stone pillar to the next, I read the names of friends who were killed in their prime. They fell in Africa, the former Yugoslavia, Central America and all the other badlands of our modern era.

I know that they would have rejected the description of themselves as heroic, but how else could I describe my dear friend Kate Peyton, shot in the back as she tried to bring the story of Somalia's terrible war to a wider public? Or James Miller, a father of two young children, shot dead in Gaza by the Israel Defence Force as he documented the lives of children caught in the crossfire?

Peyton and Miller belong to a great tradition that includes William Russell, who exposed the appalling conditions faced by troops in the Crimea, Vasily Grossman, the Russian correspondent who chronicled with such literary brilliance the struggle against the Nazis, and Martha Gellhorn, whose vivid dispatches from Spain and later from war-torn Europe helped to redefine the nature of war journalism with their vivid depiction of the suffering of civilians.

As journalists, we remind the public that the wars waged in their name are not simply a matter of guns, bullets, tanks, rockets and aeroplanes. The best of our breed never forget that war – even a war fought for the right reason – is always a debasement of humanity.

Fergal Keane is one of the BBC's most distinguished correspondents. He has published several books, including *Letters Home*, *A Stranger's Eye* and *All of These People*.

Martha Gellhorn with troops on the Italian front, 1944.

Martha Gellhorn's legacy is celebrated by a journalism prize in her name, awarded to a journalist whose work has told an unpalatable truth that exposes what she herself used to call 'official drivel'. Her war reporting has been collected in a book, *The Face of War*, which gives a from-the-ground view of twentieth-century conflict.

William Howard Russell.

William Russell's accounts of the plight of soldiers during the Crimean War inspired Florence Nightingale and helped to raise public funds for the sick and wounded. The boots he wore while reporting from the battlefield can still be viewed at London's Frontline Club, which celebrates journalism and frequently plays host to today's intrepid war reporters.

ANGELS OF THE AIR

By Georgina Reid

An RAF C-17 cargo plane swoops like a giant albatross from the skies over Afghanistan. Its mission: to rescue six critically injured soldiers from the front line after they were shot by the Afghan policeman they were training. Five of their colleagues were killed when the rogue cop turned his AK-47 assault rifle on them at a checkpoint.

The massive £130 million aircraft usually carries tanks, troops and supplies to the front line. But in just 60 minutes it has been transformed into a fully functioning intensive care ward at 30,000 feet.

And for many passengers the seven-hour trip is the difference between life and death. They are tended to by a dedicated team of doctors, consultants and nurses who are members of the RAF's elite Critical Care Air Support Team unit (CCAST).

The team includes Scots anaesthetist Martin Ruth. The forty-one-year-old Wing Commander from Glasgow has worked with CCAST for over ten years and has been in the RAF for twenty-two years. Martin has been deployed in Kosovo, Iraq and Afghanistan – all a far cry from the wards of the Royal Infirmary in Edinburgh where he spends the rest of his working life. He says, 'When people are injured in wartime it's always hellish and very distressing. But we have to give a level of intensive care you would expect in most hospitals.'

An aerial A&E swings into action.

Their patients are young soldiers – many of them victims of the Taliban's improvised explosive devices – and the C-17 almost always returns with more patients than it went out for. This flight, in March 2010, is one of the busiest the CCAST team has seen. There are eight wounded in total, with injuries ranging from double amputations to facial wounds – and at least four are critical.

The troops describe how they had to play dead after being shot to avoid being finished off by the madman. One says, 'I feel

The RAF's Critical Care Air Support Team save lives at 30,000 feet.

guilty I didn't kill him. I was last to be shot.'

Another shell-shocked soldier is asked how he copes. He answers, 'When I find a way I'll let you know.'

Martin adds, 'I think we are seeing more injured now as more are surviving due to the great work of surgeons and medical teams in the field hospitals on the ground. The biggest factor for us while we are working is our environment. The noise has an effect and there are limitations. You are in the back of an aircraft which maybe had a Chinook in it the previous trip.'

RAF Brize Norton in Oxfordshire is home to six C-17s – the most expensive pieces of kit owned by our Armed Forces. One pilot said, 'It can land just about anywhere because it is such an advanced design. It can descend at very high rates and it has a very advanced defence system too, if we do come under attack. There isn't a single member of the squadron who doesn't love this aircraft. It's the aircraft that makes the squadron what it is. Just standing in front of it makes you feel good about yourself and about coming to work.'

Flown by 99 Squadron, they are on standby 24/7 and can retrieve injured troops within thirty-six hours of an incident. 99 Squadron is also increasingly deploying soldiers to the front line and the dangers of flying into a war zone are always in the back of the medics' minds.

But Martin insists, 'We have nothing like the danger the guys at the forward operating bases are in.'

The crew and medics have been on the go for sixty-eight hours but they must be ready to return at a moment's notice.

Martin said: 'It's a real privilege to look after them. I'm proud to be able to say I do what I do.'

Flight Lieutenant Niven Phoenix adds, 'You wouldn't be human if you weren't moved. Some of the people you've taken out you could be bringing back in a few weeks. These lads are operating in a whole different sphere of bravery. I couldn't do that.'

Flight Lt Aimee Foster said: 'It is difficult sometimes to look after them and you think, "How are they going to cope with that?" But then you know the spirit of these guys and you know they'll cope.'

For the RAF teams who fly the C-17s, it's just another mission. There is still banter on the flight deck and they need to be 100 per cent focused on flying the aircraft.

- The enormous C-17 Globemaster is a state-of-the-art transport aircraft. It is designed for rapid delivery of troops and all types of cargo anywhere in the world.
- It takes 1,000 people – from air-traffic controllers to engineers – to get it in the air. The £130-million plane has a wingspan of 169 feet.
- Fifty pilots with 99 Squadron are on standby any time of the day or night – and they are immensely proud of their C-17s.
- Last year C-Cast rescued 121 critically injured patients – more than double the previous year
- The medics are RAF personnel who work within the NHS and choose to dedicate up to six months of the year to the air hospital.

One of the RAF's massive C-17 airlifters.

BRAVEST OF THE BRAVE

WILLIAM RHODES-MOORHOUSE

Few men have carried out an act of bravery as heroic and selfless as Will Rhodes-Moorhouse, the first airman to win the VC.

Already a famous flying ace before World War I, Rhodes-Moorhouse volunteered for the Royal Flying Corps as soon as war was declared in 1914.

He knew there was little chance of surviving the solo mission he was assigned on 26 April 1915, to bomb a German railway junction in western Belgium.

Ignoring advice from his flight commander to release the bomb just below cloud level, the daring flyboy refused to take any chances on such a crucial mission.

He dropped to just 300 feet – so low that fragments from his bomb tore through his wings when it exploded.

The payload scored a direct hit, but not before German machine-gunners had ripped through the underside of Rhodes-Moorhouse's plane and lodged a bullet in his thigh.

If he had landed and surrendered, the twenty-seven-year-old hero would have received the medical attention he urgently needed, but that was not his style.

Instead, he dropped to 100 feet in order to pick up speed and race for home.

At the mercy of heavy fire from the ground, he took further hits in the hand and stomach, but still managed a perfect landing back at Merville airbase and demanded he deliver his report before going to the casualty ward.

One of the fragile-looking aircraft that were deployed during World War 1.

Sadly, by the time the doctors saw the damage to his stomach, it was too late. Rhodes-Moorhouse died the next day.

The British commander called his mission 'the most important bomb dropped during the war so far', while a news report at the time praised him as 'one of those who have never "done their bit" till they have done the impossible.'

By David Willetts

More VCs were awarded during the First World War than any other conflict – 628 out of a total 1,356 that have been given out since the award was introduced.

ANDREW FITZGIBBON

One of the youngest recipients of the VC was a lad of just fifteen named Andrew Fitzgibbon.

Fitzgibbon was a hospital apprentice with the Indian Army, attached to the 67th Regiment (later the Royal Hampshire Regiment) during the Second Opium War with China of 1856–1860.

The British and French were fighting to expand their empires into China and force its rulers to legalise the highly profitable opium trade.

On 21 August 1860, the 67th Regiment attacked the North Taku Fort in north-eastern China.

Under heavy fire from the Chinese, young Andrew was ordered to dress the wound of a stretcher-bearer as the regiment advanced slowly on the fort.

But then, in an astonishing act of bravery, he spotted another wounded man in the middle of the battlefield, and ran across open ground to treat him.

He was severely wounded in the process, but survived and became one of the youngest VC heroes in British history. Another boy of fifteen years and three months, Thomas Flinn, was also awarded the VC in 1857.

By David Willetts

An attack on the Old Summer Palace during the Opium War with China.

The largest number of VCs awarded for actions on a single day was twenty-four on 16 November 1857, at the Siege of Lucknow during the Indian Mutiny. The recipients included the first black man to ever receive the VC. Able Seaman William Hall was a Canadian whose parents had escaped slavery in the United States. In the fierce battle, Hall and his lieutenant were the only survivors of their crew, and between them continued to load and fire the ship's guns until the relief of Lucknow had been assured.

CARL THOMAS

ON 10 JULY 2009, CORPORAL CARL THOMAS - 'THOMO' TO HIS MATES - SAVED THE LIVES OF SEVEN SOLDIERS DURING THE WORST SPATE OF ROADSIDE BOMBINGS SEEN IN AFGHANISTAN - AND THE BLOODIEST DAY OF HIS UNIT'S TOUR...

SUDDENLY THE DAWN IS SHATTERED BY A MASSIVE EXPLOSION.
BOOOOM!!!!...
THAT SOUNDED HUGE. AND WE'VE GOT GEEZERS IN THERE.
GAAH!
WE WERE 500 METRES FROM THE BASE WHEN WE HEARD A LOUD EXPLOSION ABOUT 50 METRES AWAY.
AAAGH!
TRAINING AND INSTINCT TAKE OVER, AS THOMO RACES THROUGH THE THICK DUST CLOUD TOWARDS THE GROANS OF INJURED MEN.
LYING AMONGST THE TORN WEBBING AND TWISTED METAL ARE LIEUTENANT ALEX HORSFALL AND AN AFGHAN INTERPRETER, BOTH BADLY WOUNDED. ALL TOLD, EIGHT MEN ARE DOWN.
OH CHRIST, THIS DOESN'T LOOK GOOD...

ALEX! AASIF! TALK TO ME! ARE YOU OK? ARE YOU HIT?
GROAN
WHAT... WHAT HAPPENED?

FROM BEHIND COMPOUND WALLS, THE ENEMY TAKE AIM AT THE STRICKEN MEN AND THE BRAVE SOULS WHO HAVE RUSHED TO THEIR RESCUE.
BRAAAAP! BRAAAP!
CHRIST, WHERE DID THEY COME FROM?!

THIS IS THOMAS. WE'VE GOT A CAT A, BLEEDING BADLY. WE NEED A CASEVAC. NOW!
IGNORING THE DANGER, THOMO CONCENTRATES ALL HIS ENERGY ON THE MEN ON THE GROUND. HORSFALL IS SERIOUSLY WOUNDED - HE'S LOST A LEG, PART OF HIS HAND AND HIS THROAT IS BADLY INJURED.

THWUP
THWUP
THWUP

BUT JUST AS THE CHINOOK IS ABOUT TO PUT DOWN...
...ONE OF THE PLATOON SPOTS SOMETHING.

WAIT! DON'T LAND HER! SOMETHING'S WRONG!

AS THE BULLETS WHIZZ PAST THE MEN'S EARS, THE TROOPS STEEL THEMSELVES FOR WHAT THEY FEAR WILL BE BAD NEWS.

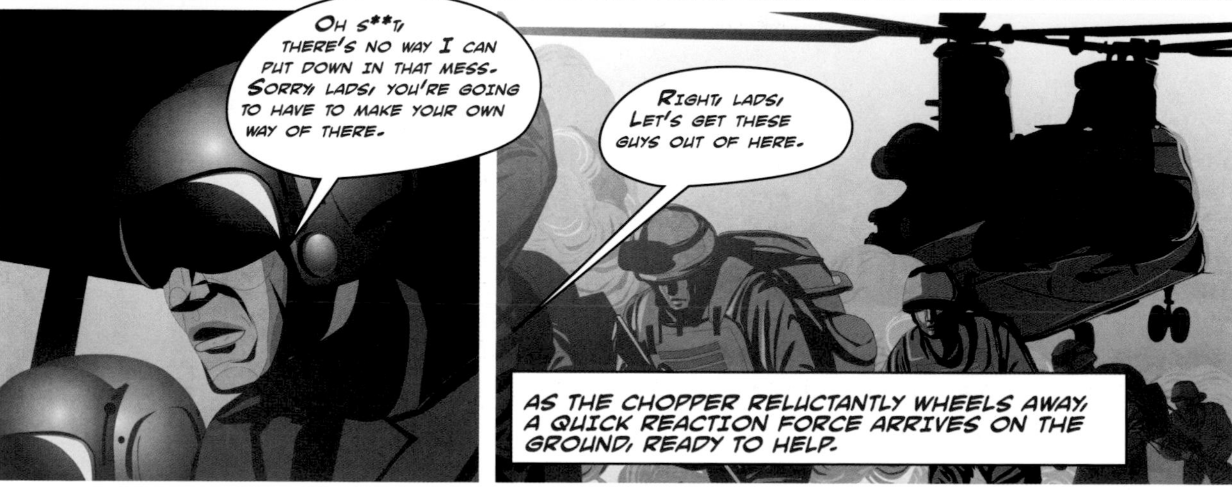

Come on, Alex, stay with me. Hang in there, mate.
While the chaos swirls around him, Thomo works desperately to save Horsfall's life, applying tourniquets and bandages, clearing his airway, doing what he can to stabilise his badly wounded commander.

As fellow soldiers return enemy fire, Thomo carries Horsfall on his back towards a quad bike.
Let's get the hell out of this mess.

But the Taliban have other ideas...

BOOOOM!!!!...
Ungh!

I SAW THE SECOND EXPLOSION TAKE MY MATES OUT...
...SO I JUMPED OFF THE QUAD TO GO BACK TO THEM...
IT WAS OBVIOUS MORE OF THEM WERE DEAD.
A SCENE OF TERRIBLE DEVASTATION GREETS HIM.
WE'VE GOT MORE MEN DOWN! WE NEED A SECOND QRT, NOW!
THOMO CAN'T AFFORD TO LOSE HEART NOW - NOT WITH HORSFALL STILL IN THE BACK OF HIS QUAD.
IF HE CAN'T SAVE THE GUYS ON THE GROUND, HE'S SURE AS HELL GOING TO SAVE THE ONE ON THE BIKE.
HE BURSTS THROUGH THE HESCO BASTION PROTECTING FOB WISHTAN, HIS PRECIOUS CARGO ALIVE - BUT ONLY JUST.
AND ONLY THANKS TO THOMO.

THE HEART-POUNDING ADRENALINE OF BATTLE SUBSIDES AND EXHAUSTION STEALS OVER THOMO AS HE WEARILY REMOVES HIS DUSTY, BLOOD-STAINED BODY ARMOUR.
CHRIST, WHAT A DAY.

ALL AT ONCE HE HEARS...
WE NEED MORE BOOTS AT THE CONTACT AREA! WE'VE GOT INCOMING!

...A CALL FOR HELP!
THOMO LEAPS ONCE MORE INTO ACTION.
THE QUAD BIKE SQUEALS BENEATH HIM AS HE RACES PAST...
...PAUSING ONLY TO SNATCH AN SA80 FROM THE ASTONISHED HANDS OF A FELLOW SOLDIER!
WHAT THE...?

THOMO, WAIT! YOUR BODY ARMOUR! YOUR HELMET! YOU'VE LEFT YOUR... DAMMIT!

BACK ON THE FRONT LINE...
WHAT THE BLOODY HELL ARE YOU DOING OUT HERE WITHOUT ARMOUR? YOU TRYING TO GET YOURSELF KILLED?!
BRAAAAK!
BRAAAKK!
...THOMO BLAZES WAY, RETURNING THE ENEMY FIRE RAINING IN FROM ALL DIRECTIONS. IN THE HEAT OF BATTLE, HE BARELY NOTICES HIS LACK OF ARMOUR.
THE DAY WAS WON - BUT AT A COST.

A CHINOOK TOOK 12 WOUNDED SOLDIERS TO HOSPITAL THAT DAY. FIVE BRAVE MEN DIED IN THE HORROR OF THE ROADSIDE ATTACK.
THWUNP
THWUNP

CARL THOMAS WON THE QUEEN'S GALLANTRY MEDAL AND A MILLIE LIFE SAVER AWARD FOR HIS HEROIC EFFORTS.
'He has seen too much, but is unshakeable, a rock whose presence is a constant reassurance. We owe him a huge debt.'
Lieutenant Alex Horsfall

The Art of War

By Sun Tzu

Translator: Lionel Giles

Sun Tzu's classic treatise *The Art of War* was written around 500 BC and is one of the most influential works ever written on warfare and military strategy. Over the centuries it has influenced many notable warriors, including Napoleon, Communist leader Mao Zedong and Ho Chi Minh, who translated the work for his officers in Vietnam to study.

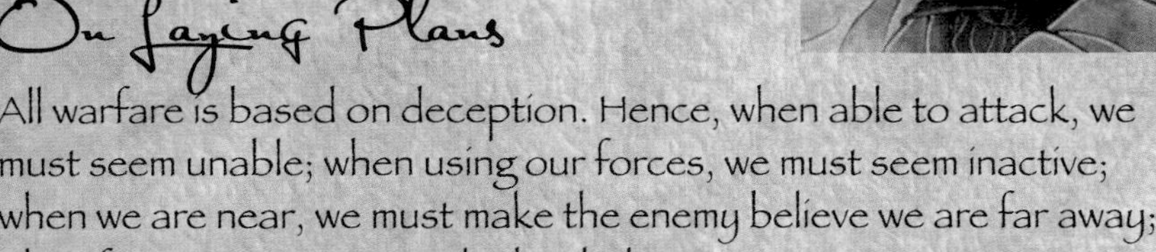

On Laying Plans

All warfare is based on deception. Hence, when able to attack, we must seem unable; when using our forces, we must seem inactive; when we are near, we must make the enemy believe we are far away; when far away, we must make him believe we are near.

On Waging War

When you engage in actual fighting, if victory is long in coming then men's weapons will grow dull and their ardour will be dampened. If you lay siege to a town, you will exhaust your strength. Now, when your weapons are dulled, your ardour dampened, your strength exhausted and your treasure spent, other chieftains will spring up to take advantage of your extremity.

On Attack by Stratagem

The skilful leader subdues the enemy's troops without any fighting; he captures their cities without laying siege to them; he overthrows their kingdom without lengthy operations in the field. With his forces intact he will dispute the mastery of the Empire, and thus, without losing a man, his triumph will be complete.

If you know the enemy and know yourself, you need not fear the result of a hundred battles. If you know yourself but not the enemy, for every victory gained you will also suffer a defeat. If you know neither the enemy nor yourself, you will succumb in every battle.

On Tactical Dispositions

What the ancients called a clever fighter is one who not only wins, but excels in winning with ease. Hence his victories bring him neither reputation for wisdom nor credit for courage. He wins his battles by making no mistakes. Making no mistakes is what establishes

On Energy

The quality of decision is like the well-timed swoop of a falcon which enables it to strike and destroy its victim. Therefore the good fighter will be terrible in his onset, and prompt in his decision. Energy may be likened to the bending of a crossbow; decision to the releasing of a trigger.

the certainty of victory, for it means conquering an enemy that is already defeated.

On Soldiers

If soldiers are punished before they have grown attached to you, they will not prove submissive and, unless submissive, they will be practically useless. If, when the soldiers have become attached to you, punishments are not enforced, they will still be useless. Therefore soldiers must be treated in the first instance with humanity, but kept under control by means of iron discipline. This is a certain road to victory.

© ASSOCIATED PRESS

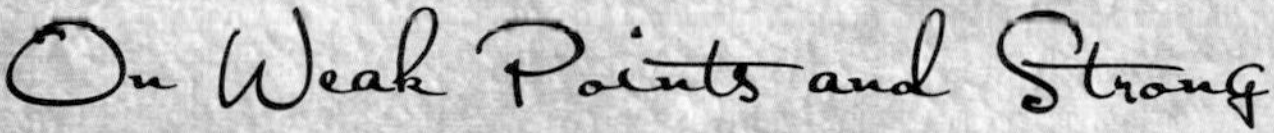

On Weak Points and Strong

Whoever is first in the field and awaits the coming of the enemy will be fresh for the fight; whoever is second in the field and has to hasten to battle will arrive exhausted. Therefore the clever combatant imposes his will on the enemy, but does not allow the enemy's will to be imposed on him.

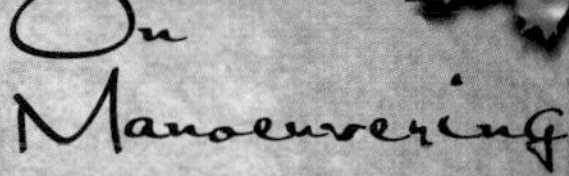

On Manoeuvering

Let your rapidity be that of the wind, your compactness that of the forest. In raiding and plundering be like fire, in immovability like a mountain. Let your plans be dark and impenetrable as night, and when you move, fall like a thunderbolt.

On Terrain

The natural formation of the country is the soldier's best ally; but a power of estimating the adversary, of controlling the forces of victory, and of shrewdly calculating difficulties, dangers and distances, constitutes the test of a great general. The general who advances without coveting fame and retreats without fearing disgrace, whose only thought is to protect his country and do good service for his sovereign, is the jewel of the kingdom.

174

You can read the full text of *The Art of War* here **http://bit.ly/cFU2Hz** or by using your smartphone to scan this code:

SERGEANT ROBERT WISEMAN

Age	28
Hometown	Stoke-on-Trent
Unit	1st Battalion, The Grenadier Guards

What is your job and what do you do?
I am a recce platoon sergeant and I administrate and help manage a platoon of thirty-two men. I've been doing this job for over a year and I have gone from acting as a multiple commander managing resupplies and casualty evacuations in the platoon in Afghanistan to carrying out public duties as a guard commander in London. It's a demanding yet rewarding job.

What was your best day?
My best day in the Army so far was finishing the Recce Commanders' Course and integrating into the platoon for Operation Herrick XI.

What was your hardest day?
The stresses of managing a team under the constant threat of attacks from IEDs and rifle fire attacks whilst navigating over unknown and uncleared areas with the heavy weight you carry in Afghanistan can drain the best of soldiers.

OPERATION HERRICK

Operation Herrick is the codename under which all British operations in the war in Afghanistan have been conducted since it began in 2002. The operation consists of the British contribution to the NATO-led International Security Assistance Force (ISAF), as well as support to the US-led Operation Enduring Freedom (OEF).

Since it began, Op Herrick has developed significantly. Between 2002 and 2003, it consisted primarily of 300 personnel based in Kabul, whose main tasks were to provide security and train members of the Afghan National Army. This deployment was expanded to battalion size when two Provincial Reconstruction Teams (PRTs) were established in Kabul, together with a rapid reaction force. In 2004, British troops were deployed to Kandahar to support OEF forces and in 2006 forces were deployed to Helmand in the south-west of the country.

The most recent deployment is Op Herrick XIII, which will last from October 2010 until April 2011. The first UK troops to enter Helmand in 2002 were 16 Air Assault Brigade – Herrick XIII will mark their fourth Afghan deployment.

Troops on the ground patrol day and night as part of Op Herrick.

What is your favourite bit of kit and why?

My self-built belt kit – it is light, comfortable and has never faltered or caused me any trouble.

Please list the last 3 films/TV programmes you watched.

1. *World Cup England v. Germany*
2. Lost *Season 6*
3. Transformers 2.

What do you miss most when away from home?

The main thing I miss is my wife and family. The rest you forget about quite quickly.

What is the best thing about being in the military?

The feeling of being part of a team, especially on operations, is unbeatable – no other job can compare to the exhilaration of being on tour as part of a platoon on operations.

Who do you most admire/who is your hero?

Ranulph Fiennes, the explorer, due to his determination and grit.

CIVILIAN COURAGE

Sometimes the bravest acts take place far from the battlefield and away from the enemy.

The George Cross is the highest civil decoration for gallantry in the United Kingdom. The civilian counterpart of the Victoria Cross, it is awarded to civilians and military personnel for 'acts of the greatest heroism or of the most conspicuous courage in circumstances of extreme danger' when not in the face of the enemy.

THE CREATION OF THE GEORGE CROSS

The George Cross was created by King George VI on 24 September 1940, at the height of the Blitz during World War II. During this time, there was a widespread desire for the many acts of civilian courage taking place to be recognised. Announcing the new award, the King said, 'In order that they should be worthily and promptly recognised, I have decided to create, at once, a new mark of honour for men and women in all walks of civilian life. I propose to give my name to this new distinction, which will consist of the George Cross, which will rank next to the Victoria Cross, and the George Medal for wider distribution.'

FIRST RECIPIENT

The first George Cross was awarded shortly after its inception to Thomas Hopper Alderson for 'sustained gallantry, enterprise and devotion to duty during enemy air raids' in September 1940. During the Blitz, Alderson

Battle of Britain: Stiff upper lips during the Blitz.

tunnelled under a demolished building in Bridlington to rescue a trapped woman. Days later, eleven people were buried alive in a cellar when two buildings were knocked down and, despite the presence of enemy aircraft overhead and the very real risk of gas leaks and flooding, Alderson tunnelled thirteen to fourteen feet under the wreckage for three and half hours to release the bomb victims. On a third occasion he again tunnelled through the wreckage of a destroyed building, ignoring a dangerously teetering wall above him and ongoing air raids, to rescue two people. Today, Alderson's George Cross can be seen on display at the Imperial War Museum.

A building burns brightly after a night-time bombing raid on London.

MALTA

In 1942, the entire island of Malta was awarded the medal in recognition of the stoicism and gallantry displayed by the islanders in their continuing resistance to German attack. The island was of vital strategic importance to the Allied North African campaign during the Second World War and came under sustained attack for two years. During the worst of the onslaught, the tiny island suffered an average of seven air raids a day. Cut off from resupplies by enemy blockades, with military resources and food rations practically exhausted, the starving islanders had only enough ammunition to fire a few anti-aircraft rounds a day in their defence.

Salvation came when Operation Pedestal was launched in a valiant effort to deliver desperately needed supplies to the besieged island. The epic attempt to run fourteen merchant navy ships guarded by sixty-four warships past enemy bombers, minefields and U-boats has gone down in military history as one of the most important British victories of the Second World War. However, it came at a cost: more than four hundred died, and only five of the fourteen merchant vessels that set sail for Malta reached the island's Grand Harbour on 15 August 1942.

King George awarded Malta the George Cross by letter, stating:

> *To honour her brave people I award the George Cross to the Island Fortress of Malta to bear witness to a heroism and devotion that will long be famous in history.*

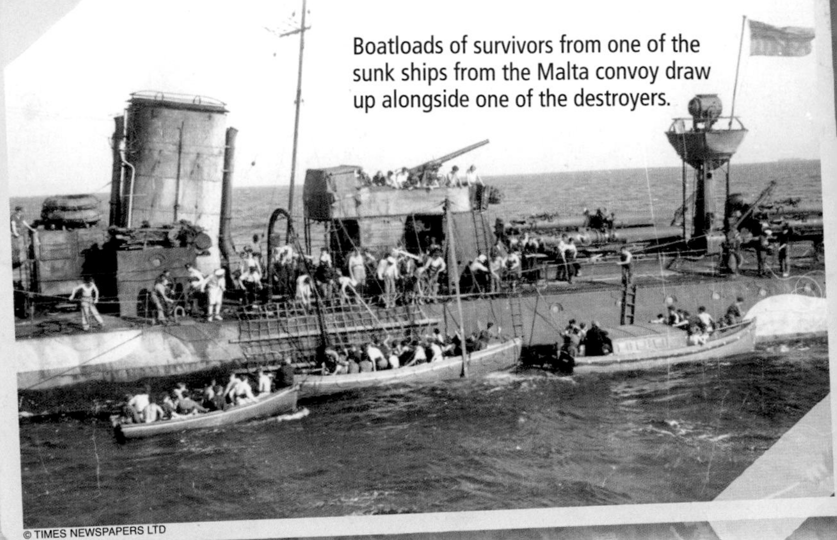

Boatloads of survivors from one of the sunk ships from the Malta convoy draw up alongside one of the destroyers.

The George Cross is now woven into the flag of Malta and can be seen wherever the flag is flown.

DURING PEACETIME

Although the majority of George Cross medals have been conferred during times of war, it is also awarded during peacetime. Air stewardess Barbara Jane Harrison is the only woman to have been awarded the medal during peacetime.

On 8 April 1968, Flight 712 took off from Heathrow Airport bound for Sydney, fully loaded with 126 passengers. Minutes into the flight, the flight deck of the Boeing 707 was rocked by a huge blast. Seconds later, the aircraft's engine caught fire and fell from the plane's wing. The pilot managed to land but a fire quickly took hold of the aircraft. When Harrison and the steward at the aft station opened the rear door of the aircraft to allow passengers to escape, the inflatable escape chute became twisted and the steward had to climb down it to straighten it before it could be used. Harrison was left alone to shepherd passengers out of the aircraft. When flames blocked the galley at the back of the plane, Harrison redirected those still trapped to other exits while remaining at her post. She was finally overcome while trying to save an elderly passenger who was seated in one of the last rows and whose body was found close to hers.

TALLER THAN THE TALLEST

Since its inception, the George Cross has been awarded to 161 individuals. Although intended initially to recognise civilian courage, the majority of awards have been made to military personnel for acts of bravery away from the enemy. Most recently, two soldiers from the Royal Logistics Crops were recognised for their astounding courage against a deadly and insidious foe: the devastating IEDs that wreak such havoc on servicemen and women in Afghanistan.

On 18 March 2010, the George Cross was awarded posthumously to Staff Sergeant Olaf (Oz) Schmid for making safe seventy improvised explosive devices while performing one of the most physically draining, mentally intense and hazardous jobs in Helmand. He was killed in October 2009 trying to disconnect three linked, buried, charges laid in an alley – the fourth device he had tackled that day. Schmid's citation states: 'His selfless gallantry, his devotion to duty and his indefatigable courage displayed time and time again saved countless military and civilian lives and are worthy of the highest recognition.' Schmid's commanding officer, Lieutenant Colonel Robert Thomson, commanding 2nd Rifles Battle Group, said, 'Staff Sergeant Oz Schmid was simply the bravest and most courageous man I have ever met. Under relentless IED and small-arms attacks he stood taller than the tallest.'

The George Cross was also awarded to Staff Sergeant Kim Hughes, who was recognized for making safe eighty improvised explosive devices on his tour of Afghanistan. In August 2009 Hughes was called on to disarm a minefield at a helicopter landing site, surrounded by the bodies of two troops and four others who had been seriously wounded. He operated without protective clothing to save time while clearing a path to evacuate the injured.

Both men were described by Air Chief Marshal Sir Jock Stirrup, the Chief of the Defence Staff, as the bravest of the brave. 'They are true heroes and I salute them both,' Stirrup said.

Staff Sergeant Olaf 'Oz' Schmid, RLC

Staff Sgt Kim Hughes, RLC, speaks with former Defence Secretary Bob Ainsworth, right, and former Home Secretary Alan Johnson.

Homeward Bound

After a tour of duty on the front line the transition between life in the field and life on civvy street can be hard. Today, men and women returning from Afghanistan and other war zones have access to help and support from a number of organisations set up to cater to the needs of veterans and serving soldiers returning from the front line. Veterans UK provides information about the medical support available, as well as mental healthcare and dealing with pensions and compensation. The Royal British Legion sponsors a website, www.civvystreet.org, which provides information and support for returning soldiers on getting back into work, settling back into civilian life, and the training and support available.

Today a soldier is not alone when he returns home, but it was not always the case.

Stranger in the House: Back from the Wars

By Julie Summers

The Second World War ended during 1945. Over that summer and autumn and on through the spring and summer of 1946, four and a half million men were demobbed and returned home. For many it was a serious challenge, for 'home' was no longer familiar. For a fortunate few nothing much at home had changed. But these men had.

After years in service, men were uneasy with their freedom from order and military discipline, thrown into a state of uncertainty about how they would readjust to civilian society. They were confused by women who had grown older, who had become independent. Then there were the children who didn't recognise their fathers, who sometimes didn't even know their fathers as they had been born while the men were away, who were jealous of the attention now lavished on their mothers.

Where before there had been a certain harmony and rhythm at home, even during the difficult economic times of the 1930s, there was now only disruption and confusion. How could someone who had never witnessed the front lines ever understand what a soldier had experienced? How could a returning man ever comprehend what a woman had been through waiting for him to come home? So much was unfamiliar and some things had moved on while others had stood still. All of this simmered away in family homes in cities, towns and villages throughout the country.

Kenneth Laing wrote in an article for the Prisoner of War Relatives Association news sheet in June 1945: 'A completely new generation has arrived. Strange people turn up among your acquaintances and you realise you left them as children. Now they're around everywhere. They're bewildering. They seem to have skidded out into life rather than to have grown up. They're a mixture of sheer worldliness and complete childish innocence.'[1]

There is a popular belief that the government and army had made no provision for helping men to get back into the swing of civvy street, but in fact there were plans galore. As the end of the war drew closer a whole conflation of documents and leaflets was published by the War Office, the Ministry of Labour and the Armed Forces. The HMSO Release and Resettlement advice booklet was handed out to every returning serviceman, urging them to contact their local Resettlement Advice Office.

---

1. *W. Kenneth Laing, IWM Con Shelf, unnumbered MS.*

The weak point in the plan was the human element. Despite the experiences of the post-First World War era, no account was taken of the traumatic psychological effect of the war on men and women.

There was little help offered to families who found themselves with marital difficulties as they sought to readjust to married life and the experiences that doctors encountered were not solved by the well-intentioned official advice. The men and women who worked in the resettlement centres did not feel themselves able to cope with intimate personal problems and men were often referred to voluntary bodies such as the British Legion, the Salvation Army and the Church. Novelist Dame Barbara Cartland, who worked as a welfare officer during the war, was dismissive of individual padres' abilities to deal with the delicate questions concerning sex and she told them so quite bluntly. 'Couldn't you speak to the men and tell them not to be upset if their married relationship is not quite normal – tell them that with patience and returning health things will adjust themselves?' she asked two priests in Bedfordshire, where she visited a group of returned prisoners of war from Germany. 'The padres looked at me goggle-eyed,' she continued. '"We wouldn't have time to say that," one remarked at length primly. What he meant was that he didn't want to talk about such things.'[2]

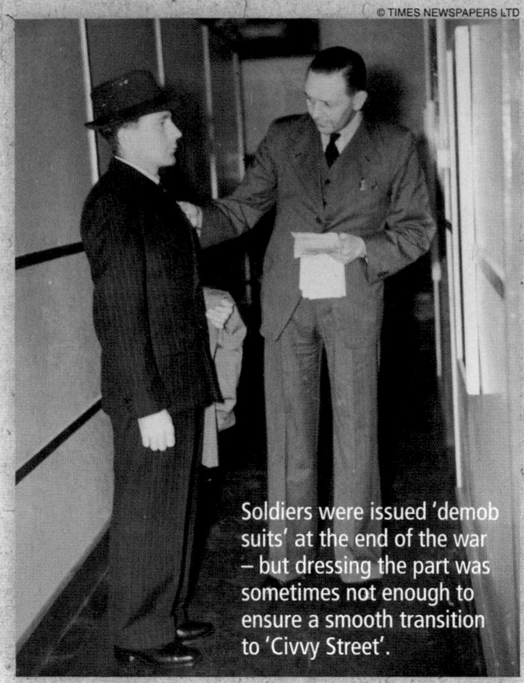

Soldiers were issued 'demob suits' at the end of the war – but dressing the part was sometimes not enough to ensure a smooth transition to 'Civvy Street'.

One group of returning men who were particularly hard hit were those coming back from the prisoner-of-war camps in the Far East. They came home to a world they barely recognised. Their war had ended so suddenly after the dropping of the atomic bombs on Hiroshima and Nagasaki that their initial reaction was one of shocked surprise. This was summed up by Lieutenant Colonel Philip Toosey, who had been in charge of the officers' camp in Kanchanaburi in Thailand:

'My reaction? I was stunned. Stunned. You have to remember what we'd gone through. And then to be told, just like that, out of the blue, the whole thing was over. My feelings had been so numbed by some of the dreadful things that had gone on that I wasn't particularly easily moved by anything by then.

But gradually my mind reacted to it and then it was a feeling of tremendous joy.'[3]

That joy was tempered by the fact that many of his men would not be coming home with him. Nearly a third of prisoners taken by the Japanese had died during captivity. Fit, fighting men, reduced to physical and mental shadows of their former selves, they had watched their colleagues die of disease and neglect in their thousands.

Quite apart from the shock of what they had witnessed in the fighting and as prisoners, these men had been away for so long that the developments that had taken place in the meantime bewildered them: 'We are completely foxed by expressions such as D Day, VE Day, VJ day, SEAC, Alligators, Ducks, Pythons, RAPWI, buzz bombs, atom bombs, bazookers, etc. Neither do we know who are Montgomery, Supremo, Ike or Bill Slim. I suppose we shall

2. *Cartland, Barbara,* The Years of Opportunity, *1939–45.*

3. *Toosey, Brigadier Sir Philip, unpublished MS 1974.*

find out bit by bit,' wrote Lieutenant Louis Baume in mid-September 1945 as he became a free man again[4].

The war had not been terrible for all men. Many had found it a positive experience and their lives were enhanced by the camaraderie and excitement of their time in the services. They had travelled and had their horizons broadened and formed friendships that lasted a lifetime. Many described the war as the best time in their lives.

For some women the thrill of having their sons, husbands, fathers home outweighed the initial surprises and life settled quickly. For those who did not find it easy to adjust there was little in the way of marriage guidance. They had to rely on the family, on the community, on their own internal strength. But the fact that everyone was going through similar experiences in a time of shared austerity made it easier in many ways for people to find a balance, albeit an uneasy one.

Today there is more help available for returning servicemen and -women. Issues of reconciliation and readjustment are discussed far more openly than ever they were in the late 1940s. Still, the homecoming is not always easy. It cannot be. Many returning servicemen and women feel ignored or misunderstood by the general public. They are returning from conflicts that have been high profile in the media but of which a section of the public does not approve. Their problems are different, but the readjustment to family life is just as important. Sights seen, experiences endured, comrades lost – those do not change from war to war. From recent global conflicts, like the war in Afghanistan, we have a lot to learn both in order to understand the past and to prepare for the future.

Julie Summers is a biographer and historian living in Oxford.

4. *Baume, Louis, diary entry 1 September 1945. Baume lists a series of acronyms and nicknames of organisations, weapons and dates that were familiar to Britons but not to the POWs who had been cut off from the outside world for 3 ½ years. Similarly they did not know the names of the military leaders who had risen to fame in the latter half of the war.*

'When you come back, there's often a bit of a low. One minute you're out in Afghanistan [making] front-page news, and suddenly you come back and you're a no-one....It probably took me a good few months to respond to the changes that come about with not being on operations any more, when all of a sudden you're not doing things that are important and every decision isn't potentially life changing.'
Capt Matt Clamp, 3 Para

CHARLES LUCAS

Seaman Charles Lucas became the first ever recipient of the Victoria Cross after he refused to allow a Russian shell to blow his warship to smithereens.

The VC medal had not even been invented when twenty-year-old Lucas, a mate on the HMS *Hecla*, risked life and limb to save his fellow seamen on 21 June 1854.

It was the height of the Crimean War, with Britain and France battling the Russians for control of the Middle East.

HMS *Hecla* was dispatched to blockade the Russian Baltic Fleet. On the night of the 21st, it attacked a Russian fortress in the icy waters around Finland, along with two other wooden battleships.

Charles Lucas, holder of the very first VC.

A contemporary illustration of Lucas's heroic action.

Ships and equipment at the wharf during the Crimean War.

A brutal and bloody battle ensued, with Russian guns mercilessly pounding the British ships from the fortress. At the height of the action, a live shell, its fuse still hissing, came crashing down on the upper deck of the *Hecla*.

The men were ordered to hit the deck, but Lucas leapt over to the shell, grabbed it and threw it over the side. There was barely a second to spare: the shell exploded before even hitting the water.

The young seaman's brave actions saved the ship and his brothers in arms, and made Lucas a legend back home. His story helped convince the government there should be a bravery award open to every rank in the armed forces. Lucas was one of the very first servicemen to receive a VC from Queen Victoria herself, on 26 June 1857. He later achieved the rank of rear-admiral.

By David Willetts

The VC was introduced on 29 January 1856 by Queen Victoria to reward acts of valour during the Crimean War. The traditional explanation of the source of the gunmetal from which the medals are struck is that it derives from Russian cannon captured at the siege of Sebastopol.

SANGIN

THE CRUCIBLE OF COURAGE

On 20 September 2010, British Forces handed hard-won control of the town of Sangin over to American troops. Colonel Stuart Tootal, commander of the first battle group sent into Sangin, reflects on what has been achieved in just over four years of occupation – and at what cost.

On 18 June 2006, 100 paratroopers of A Company, 3 Para, air assaulted into the town of Sangin in northern Helmand Province in three heavy-lift Chinook helicopters. It started as a rescue mission to pick up some Afghan Government supporters and provide temporary reinforcement to prevent the town's district centre from falling to the Taliban. As the first UK battle group to be sent into southern Afghanistan, holding the district centres in Musa Qaleh and Nowzad, as well as the Kajaki Dam, our resources were already strained. Consequently, the paratroopers had expected to stay in Sangin for no more than three days, until Afghan National Policemen could be sent to bolster the beleaguered Afghan garrison.

Soldiers from 3 Parachute Regiment return to Camp Bastion after fierce fighting in Sangin.

Instead, we ended up spending ninety-five days defending the district centre against relentless attacks by an enemy hell-bent on driving out the British. It resulted in what has been described as the most intense level of sustained combat experienced by the British Army since the Korean War. It ended this year, after just over four years of occupation by UK Forces, and it cost the lives of over 100 soldiers and Royal Marines.

Sangin's district centre lies on the east bank of the Helmand River on the town's outskirts. In 2006 it consisted of a compound of administrative buildings and a small orchard surrounded by a crumbling mud wall. A partially completed two-storey building was attached to the northern part of the compound, offering a vantage point that overlooked an open-air bazaar of stalls and goat traders in a dry wadi (river bed) running into the western part of the town. The town itself formed the hub of the province's opium trade and a meeting point for competing Pashtun tribes; dynamics that made it a hotbed of Taliban activity and a key location in the battle for Helmand.

As the single battle group in Helmand, 3 Para's resources were already stretched to breaking point. Consequently, we could only ever station a single company in Sangin at any one time. However, it became the hub around which the first six-month tour centred – virtually all the battle group's elements rotated through Sangin and drew combat duty there. Attacks came in as often as five or six times a day, as the Taliban launched continuous assaults on the district centre's perimeter and rained down RPG and mortar attacks on its defenders. Helicopters came under enemy fire as they brought in supplies and attempted to remove casualties. On occasion, the risk to the inserting Chinooks was so great that water and rations were exhausted and ammunition stocks ran perilously low.

The constant attacks were fought off by heavy machine gun and rifle fire, combined with the use of claymore mines and mortars. British artillery, Apache

SANGIN STATS

- Sangin has a long history of conflict with British troops. It was the scene of the first major military engagement in the south of Afghanistan during the second Anglo-Afghan war of 1878, when the British fought a cavalry battle against 1,500 fighters.
- Today, Sangin is the most dangerous place in the world for UK troops.
- Over a third of British casualties in Afghanistan have taken place in Sangin.
- In 2010, British troops in Sangin suffered more than twelve times the average casualty rate for Nato troops in Afghanistan.
- During its tour of duty, the 3 Rifles battle group – which represented only 0.8 per cent of the total Nato Force in Afghanistan – suffered more than 10 per cent of the daily casualties suffered by Nato forces.
- Out of over 330 British service personnel to have died in Afghanistan since 2001, more than 100 were killed in Sangin.

Stuart Tootal, former commanding officer of 3 Para.

© AP PHOTO / RAFIQ MAQBOOL

A British soldier of the 2nd Royal Regiment of Fusiliers looks through his gun sight during a patrol in Sangin.

helicopter gunships and US A-10 tank-buster aircraft delivered 'danger close' fire around the perimeter, their cannon shells and precision-guided bombs often detonating within fifty metres of our defending positions, sometimes close enough to blow men out of their sand-bagged bunkers. The troops also conducted fighting patrols into the town and surrounding fields of high-standing maize. The close nature of the mud-walled alleyways, irrigation ditches and dense vegetation through which we patrolled meant that ambushes and contact with the enemy occurred during almost every patrol, often at distances of only a few metres, resulting in bitter close-quarter fighting. One such patrol resulted in the posthumous award of the Victoria Cross to Corporal Bryan Budd of A Company, who made a lone assault on a Taliban position after almost every member of his section had been hit.

After 3 Para's tour, subsequent battle groups were able to station more troops in Sangin as the number of British Forces in Helmand increased. By 2010, a complete British battle group of 1,400 troops was based there. They also operated with increasing numbers of the Afghan National Army and Afghan policemen. Working together, they gradually began to expand the footprint of security beyond the confines of the compound by establishing more bases and checkpoints within the town and so pushing the Taliban out of Sangin. This allowed the population to reopen their shops and markets, and prompted the initiation of development projects building clinics, schools and roads. But while concerted attacks against the district centre became a thing of the past, Sangin remained a lethal place. Although pushed to the fringes of the urban area, the Taliban continued to shoot at British Forces and began to use an ever-increasing number of deadly roadside bombs, the latter accounting for over 60 per cent of all British casualties. During its tour there in early 2010, 3rd Battalion, The Rifles,

Paratroopers mount a clearing operation in Sangin. The men smash holes in mud walls to open up the town and allow them to pursue Taliban fighters. These pictures are from a cockpit video at altitude.

© NO CREDIT INFO GIVEN

© NO CREDIT INFO GIVEN

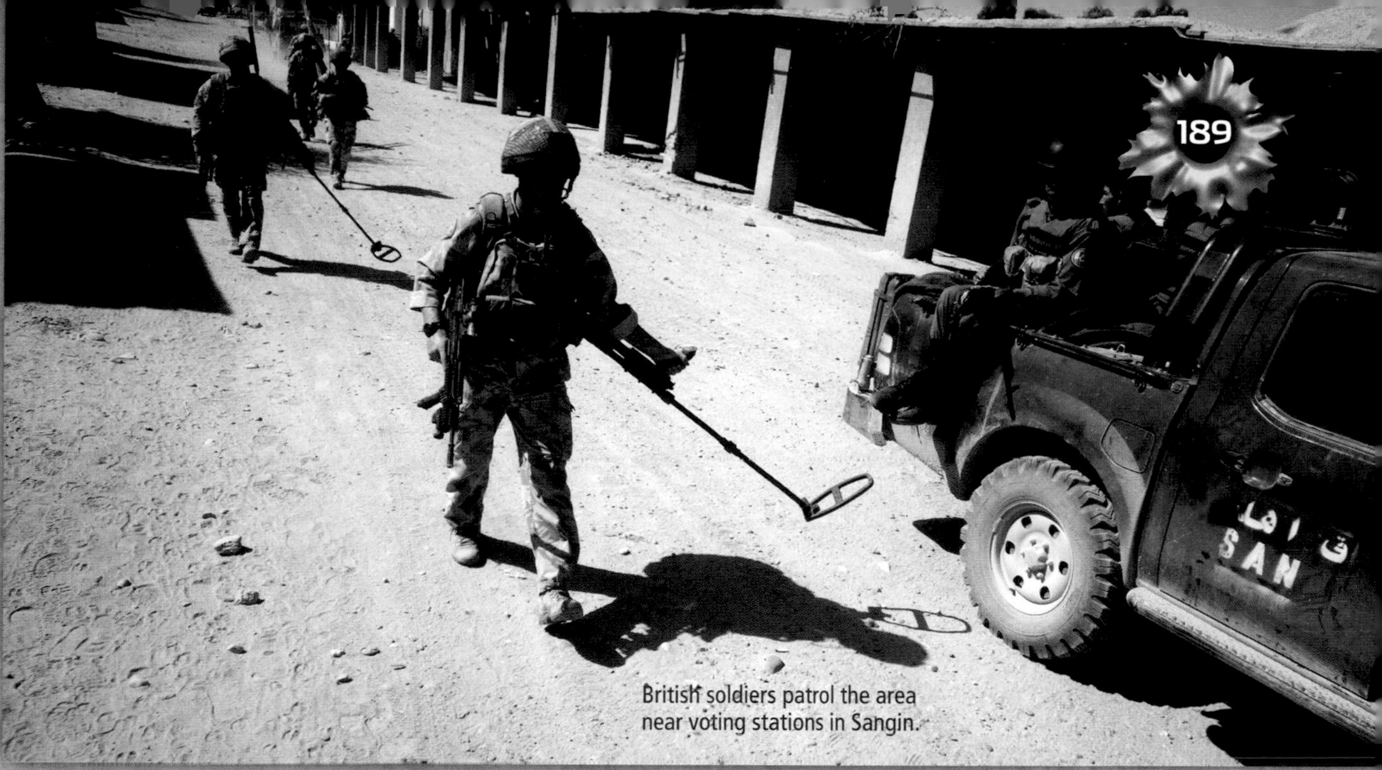

British soldiers patrol the area near voting stations in Sangin.

© EROS HOAGLAND / THE TIMES

lost thirty soldiers and many more were badly wounded. Later the same year, the casualties of 40 Commando Royal Marines, the last British battle group to be stationed in Sangin, also ran into double figures.

With the recent American surge of thousands of extra troops into Helmand, Sangin is now part of the US area of operations. With practicalities of logistics and command structures in mind, it made sense to hand over responsibility for the security of the town to American Forces. This has allowed British troops to be relocated to towns further to the south, where the rest of the UK brigade in Afghanistan now concentrates its main effort.

After four years, the investment of British blood in Sangin has been high. But it is a cost that has made a valuable contribution to the Nato campaign to bring stability to Afghanistan. All subsequent British units who served there after 3 Para, such as the Marines, 2 Para and The Rifles, have done so with equal distinction and valour. They often had to operate in the most difficult of circumstances, facing danger and privation on a daily basis. To anyone who has served in Sangin, it is a badge of courage and something that all those who fought there should wear with immense pride and honour.

By Colonel Stuart Tootal, DSO OBE

© NO CREDIT INFO GIVEN

© NO CREDIT INFO GIVEN

© NO CREDIT INFO GIVEN

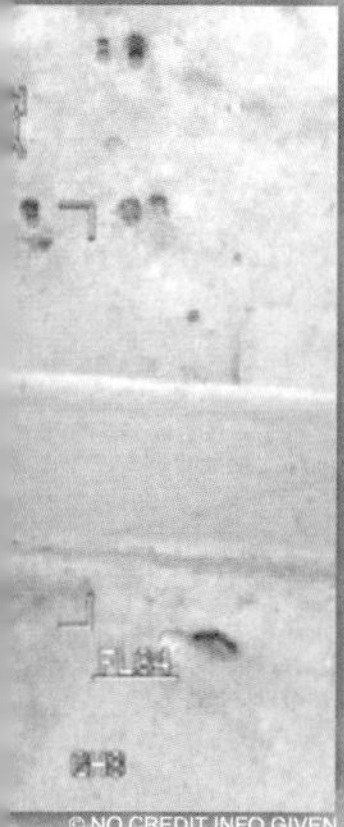

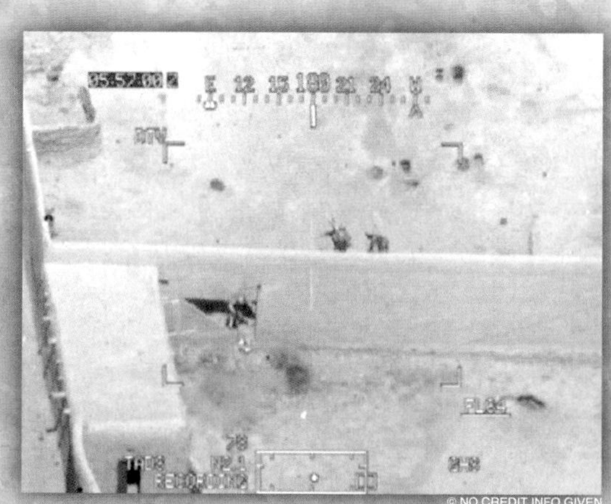

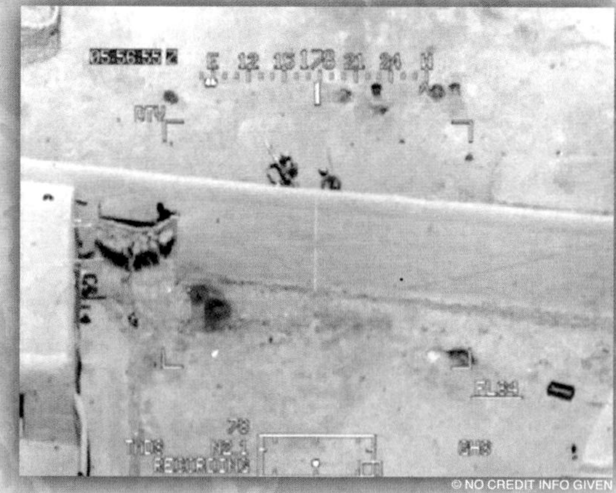

OUR LOSSES ARE NOT IN VAIN

3rd Battalion, The Rifles, returned from their Afghan deployment in May 2010. Here, their commander, Lieutenant Colonel Nick Kitson, describes recent developments in Sangin and what serving there has meant to the troops under his command.

I'm writing this from the comfort of home, the tour in Afghanistan now over. How do I feel? A sense of release, of course, but a little nostalgia too.

The final two months of the battalion's tour were very hard – but we know for sure that they were harder for the insurgents. We know our comrades from 40 Commando Royal Marines, who relieved us at the end of our tour in March, will have wasted no time in carrying our work forward.

Thanks to the hard-won achievements of those who fought before us in Sangin we were able to make the leap of faith and spread ourselves out more. This has undoubtedly been effective; it's also presented many challenges.

It is logistically more of a burden, and has created more bases to equip and resupply, which in itself brings extra risk with every move. It has demanded more of our junior commanders – young officers, corporals and sergeants in their twenties – out on their own in smaller groups, separated and thus potentially more vulnerable; having to know and read their own patch and to make their own plans and their own instinctive life and death decisions.

They have risen to these challenges in a way that should give us all the utmost pride in our young leaders.

Earlier in our tour, which began in October 2009, we were effectively corralled into a small number of large, obvious, observable bases. Mainly on the fringes of the population, we patrolled in strength, due to the distance we had to travel to our objectives, whether they were known or suspected concentrations of enemy combatants (who would see us coming) or pockets of the local community with whom we would never be able to linger for long.

A Royal Marine of 42 Commando keeps watch in Sangin.

AGLAND - THE TIMES

British soldiers cautiously patrol Sangin, which has become a veritable minefield as the Taliban plant hundreds of IEDs on routes favoured by ISAF soldiers.

Rather like the pair of enemy sentries pacing up and down outside the HQ in an old Second World War film, the security we were providing was predictable, temporary in any given area and easily avoided or attacked. It was also not quite the sort of presence with which the locals felt inclined to engage. Even if they overcame their nervousness at such intimidatingly large fighting patrols, which inevitably attracted trouble, their co-operation would be immediately apparent to the ever-watchful Taliban and a price would undoubtedly be paid.

With more bases, we were able to mount many more patrols – more frequent, less predictable and more amongst the people. With more presence amongst the people, and an unflinching determination to do the job despite the risks, the soldiers of the battle group were in a far better position to protect the population from Taliban intimidation and exploitation.

They could at least give some of the locals the confidence to side with and spread the influence of the Afghan Government. Most importantly of all, they were maintaining the initiative and, despite casualties, demonstrating to the people an inexorable forward momentum which was, albeit slowly and painfully, squeezing the Taliban out.

We had been told since before we deployed that our mission was about 'winning the argument', and we left a situation where the argument is most definitely being had – and it is a socio-political argument, not a fighting argument. We have paid a desperately high price in Sangin but not one of us has failed to notice the clear progress that has been made. Nothing can make up for our losses but they have not been in vain. While the local population may not quite yet be at the stage of throwing flowers at the feet of ISAF Forces, our Afghan partners, military and civilian, bade us farewell with genuine and deep gratitude for the small steps we enabled on the long path to solving their problems.

By Lieutenant Colonel Nick Kitson, Commanding Officer of 3rd Battalion, The Rifles

© SEAN POWER / THE TIMES

British troops who have served in Sangin leave behind a proud tradition of determination, discipline and courage.

An Afghan National Army patrol heading back to camp.

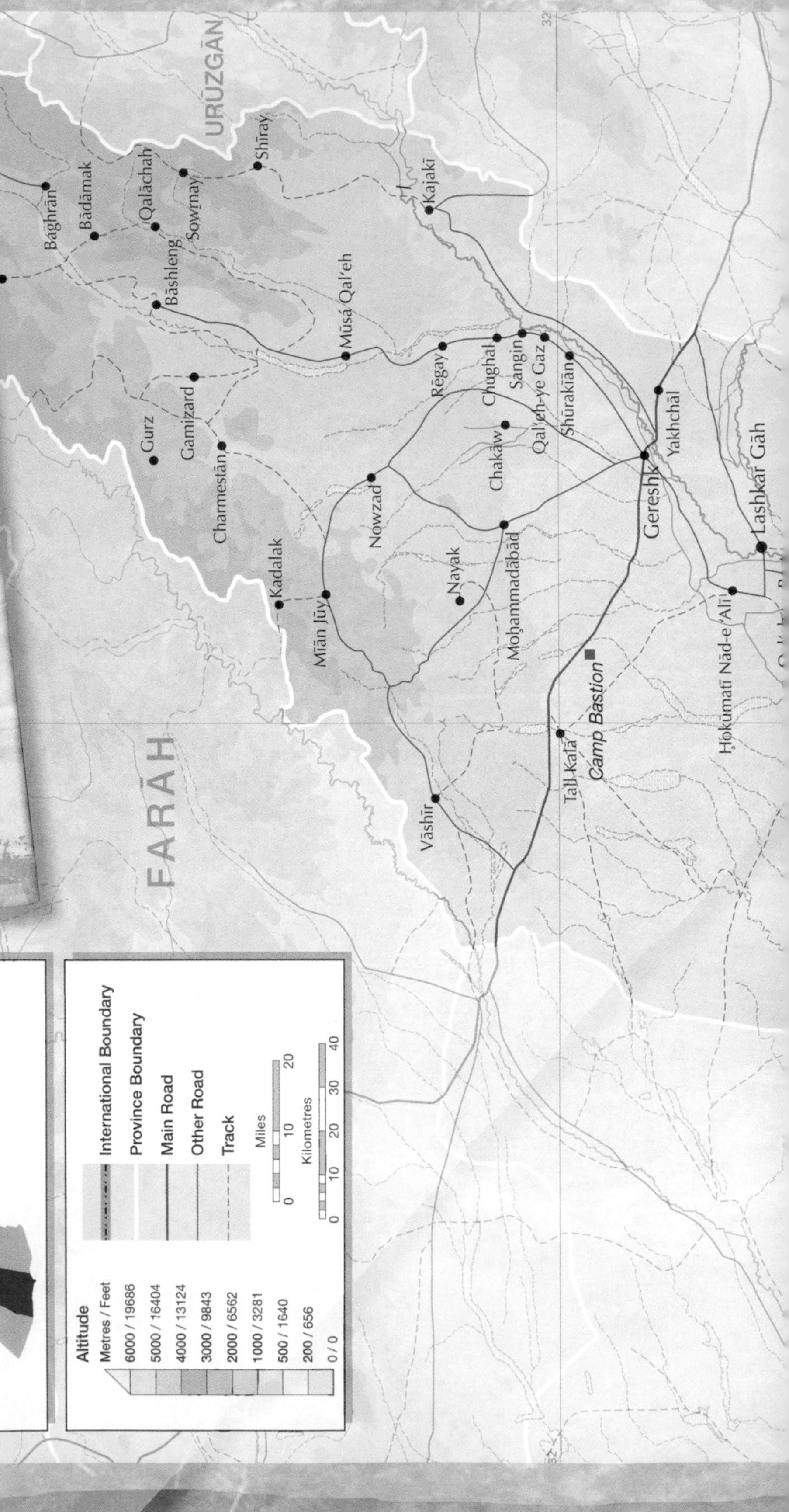

HELMAND PROVINCE

- Helmand is one of 34 provinces in Afghanistan.
- It is in the southwest of the country. Its capital is Lashkar Gah.
- The Helmand River flows through the mainly desert region, providing water for irrigation.
- Helmand has a population of over 1,400,000, spread over 58,584 km² – an area a quarter of the size of Great Britain, occupied by only one-fifth of the population of London.
- Helmand is the world's largest opium-producing region, responsible for 42 per cent of the world's total production. This is more than the whole of Burma, which is the second-largest opium-producing nation after Afghanistan.

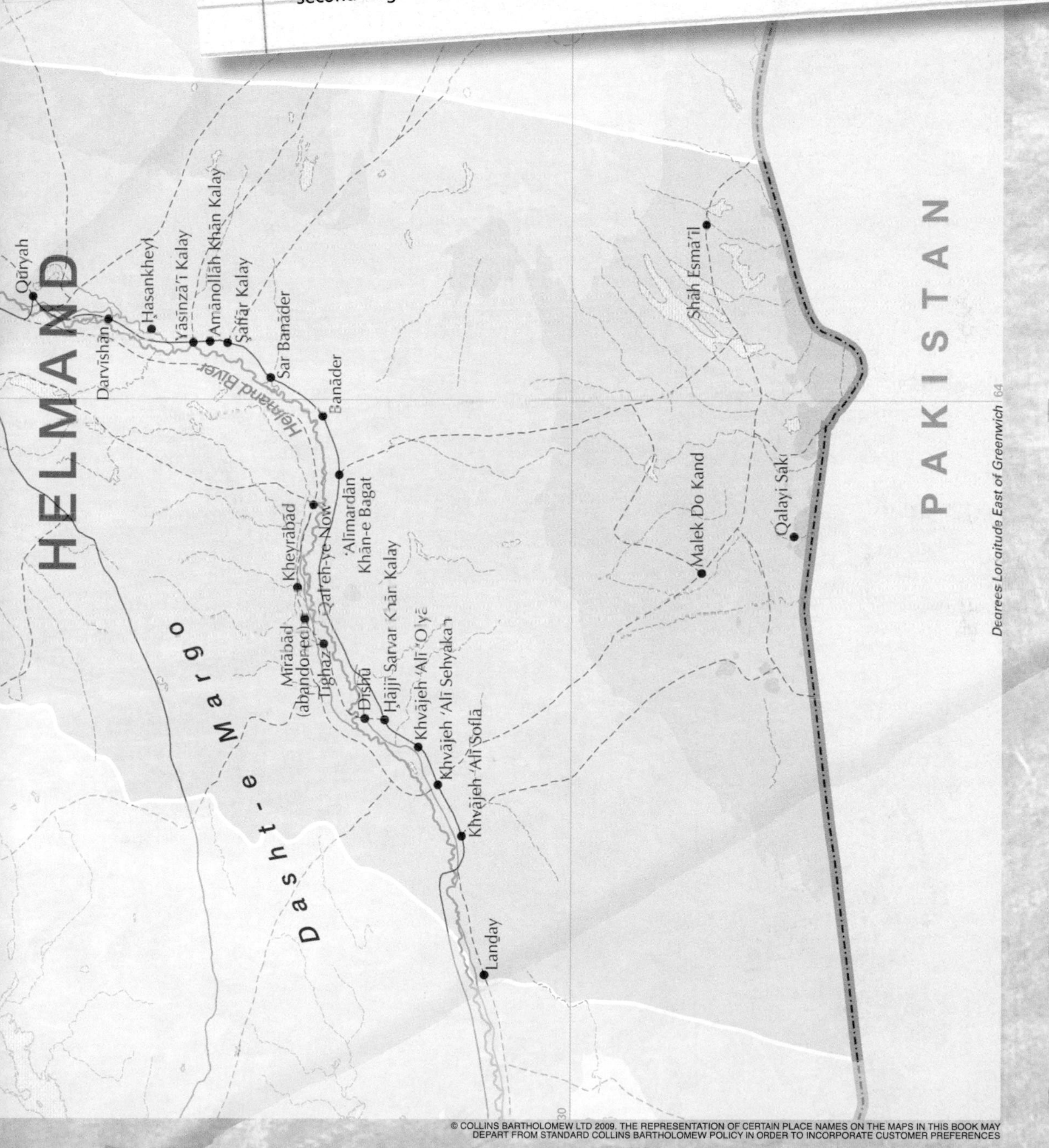

By Duncan Larcombe, *Sun* Defence Editor

GLOBAL HOT-SPOTS

The war in Afghanistan divided military leaders and ripped up the book on theories of modern warfare.

Before 11 September 2001, there were those who felt the end of the Cold War and the collapse of Communism meant the world was a safer place. A place where 'history had ended' and capitalism had triumphed. The war in Afghanistan has silenced these voices. It came as an ugly reminder that the world will always be a dangerous place to live. Hundreds of billions of pounds have been spent trying to see off the Taliban but their resistance remains and, although the Prime Minister is now discussing the possibility of pulling out UK forces, there is no immediate end in sight to the conflict.

But Afghanistan isn't the only threat facing the UK. Military leaders trying to equip themselves for future wars must predict where future threats are likely to come from in order to be ready and able to fight back as and when the need arises. In this new climate of global terrorism, few can even agree on who our future enemies will be. Does the threat come from China, North Korea, Pakistan or Iran? Or will future conflicts mean fighting wars with individual terrorist groups, rather than country against country?

The head of the Army, General Sir David Richards, has warned that lessons must be learned from Afghanistan. He believes it is dangerous to invest billions of pounds in state-of-the-art technology without spending money on troops that can go in and get the job done. 'While Afghanistan is not the template on which to base the future,' he says, 'it is most certainly a signpost for much of what that future might contain. There must be a balance between current operational priorities and future capabilities.'

General Peter Chiarelli, Vice Chief of Staff of the US Army, agrees: 'I readily admit I don't know what the next war will look like but I believe it will look more like this war than the last war.' He said future conflicts would not have a battle front on which to fight and there would be no going back to a 'simpler age'.

So who is tomorrow's enemy?

While it is impossible to predict where the next conflict will take place, there are several hotspots of tension which could be cause for concern.

PAKISTAN

Full Name: Islamic Republic of Pakistan

Head of State: President Asif Ali Zardari, Pakistan People's Party

Population: 170 million

Religion or ideology: Islam (Sunni majority, Shia minority)

Nuclear Status: Active nuclear strategy in case of war

Bordered By: Afghanistan, Iran, India, China

UK Prime Minister David Cameron greets President Zardari during a visit intended to smooth relations between the two countries.

Political Situation: While Pakistan is part of the Allied Forces in the war in Afghanistan, it is also home to countless terrorist 'training camps' where radical Islamic extremists foster terrorism to export around the world. The country has a highly unstable history and in recent years a surge in both home-grown terrorist organisations, such as Lashkar-e-Taiba, and foreign terrorist groups, such as the Taliban and al-Qaeda, has meant the country is now one of the most volatile in the world. This delicate situation, which the Pakistan Government has been unable to control to date, could explode into an even more deadly conflict.

IRAN

Full name: Islamic Republic of Iran

Head of State: President Mahmoud Ahmadinejad, Alliance of Builders of Islamic Iran

Population: 74 million

Religion or ideology: Islam (Shia majority, Sunni minority)

Nuclear Status: Active and expanding

Bordered By: Afghanistan, Pakistan, Turkey, Russia, Armenia, Azerbaijan and Turkmenistan

Political Situation: Iran's nuclear programme has long been a source of concern for the United Nations and the threat the country poses is becoming more serious. In 2002, in his State of the Union address, Former US President George W. Bush declared Iran part of an 'axis of evil' which was seeking to develop weapons of mass destruction. In 2007, the United Nations Security Council imposed a series of sanctions on the country after President Ahmadinejad refused to comply with its demands to suspend the enrichment of uranium. In January 2010, the UN stepped up its sanctions and imposed a complete arms embargo on Iran and a travel ban on certain key Iranian figures. Ahmadinejad replied by declaring his country a 'Nuclear State' in February 2010. If Iran's nuclear programme expands to produce nuclear weapons, the world's powers will have to act decisively in response.

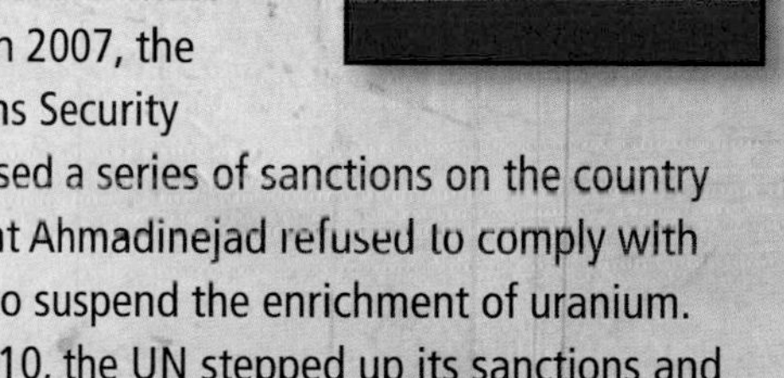

Iranian President Mahmoud Ahmadinejad (second from left) watches as a rocket is paraded by the Iranian Army.

NORTH KOREA

Full name: Democratic People's Republic of Korea (DPRK)

Head of State: Kim Jong-Il, Korean Workers' Party

Population: 23 million

Religion or ideology: Juche philosophy, some Buddhism and Confucianism

North Korean troops.

Nuclear Status: Active nuclear and ballistics missile weapons programmes

Bordered By: China, Russia, South Korea

Political Situation: One of the most secretive regimes in the world, the North Korean Government runs a single-state dictatorship based on a cult of personality where any dissention is quickly stamped out. Kim Il-Sung, the first (and only) President of North Korea, ruled the country from its inception in 1948 and was granted the role of Eternal President of the Republic on his death in 1994. He was succeeded by his son, Kim Jong-Il who has ruled as Supreme Commander ever since. North Korea's threat to the rest of the world lies in its nuclear weapons programme, which it refuses to abandon. Tensions have run high over recent years as North Korea has tested several nuclear missiles, moves which have been seen as acts of aggression by the rest of the world, in particular its closest neighbour and oldest enemy, South Korea. Kim Jong-Il seems impervious to sanctions against his country and is a dangerous and unpredictable leader. Recently, he announced as his successor his youngest son, Kim Jong-Un.

CHINA

Full name: People's Republic of China

Head of State: President Hu Jintao, Premier Wen Jiabao, Communist Party of China

Population: 1.3 billion

Religion or ideology: Not permitted officially; Buddhism and Taoism unofficially

Nuclear Status: Emerging nuclear superpower

Bordered By: Vietnam, Laos, Burma, India, Bhutan, Nepal, Pakistan, Afghanistan, Tajikistan, Kyrgyzstan, Kazakhstan, Russia, Mongolia and North Korea.

Political Situation: China has changed hugely over the past decade. What was an extremely insular and secretive nation is now much more open. It has benefitted from a relaxation in trade which has meant its economic power has grown enormously. But it is still ruled by the Communist Party of China and they are still intent on growing their nuclear weapons programme. Intermittent nuclear weapons testing by the superpower puts the rest of the world on edge and the sheer scale and size of China makes it a nation to be reckoned with.

Modern China is not afraid to parade its strength.

TERRORIST ORGANISATIONS

TALIBAN

A Sunni Islamist political terrorist organisation which ruled Afghanistan until it was overthrown by the Allied Forces in 2001, the Taliban are now one of the most dangerous terrorist groups in the world. Embedded in the Pakistan–Afghanistan borderlands, the Taliban are fighting back hard against the Allies with, some claim, support from Pakistan and Iran, although this is denied by both governments. Taliban fighters are responsible for hundreds of suicide attacks against both military and civilian targets in Afghanistan and Pakistan. They are also responsible for training terrorists and suicide bombers from around the world and have been behind a number of attempted attacks in the UK and the US. What makes the Taliban so dangerous is not only their access to weapons and explosive devices but also their seeming determination to stop at nothing to achieve their aims.

Masked Taliban fighters.

AL-QAEDA

A global Islamic terrorist network of extremists calling for Jihad (holy war) on the non-Muslim world, al-Qaeda is behind the worst terrorist outrages of the twenty-first century. After carrying out the World Trade Center attacks of 11 September 2001, al-Qaeda has continued its attacks on the West, and has claimed responsibility for and links with the suicide bombers who attacked London in July 2005. Other attacks planned by members of the organisation have been foiled by UK and US authorities, but they remain a very real threat.

Thousands of protesters display a portrait of Osama bin Laden during a rally in Karachi.

TROOPER ADAM HANGER

Age	22
Hometown	Eastbourne
Unit	Household Cavalry Regiment

What is your job and what do you do?
I'm a CVR(T) driver in the Household Cavalry Regiment.

What was your best day?
The best was the first contact we had, although it was scary. The adrenaline takes over and the rush you get is hard to beat. There is nothing quite like it in the world.

What was your hardest day?
The hardest days were because they were long and there was little time for sleep. We get up early, go on patrol, then work on the vehicles, go on guard duty and patrol again in the afternoon. We carry on working on the vehicles then carry out a night patrol until the early hours.

What is your favourite bit of kit and why?
As a CVR(T) driver I would have to say the thermal driver's screen. It makes driving at night a gift and it picks up heat signals easily, which is essential for recce and spotting IEDs.

LANCE CORPORAL MICHAEL PRITCHARD

Lance Corporal Pritchard of the 4th Regiment Royal Military Police was twenty-two when he was killed in Afghanistan.

Born in Maidstone, Kent, Lance Corporal Pritchard grew up in Eastbourne, Sussex. After finishing school and college, he enlisted into the Adjutant General's Corps (Royal Military Police). He deployed to Kenya as part of the training for Operation Herrick XI and arrived in Afghanistan in October 2007 attached to 4th Battalion, The Rifles.

Lance Corporal Pritchard was killed by friendly fire in the Sangin area of Helmand Province. After his death, his family paid the following tribute:

'With great sadness we say goodbye to our beloved son, a lover of life who has lived life to the full and has brought great joy to all those who were lucky enough to know him. A light that shines brightly, our precious son, brother, grandson, boyfriend and special friend to all, we are very proud of you in all that you have done and achieved and you will always be in our hearts now and evermore. God bless our darling boy, from all of your family and friends.'

Please list the last 3 books/magazines you read.

1. Front Magazine
2. The Road by Cormac McCarthy
3. Without Fail by Lee Child.

Please list the last 3 films/TV programmes you watched.

1. Crazy Heart
2. Superbad
3. Sherlock Holmes.

Sophisticated night-vision technology shows remarkable detail that would be invisible to the naked eye.

What do you miss most when away from home?

It's a close one between family and friends and booze, but just in case they are reading this I'd better say family and friends!

What is the best thing about being in the military?

Without a shadow of a doubt the camaraderie. There is nothing like having a friend there every time you turn your head.

Who do you most admire/who is your hero?

My best mate, the late Lance Corporal Michael Prichard of the 4th Regiment Royal Military Police. He laid down his life in the line of duty and his country. Heroes don't come much bigger than him.

INVISIBLE BATTLE SCARS

Coming home from a war zone often evokes mixed feelings for those in the military. While a return to loved ones and civilian life can be welcome after years coping with the pressures of military action, the adjustment is difficult for many.

POST-TRAUMATIC STRESS DISORDER

There are invisible psychological scars that can accumulate in a theatre of war. The most common of these is Post-Traumatic Stress Disorder (PTSD). PTSD can occur after any traumatic event, such as being in danger, having your life threatened, or seeing other people dying or being injured – all common occurrences in military combat. The symptoms of PTSD can start immediately or after a delay of weeks or months. The common symptoms are:

- Flashbacks/nightmares – these can occur whilst awake or asleep and they often involve reliving an event. Everyday things can trigger flashbacks. For instance, if a soldier was involved in a traumatic event involving an explosion, a loud bang might trigger a vivid episode.
- Being 'on guard' – victims of PTSD find that they stay alert almost all the time, as if expecting danger, in a state of 'hypervigilance'. As well as finding it difficult to sleep, victims can be jumpy and irritable.
- Avoidance and numbing – to distract from flashbacks and nightmares victims will go

Isaiah Schaffer shops with his service dog Meaghan.

CASE STUDY:
ISAIAH SCHAFFER

Isaiah Schaffer at home with his service dog Meaghan.

© EVELYN HOCKSTEIN / POLARIS

Former Marine Corps lieutenant Isaiah Schaffer was diagnosed with PTSD after serving three tours on the front line in Iraq. When he returned home, he became a virtual recluse: 'I came to Walmart one time and suddenly there was a baby crying. My mind leapt back to the sound of a baby in Iraq, lying in the middle of the road, screaming. Its parents had been shot and we were in a firefight all around it. I don't even remember noticing it at the time, but your mind stores up these things and unleashes them on you later.' Schaffer began shaking uncontrollably in the aisle of the shop. 'I peed myself – literally,' he says.

But Schaffer is one of the lucky ones. His symptoms were diagnosed and he was given Meaghan, a dog from Puppies Behind Bars, an organisation which works with convicted prisoners who train guide dogs to live with people suffering with blindness, epilepsy, physical disabilities and, in the past three years, soldiers with PTSD.

Meaghan helps Schaffer deal with his paralysing anxiety attacks – when Schaffer suffers nightmares or flashbacks, she senses his terror and wakes him by licking his face. In the morning, she fetches his tranquillisers, painkillers and anti-depressant pills. 'She's my miracle dog,' he says. 'I used to take a slew of stronger meds but those have been reduced and I've halved the main anti-anxiety drug that I take.'

Meaghan, a highly trained service dog, opens the refrigerator for her companion Isaiah Schaffer.

© EVELYN HOCKSTEIN / POLARIS

Following the success of Puppies Behind Bars, the Ministry of Defence has already shown interest in the new study: 'The Defence Secretary is very, very keen to do more on the mental health issues; it's a big personal project,' an MoD spokesman says of the newly installed Liam Fox. 'He will be talking about it when he next goes to the US and I wouldn't be at all surprised if the subject of service dogs comes up.'

to great lengths to avoid places and people that remind them of the trauma, keeping their mind busy on other things, often hobbies or working very hard. In many cases this leads to communicating less with other people.

- Other symptoms include: muscle aches and pains, irregular heartbeats, violent temperaments, depression, headaches, feelings of panic and fear, diarrhoea, alcoholism and drug use (including painkillers).

There are various places that retired army personnel suffering from PTSD can get help, with charities and organisations such as Combat Stress, the Braveheart Programme and the Royal British Legion.

UNEMPLOYMENT

Ex-servicemen leave the armed forces having acquired specialist skills that can't always be used when they return to civilian life, and this can be incredibly frustrating for them. A large number also find it hard to relate to people who haven't shared their military environment.

Some soldiers join the Army from difficult backgrounds – in some of the poorest parts of society high unemployment is one of the key reasons to sign up to the armed forces. When they return at the end of their military career, they return to the same set of difficult circumstances.

There is help – the Forces Recruitment Services specialises in finding jobs for UK Armed Forces' personnel, involving retraining and adjusting to different types of work.

CRIME

The effects of PTSD and readjusting to civilian life can sometimes have disastrous consequences. A 2009 study by the National Association of Probation Officers claimed that an estimated 20,000 army veterans were in the criminal justice system, with 8,500 in prison – that is 8.5 per cent of the prison population, with the figure rising more than

CASE STUDY:
STEVE GIBB

Thirty-nine-year-old Stevie Gibb served in Iraq as a member of the Royal Highland Fusiliers. He left the army in 1994 and, like many others, found it difficult to adjust to civilian life. He turned to drink to fill the void left by the armed forces.

Now he has discovered Hollybush House and Gardening Leave, a horticultural therapy centre set up two years ago by Anna Baker Cresswell in an estate near Ayr, in southwest Scotland. Gardening Leave is the only centre in the country to offer therapy through horticulture and Baker Cresswell believes it is highly beneficial to the ex-service personnel. The men take on different gardening jobs; the work is calming and methodical, and they have control over the task – something they may have found missing in civilian life. 'It is also diversionary, as you have to concentrate hard,' says Baker Cresswell. 'Planting bulbs can help people's attention span, as you can break the activity down into small, achievable tasks, such as finding the pots and getting the crocks for the bottom.'

Just the act of driving there is positive for Steve: he can get away from his flat and away from the temptation to drink. 'It is a sense of achievement that you've done something with your day,' he says. Each man can take on as much or as little as they need and, although Steve is not as hands on as some of the veterans, he designed the charity's stand at the Ayr Flower Show (it won silver) and helps with the charity's newsletter.

30 per cent in the last five years, due to the conflicts in Iraq and Afghanistan. The majority of convictions were for violent offences, particularly domestic violence.

These figures suggest that, despite the efforts of many organisations, not enough is being done to address the mental health of ex-servicemen.

Part of the reason for these statistics are the strict codes of conduct that are adhered to in the armed forces; upon a return to civilian life those codes no longer exist. Another reason is that, due to the nature of warfare, soldiers become desensitised to the violence around them. Many of the symptoms listed above, such as violent temperaments, alcoholism and drug use, can lead down the path to a prison sentence.

Similarly with unemployment, returning home to an area struggling with poverty and crime, the chances of returning to the way of life that the armed forces initially offered a way out of are increased.

By Michael Upchurch

Neil Christie on duty.

CASE STUDY: NEIL CHRISTIE

Royal Marine Captain Neil Christie developed PTSD after being posted to Afghanistan in 2006. His time on the front line affected him deeply and what he saw stayed with him. After an incident of friendly fire, he was asked to identify a fellow soldier who had been killed: 'His face was all gnarled, his back had been ripped apart and mutilated.'

© MIKE WALKER, M AND Y PORTSMOUTH

Today, Neil Chrsite helps others who have suffered similar experiences.

A convoy of his comrades were hit by a suicide bomber and Christie said, 'One of my friends had his throat ripped out. We had to wash the blood from their vehicles and equipment afterwards.'

His abiding memory was of Afghan children treated at Camp Bastion after sustaining injuries by walking into mines: 'I can never forget their faces, some of them were as young as five or six and they had lost limbs.'

'I had been to hell and couldn't process all the mental and emotional shit that went with that.' Christie received intensive counselling from Talking2minds, a charity for traumatised soldiers. He now works for it as a counsellor.

RORKE'S DRIFT

The most Victoria Crosses awarded for a single military action came from the Battle of Rorke's Drift in southern Africa, one of the most heroic defences in military history.

Eleven VCs were awarded for the events of 22–23 January 1879, when a plucky group of 139 Brits held off an onslaught by 4,000 Zulu warriors.

The battle was immortalised in the classic Michael Caine film, *Zulu*.

The mission station at Rorke's Drift was little more than a supply depot and hospital, manned only by a small force from B Company, 2nd Battalion, 24th (2nd Warwickshire) Regiment of Foot and the Royal Engineers. Around thirty-five of the men stationed there were not even fit for active duty.

When they found themselves under siege, the men of Rorke's Drift used anything they could get their hands on to defend the station, including maize bags, biscuit boxes and old furniture.

The Zulus attacked just after 4p.m. At first, the Brits were able to hold them off thanks to superior firepower and training, but the sheer number of Zulus soon forced the Brits to fall back from the main barricade.

This left the hospital unprotected, with only six troopers defending the patients. They soon ran out of ammunition, but bravely held firm with their bayonets as the Zulus beat down doors, swarmed through windows, and set the thatched roof on fire.

The courageous troopers refused to leave the base and the wounded, and instead hacked

Winners of the Victoria Cross at Rorke's Drift (from left): Lt John Chard VC, Lt Gonville Bromhead VC, Pte John Williams VC and Pte Alfred Hook VC.

Lieut. John Chard VC.

Lieut. Gonville Bromhead VC.

Pte. John Williams VC.

Pte. Alfred Hook VC.

their way through walls with just one pickaxe, holding each room as long as possible to help the injured escape.

Two of the men were speared to death. At least one had his stomach ripped open, as was Zulu custom at the time.

Just as the roof of the building collapsed, the remaining four rescuers and fourteen patients made a desperate dash across the courtyard to the new line of defence.

The Brits held their position for eight hours against repeated assaults before the fighting began to ease around midnight.

At dawn, they found 350 Zulu dead while the Brits had lost only 17 men.

VCs were awarded to Corporal William Wilson Allen, Lieutenant Gonville Bromhead, Lieutenant John Rouse Merriott Chard, Acting Assistant Commissary James Langley Dalton, Private Frederick Hitch, Private Alfred Henry Hook, Private Robert Jones, Private William Jones, Surgeon Major James Henry Reynolds, Corporal Christian Ferdinand Schiess and Private John Williams.

By David Willetts

An engraving of the battle shows the entrenched position in which the heores of Rorkes' Drift found themseleves

Pte Robert Jones was among those awarded the VC in 1879 for the historic defence of the Missionary Station at Rorke's Drift.

The question of whether recommendations could be made for colonial troops not serving with British troops was asked in 1881 in South Africa. Surgeon John McCrea, an officer of the South African Forces. was recommended for gallantry during hostilities which had not been approved by British Government. He was awarded the Victoria Cross and the principle was established that gallant conduct could be rewarded independently of any political consideration of military operations. More recently, four Australian soldiers were awarded the Victoria Cross in Vietnam, although Britain was not involved in the conflict.

The young Princess Mary was the first to suggest presents for the troops.

Serving in the Army often means spending time far away from your loved ones. This is never easy, but at Christmas it's especially hard. At a time when families are meant to be together, members of the Armed Forces find themselves in dangerous, foreign lands, many thousands of miles away from home.

To make things a little easier for them, the charity uk4u Thanks! was established. The charity provides Christmas boxes, affectionately known as 'square stockings', filled with presents from the nation which are sent to serving members of the Armed Forces on Christmas Day.

The initiative was inspired by the 1914 Christmas Gift Fund, established by Princess Mary, the daughter of King George V, during the First World War. She wanted to pay, from her own private allowance, for a gift for every soldier and sailor away from home on Christmas Day. This was deemed impossible, so instead it was proposed that the seventeen-year-old princess lend her name to a public fund, which would raise the necessary money

Christmas Boxes

uk4u's Christmas boxes are greeted with anticipation.

Soldiers serving at Camp Bastion show off their gifts from uk4u at Christmas dinner.

© PETER JORDAN / THE SUN

A Piece of Home on the Front Line

to ensure that a 'gift from the nation' was provided for everyone wearing the King's uniform and serving on Christmas Day. To make sure this happened, the princess sent out a plea to the nation:

> I want you now to help me send a Christmas present from the whole of the nation to every sailor afloat and every soldier on the front. I am sure that we should all be happier to feel we had helped to send our little token of love and sympathy on Christmas morning, something that would be useful and of permanent value, and the making of which may be the means of providing employment in trades adversely affected by the war. Could there be anything more likely to hearten them in their struggle than a present received straight from home on Christmas Day? Please will you help me?

These first Christmas boxes were made of brass and were embossed with an image of Princess Mary. They contained a pipe, lighter, tobacco and twenty cigarettes. Today's Christmas parcels are still delivered in tin boxes but are now filled with very different gifts, from useful items such as torches, padlocks and sewing kits, to more luxurious treats like pillows and eye masks and presents purely for fun, such

Jamie and his handler open his presents.

© CROWN COPYRIGHT

JOHN EVANS AND JAMIE THE SNIFFER DOG

Just before Christmas 2008, Allan Sims, one of uk4u Thanks!'s trustees, received a shoebox-sized parcel addressed to Jamie the Springer Spaniel Sniffer Dog – somewhere in Afghanistan. The box had arrived at Allan's home in West Chiltington, Sussex and the sender had put his name and address as John Evans, Abergele.

Although the charity does not send on boxes which have been supplied by the general public, Allan (being a dog lover) decided that he would do his best to trace this mystery dog. In his work with the charity, Allan gets many phone calls from people returning from Afghanistan who want to say thank you for the boxes they have received and he set about asking each caller if they had any knowledge of the whereabouts of this dog. The answers were never quite right – several sniffer dogs were known, most with different names, and one called Jamie who wasn't a Springer Spaniel.

The task seemed impossible until one day, over two months later, an RAF group captain sent an e-mail to Allan saying he had found the dog at last and would forward details of the name and address of the handler, a lance corporal serving in Afghanistan.

Allan decided to find the telephone number of John Evans in Abergele and tell him the great news, expecting the man to be as thrilled as he was. Allan's wife, knowing the efforts that had been made, wanted the phone on loudspeaker so that she too could hear his reaction.

The phone rang, a woman answered and Allan asked to speak to John. There was silence. Allan asked again and heard a sound like a stifled sob before the woman enquired what he wanted to speak to John about. Allan explained about the parcel addressed to the Springer Spaniel and was devastated to be told, 'I'm sorry, but John is dead'.

After a short period of utter confusion and bewilderment, the woman, Barbara – John's widow – composed herself and spent the next twenty minutes recounting the story of the box.

A few days before Christmas 2008, a story was relayed on BBC radio about a Springer Spaniel sniffer dog called Jamie who had been sent to Afghanistan to assist British troops in detecting explosives. The story stated that Jamie had gone on his heroic mission without any toys – not so much as a tennis ball to play with. John Evans had listened to this programme at home in Abergele whilst suffering from pneumonia. Being a dog lover, and seeing all the toys his own dogs had, he was so moved by the story that, in spite of his dreadful condition, he asked his wife Barbara to put together a box of toys and send them to relieve the dog's plight.

Barbara duly made up a box of toys but had no idea where to send them. She had heard of a charity that sent Christmas boxes to the troops, so searched the internet and discovered the address for uk4u Thanks!

Barbara then got John to put his name and his old RAF service number on the box and addressed it to 'Jamie, the Springer Spaniel Sniffer Dog – somewhere in Afghanistan c/o uk4u Thanks!, West Chiltington, RH20 2JY'. A short while later John passed away, having first made sure that the parcel had been sent.

The box arrived at the home of Allan Sims and the rest of the story you now know.

When the phone conversation ended, Allan turned to his wife, who was in floods of tears, as he was himself.

The box was sent to Afghanistan where it was received by Jim, the handler, and unwrapped by Jamie, who enthusiastically tore into his box of goodies. Barbara now cherishes pictures of the happy pooch, whose loyal and courageous service is a fitting tribute to her late husband, his love of animals and his dying wish.

209

as Frisbees and juggling balls. In 2009, uk4u Thanks! send out 23,000 parcels to serving men and women – generous gestures of support for those far from home.

This year, as last, the Armed Forces are asking that members of the public keen to show their support refrain from sending unsolicited parcels addressed to 'A Soldier' or 'A Commander' on the front lines. Though the sentiment behind these missives is welcome and never fails to boost morale, unsolicited mail can create all kinds of logistical difficulties on the front lines. Around Christmas time, unsolicited post can flood the Royal Mail, blocking packages and letters from family members and friends, and even interfering with the delivery of other priority supplies that have to be moved forward. Two years ago, Prince Harry, who was serving in Afghanistan, declared the system 'pants' after a Christmas card from his father arrived two months late!

To prevent these delays, uk4u Thanks! works with the Ministry of Defence to transport the boxes outside the postal system, using spare space in its own military transport. Because of this and because they're reliant on spare space, uk4u Thanks! start sending their boxes as early as September.

uk4u Thanks! doesn't receive any public money and depends on donations to fund its efforts.

Actor Ross Kemp is one of many celebrities to support uk4u.

Girl group and Armed Forces supporters The Saturdays also back the charity uk4u Thanks!

210

More information about uk4u can be found at **www.uk4u.org** or by using your smartphone to scan this code:

ACKNOWLEDGEMENTS

Grateful thanks are due to the following who gave generously of their time, efforts and goodwill, and without whom this book would not have been possible.

Mark Alden & SAM Medical Products
Major Lucy Anderson
Angie Avlianos & CSE
Jonathan Baker & Seagulls Design
Henry Biggs
Grenadier Guardsman Scott Blaney
Helena Caldon
Major Nick Cavill
Sergeant Robert Chester
Lance Corporal Sally Clarke
Jeremy Clarkson
Sarah Corn & the East Grinstead Museum
Essie Cousins
Captain Simon Cupples
Flight Lieutenant Alexander Duncan
Flying Officer Robin Fowler
Sophie Goulden
Alan Grace
Corporal Ronnie Gregory
Trooper Adam Hanger
Major Tim Harris
Lori Heiss
Patrick Hennessey
WO2 Matthew Campbell Henry
Clare Hey
Major Bob Hobbs
Richard Holmes
Yibi Hu
Julian Humphries
Fergal Keane
Colonel Richard Kemp, CBE
Lieutenant Colonel Nick Kitson
Duncan Larcombe
Sam Lister
The Lockett family
Ed Macy, MC
Bob Marchant & the Guinea Pig Club
Joe Marshall
Paul McNamara
Michael Moran
Captain Wayne Owers
Bryn and Emma Parry and Help for Heroes
Tom Parry
Tom Percival
Shaun Pickford
Martin Phillips
Georgina Reid
Tony Rosser & the British Library
Lieutenant Aran Sandiford
George Shepherd
Allan Sims & uk4u
Nigel Steel & the Imperial War Museum
Julie Summers
Natasha Tanczos
Corporal Carl Thomas
WO Matthew Tomlinson
Colonel Stuart Tootal, OBE
The Trustees of George Macdonald Fraser
Michael Upchurch
Sergeant Liam Varley
Lance Corporal Chris Walton
Geoff Webster
Chris Whalley
Katy Whitehead
David Willetts
John 'Lofty' Wiseman
Sergeant Robert Wiseman
Kathryn Wynn

While every effort has been made to trace the owners of copyright material reproduced herein, the publishers would like to apologize for any omissions and would be pleased to incorporate missing acknowledgements in future editions.